S. Anne Teaches the Virgin to Read.

Dedications & Patron Saints
of English Churches

ECCLESIASTICAL SYMBOLISM
SAINTS AND THEIR EMBLEMS

BY

FRANCIS BOND, M.A.

F.G.S., Hon. A.R.I.B.A.

Author of "Gothic Architecture in England," "Cathedrals of England and Wales,"
"Screens and Galleries in English Churches," "Fonts and Font Covers," "Stalls
and Tabernacle Work," "Misericords," "Westminster Abbey," "Introduction to
English Church Architecture"

WITH 252 ILLUSTRATIONS

HUMPHREY MILFORD
OXFORD UNIVERSITY PRESS
London, New York, Toronto, Melbourne, and Bombay
1914

M. L.

S. John Baptist.
All Saints' North Street, York.

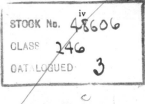

PREFACE

THIS book should be pleasant to read, for it has been pleasant to write. It grew out of a perusal of Miss Arnold-Forster's *Studies in Church Dedications* (3 vols., Skeffington, 1899). Of this the third volume is composed of statistics, and gives the first and only complete list of saints commemorated in the dedications of English churches. These include modern as well as mediæval dedications. It seemed worth while to strip off all dedications of the eighteenth and nineteenth centuries, leaving only those of more ancient date. The next step was to arrange these earlier dedications in order of frequency of occurrence, as a key to the respective popularity or unpopularity of the various saints. The results, both as to popularity and unpopularity, were so surprising that it was hardly possible not to pursue the inquiry further, and endeavour to ascertain how the old churchmen came to have such very different ideas from our own as to the merits or demerits of the saints. The inquiry turned out not to be easy, as may be judged from the long list of books in the bibliography (see below) which it was necessary to read and digest. Then some sort of order or system of arrange-ment had to be devised. It would not have been very profitable to discuss haphazard, just as they happened to occur in order of frequency, saints of such diverse characteristics as S. Andrew, S. Nicholas, S. Margaret, S. Helena, S. Thomas of Canterbury, and the rest ; it would be to compare chalk with cheese. It was necessary to divide them up into various categories. Of these evidently the first category was of those saints whose biography, or part of it, appears in the New Testament. Even here the results of the order of merit, if it may be so termed, of the Biblical saints required considerable inquiry and discussion. How did it come about, for instance, that SS. Andrew and Matthew should have such overwhelming popularity as against other apostles and evangelists? It is only by delving down to the fifth century legend of the happenings at Wrondon, the City of Dogs (page 154), that the key to the mystery was at length

v

discovered. After discussion of the anomalies of the popularity of Biblical saints, there still remained the far larger crowd of non-Biblical saints. Of these by far the most numerous are Celtic saints of Cornwall and Wales, of whom little is said in this volume, because of most of them little is known, and of several nothing at all (see pages 10-12, 25-27, 192, 193). These being expunged from the list, there still remained a very large number of non-Biblical saints, whose respective merits and demerits it was desirable to examine. These have been divided into classes. Of these the first is composed of saints of royal blood, chiefly of Anglo-Saxon dynasties, but headed by the great Roman empress, Helena (pages 72-83). Then follows a consideration of saints distinguished by their theological scholarship as compared with those who won greater acceptance by austerity and asceticism of life (pages 84-91). There follows a list of the chief saints, not excluding the charming legends of S. Bridget of Kildare, to whom was due the evangelisation of Western Europe and Ireland (pages 92-100). These are followed by the saints who brought about the conversion of the Anglo-Saxon kingdoms; special attention being directed to the position occupied by women in the Anglo-Saxon church (pages 101-108). The largest category is that of the "white-robed army of Martyrs," which, beginning in the first century and extending with breaks up to the execution at Whitehall in 1629, is largely a synopsis of the history of Church History in Western Europe through seventeen centuries (pages 109-136). A list of other good men is given, who though never formally canonised, or if canonised, not commemorated in dedications, nevertheless were popular saints with common folk (pages 137-145 and 194-200). The categories are now complete. Each contains strange anomalies. An attempt had to be made to explain the indifference felt by the old churchmen to some saints, their love and admiration of others. Some sort of explanation, or rather a series of explanations, is offered in the twelfth chapter, *e.g.*, that a particular saint was specific against some common danger or malady, or that his story lent itself readily to representation in pictorial art, or that his relics were widely diffused, or that the legend was in praise of virginity, or of loving-kindness to poor people, and the sick, and cripples, and lepers, and captives, and little children, and the birds and beasts of the forest; but far away above all, that the biography had been written up by mediæval men of letters, in whose hands, then as now, lay the gift of immortality (pages 146-182). Finally, it is asked how far these diverse biographies are veracious, and an attempt is made to set forth canons of credibility of legendary lore (pages 183-

188). So far Hagiology in general had been dealt with, but it seemed interesting also to inquire how far local Hagiology agreed with or differed from it ; test counties, therefore, were examined for the purpose, and the results are given in Chapter XVI. A comparison also has been made of the popularity of saints as shown in church dedications, and as shown in church bells and calendars ; the calendars of Bede and Sarum are given at length. Also a chapter is added on the consecration services of churches in Celtic, Anglo-Saxon, and mediæval times.

The second part of the book is devoted to an explanation of the symbolism which occurs so abundantly in every branch of mediæval church art (pages 243-291).

The third part consists of an alphabetical list of emblems to facilitate the identification of representations of the saints. This is followed by an alphabetical list of saints—chiefly those commemorated in the dedications of English churches—followed by the emblems characteristic of each. These two lists should be of use to the archæologist, but still more to a traveller who, like the present writer, has been visiting this summer the stained glass of Chartres and Le Mans, the pictures galleries of Florence, Milan, and Venice, and the churches of Brittany with their wealth of images. By the aid of these lists the identification of English saints represented in sculpture, pictorial art, stained glass, ivories, and the like, may in most cases be readily accomplished.

For the illustrations of the book the writer is indebted to the kindness and co-operation of many friends. For photographs, drawings, or blocks, acknowledgments are due to Mr S. Ambler, Mr E. W. Andrew, Rev. T. N. Baxter, Mr H. C. Beckett, Dr G. G. Buckley, Mr P. B. Burroughs, Miss Kate M. Clarke, Mr F. H. Crossley, Mr W. Davidson, Messrs Dawkes and Partridge, Mr W. Marriott Dodson, Mr J. F. East, Mr W. Eaton, A.R.I.B.A., Rev. J. T. Fowler, D.C.L., Mr A. Gardner, F.S.A., Mr S. Gardner, Mr Cecil Gethen, Mr Harry Gill, Mr Advent Hunstone, Mr F. Jenkins, Miss Mabel Leaf, Rev. Walter Marshall, F.S.A., Mrs E. M'Clure, Dr Philip Nelson, Mr C. F. Nunneley, Mr A. Y. Nutt, Mr W. T. Oldrieve, F.R.I.B.A., Mr T. Phillips, Mr H. Plowman, Miss E. K. Prideaux, Rev. C. O. Raven, Mr E. A. Reeve, Mr. A. W. Searley, Mr S. Smith, Mr W. S. Weatherley, F.R.I.B.A., Mr D. Weller, Mr G. H. Widdows, A.R.I.B.A., Rev. W. E. Wigfall, Mr W. Percival-Wiseman, Mr W. P. Young ; reproductions of the above are distinguished by the initials of the owner of the photograph or block. The following books also have been drawn on for illustrations : *Calendar of the English Church,* by permission of Messrs Parker ; *Rood Screens and Rood Lofts,* by Mr F. Bligh Bond, F.R.I.B.A., and Dom Bede Camm, by

permission of Messrs Pitman and the joint authors; the new
series of the *Reliquary*; the drawings of the *Ranworth Rood
Screen*, by Mr C. J. Winter; *Mediæval Figure Sculpture in
England*, by Professor E. S. Prior and Mr Arthur Gardner, by
permission of the Cambridge University Press and the joint
authors; and the volumes in the *English Church Art Series* by
the present writer on *Westminster Abbey* and *Rood Screens and
Galleries in English Churches*.

Valuable information has been kindly supplied from various
sources; special acknowledgments are due to the Right Reverend
G. F. Browne, Dom Bede Camm, Miss Kate M. Clarke, Mr G.
C. Druce, Rev. J. T. Fowler, D.C.L., Mr C. E. Keyser, Dr
Montague James, Mrs E. M'Clure, Mr W. J. N. Millard,
A.R.I.B.A., Mr C. F. Nunneley, Dr Philip Nelson, Miss E. K.
Prideaux, Mr H. B. Walters, Rev. W. A. Wickham.

The text has had the advantage of revision by Rev. G. C.
Niven, Rev. G. W. Saunders, and Mr F. B. Walters, F.S.A. A
bibliography has been prefixed to the text, and indexes will be
found at the end of the volume, together with alphabetical lists
of Saints and their Emblems. The writer will be glad to receive
corrections and suggestions through his publisher, Mr Humphrey
Milford, Oxford University Press, Amen Corner, London, E.C.

CONTENTS

b

BIBLIOGRAPHY

IT should be clearly understood, says Mr Bates,[1] that there is no authoritative list of English dedications in existence. Among the public Records are two works known as Pope Nicholas' *Taxatio* of 1291 and the *Valor Ecclesiasticus* of 1536, containing the names of all parishes in England and Wales; these were drawn up primarily to ascertain the value of the benefices, and only incidentally, as in the case of a town with many churches, are the dedications added. The latter work, known as the *Valor Ecclesiasticus* or *Liber Regis*, was first printed in 1711 by John Ecton. It was not till 1742, after the death of Ecton, that an edition was published, in which the dedications were added, as far as he was able to obtain them, largely from hear-say and fishing inquiries, by the well known antiquary, Browne Willis. In 1786 John Bacon brought out a new edition of the *Liber Regis*, based on the the labours of Ecton and Willis, but omitting all mention of their names from the title page.

The following are the chief authorities on the dedications of English churches :—

BACON. *Liber Regis, vel Thesaurus Rerum Ecclesiasticarum.* 1786.

ECTON. *Thesaurus Rerum Ecclesiasticarum.* 2nd edition. 1754.

LAWTON. *Collectio Rerum Ecclesiasticarum de diocesi Eboracensi.* 1840.

—— *Clergy List.* Published annually.

—— *Diocesan Calendars.* Published annually.

MACKESON. *Guide to the London Churches.* Published annually.

For general purposes Miss Arnold-Foster's *Studies in Church Dedications* or *England's Patron Saints* (London, 1899), will be found all sufficient.

CELTIC SAINTS

Round the dedications of Celtic saints a considerable literature has gathered. The following are among the most important works :—

REES, Rev. RICE. *Essay on the Welsh Saints.* London, 1836.

BORLASE, W. C. *Age of the Saints.* Truro, 1878.

[1] Rev. E. H. Bates in *Somerset Archæological Proceedings*, li. 105.

REES, Rev. W. J. *Lives of the Cambro-British Saints;* translated. Published by the Society for the Publication of Ancient Welsh Manuscripts.

NEWELL, E. J. *A Popular History of the Ancient British Church.* 1887. *Truro Diocesan Kalendar.*

FORBES, BISHOP. *Kalendars of the Scottish Saints.* 1872.

BARING-GOULD, S. *A Catalogue of Saints connected with Cornwall, with an Epitome of their Lives and List of Churches and Chapels Dedicated to them. Royal Institute of Cornwall,* xiii. 439 ; xiv. 25, 260 ; xv. 17, 256, 347 ; xvi. 144, 279, 395 ; xvii. 155.

EVANS, J. T. *Church Plate of Pembrokeshire, with Notes on the Dedications of Pembrokeshire Churches.* London, 1905.

KERSLAKE, THOMAS. *The Celt and the Teuton in Exeter. Archæological Journal,* xxx. 211.

—— *Vestiges of the Supremacy of Mercia. Translations of the Bristol and Gloucester Archæological Society,* 1872.

—— *The Welsh in Dorset.* Dorset Field Club, iii. 74.

BARING-GOULD, S., and JOHN FISHER. *The Lives of the British Saints, the Saints of Wales and Cornwall, and such Irish Saints as have Dedications in England.* London, 4 vols., 1907-1914.

STOKES, WHITLEY. *Three Middle-Irish Homilies on the Lives of Saints Patrick, Brigit, and Columba.* Calcutta, 1877.

STANTON'S *Menology of England and Wales* contains three appendixes as follows :—

(*a*) An alphabetical list of Welsh saints, to whom churches are dedicated, or whose names appear in some ancient calendar.

(*b*) A list of other Welsh saints, or eminent persons sometimes called saints, but to whom no churches are known to have been dedicated, and many of whom, it is probable, have never in fact been honoured as saints.

(*c*) A list of Cornish saints, not only those named in the above *Menology,* but others to whom churches have been dedicated, or who have given their names to places, but have left no sufficient record of their lives.

DEDICATIONS

The following deal with the subject of dedications generally:—

BINGHAM, J. *Antiquities of the Christian Church.* New edition, 10 vols. Oxford, 1855.

BRIGHT, CANON W. *Chapters of Early English Church History.* Oxford, 1878.

BROWNE, CHARLES. *Transactions of St Paul's Ecclesiological Society,* vol. i., v. 267.

PEACOCK, EDWARD. *Archæological Review,* ii. 269.

HARINGTON, E. C. *The Rite of Consecration of Churches.* London, 1844.

The following deal with the dedications of the churches in particular counties or districts :—

VENABLES, PRECENTOR. *Dedications of the Churches of Lincolnshire as Illustrating the History of the County. Archæological Journal*, xxxviii. 365.
—— *Dedications of the Parish Churches of Nottinghamshire. Associated Societies' Reports*, v. 10 and xvii. 1.
RAINE, CANON. *Dedications of the Nottinghamshire Churches, as shown by Wills. Associated Societies' Reports*, xvi. ii. 231, 239.
—— *Dedications of the Yorkshire Churches. Yorkshire Archæological Journal*, vol. ii. 180.
JACKSON, J. E. *Names of Wiltshire Churches. Wilts. Archæological Magazine*, xv. 98.
GREGORY, J. V. *Dedication Names of Ancient Churches in Durham and Northumberland. Archæological Journal*, xlii. 370.
BATES, E. H. *Dedications of the Churches of Somerset. Somerset Archæological Society*, li. 105.
DUNCAN, LELAND E. *Dedications in the Diocese of Rochester. S. Paul's Ecclesiological Society*, iii. 241.
—— *Ecclesiological Notes concerning the Deanery of Shoreham, Kent. Archæologia Cantiana*, xxiii. 134.
—— *Parish Churches of West Kent. Testamenta Cantiana.* 1907.
HUSSEY, ARTHUR. *Dedications in East Kent. Testamenta Cantiana.* 1907.
ATTREE, F. W. T. *Some Hampshire Dedications gathered from Pre-Reformation Wills. Hampshire Field Club Papers*, ii. 331
AUDEN, H. M. *Shropshire Dedications to Celtic Saints. Shropshire Archæological and Natural History Society*, iii. i. 284.
CLARK-MAXWELL, W. G. *Some Local Dedications in their bearing on Local Church History. Shropshire Archæological and Natural History Society*, iv. i. 363.
GIBBON, C. *Dedications of the Churches and Chapels in the Rapes of Chichester, Arundel, and Bramber. Sussex Archæological Collections*, xii. 61.
ROWE, J. B. *Dedications of the Ancient Parish Churches, Chapels and Religious Houses of Devon. Devonshire Association*, xiv. 93.
OLDHAM, D. W. *Church Dedications in Devonshire. Devonshire Association*, xxxv. 746.

LIVES OF THE SAINTS

For the LIVES OF THE SAINTS the chief authority is the *Acta Sanctorum*, compiled by the Bollandists. Their object was to print the best text; for the authenticity of the legends they are in nowise responsible. Over sixty volumes have appeared, and it is still incomplete.

BAILLET J. *Vie des Saints.* 1739.

BUTLER, ALBAN. *Lives of the Saints.* 12 vols. London, 1812, 1813 ;
this contains also lists of the relics of the saints, and of the places
where they are to be found.

BARING-GOULD, S. *Lives of the Saints.* 16 vols. 2nd edition. 1877.

NEWMAN'S *Lives of the Saints.* 6 vols. 1901. This series was
prepared by various hands at the suggestion of Cardinal Newman,
and was never completed.

SMITH and WACE'S *Dictionary of Christian Biography.* 3 vols. The
articles are by eminent scholars, and are of high critical value.
4 vols. London. 1877-1887.

Miss ARNOLD-FORSTER in *Studies in Church Dedications,* vols. i. and ii.,
gives a critical account of the lives of saints who are commemorated
in dedications.

JAMESON, Mrs. *Sacred and Legendary Art.* The legends of the
saints are mainly considered from the point of view of their representation in mediæval and modern art : the book consists of three
parts :—

    I. *The History of Our Lord and of Old and New Testament
        Personages.* 2 vols. 1864.
    II. *Legends of the Madonna.* 2nd edition. 1857.
    III. *Legends of the Monastic Orders.* 2nd edition. 1852.

JACOBUS DE VORAGINE (Venice, 1480). *The Golden Legend.* Translated
by William Caxton. Reprinted by William Morris. 1892.

Calendar of the English Church. Illustrated. Parker. 1851.

HARCOURT, C. G. V. *Legends of S. Augustine, S. Anthony, and S.
Cuthbert, painted on the back of the stalls in Carlisle Cathedral.*
Illustrated. Carlisle, 1868.

WEAVER, F. W. *On the Cult of S. Barbara.* Somerset Archæological
and Natural History Proceedings. 1893.

HORSTMAN, CARL. *Nova Legenda Angliæ.* As collected by John of
Tynemouth, John Capgrave, and others, and first printed, with *New
Lives,* by Wynkyn de Worde in 1516. 2 vols. Oxford, 1901.

STANTON, RICHARD. *Menology of England and Wales.* 1887.

EMBLEMS OF THE SAINTS

On the emblems of the saints the chief English authority is Husenbeth's
Emblems, 3rd edition, edited by Dr Jessop.

On the paintings of saints on the rood screens of Norfolk see G. E.
Fox in *Victoria County History of Norfolk,* ii. 529 ; and ditto,
Notes on Painted Screens and Roofs in Norfolk (*Archæological
Journal,* xlvii. 65) ; and on those of the Devonshire screens see
Rood Screens and Rood Lofts, London, 1909, by F. Bligh Bond
and Dom Bede Camm. On screens generally and their paintings
see bibliography prefixed to *Screens and Galleries,* by Francis
Bond, London, 1908.

KEYSON, C. E., on *Panel Paintings of Saints on Devonshire Screens,* in
Archæologia, lvi. 183.

WILSON. *English Martyrologe.* 1608.

CHALLONER. *Britannia Sancta.* London, 1745.

BLAISE. *Vie des Saints.* 2 vols. Paris, 1825.

KEYSER, C. E. *Notes on some Fifteenth Century Stained Glass in the Church of Wiggenhall St Mary Magdalen. Norfolk and Norwich Archæologial Society,* xvi. 306-319.

NELSON, PHILIP. *Ancient Painted Glass in England.* London, 1913.

WINTER, C. J. W. *Rood Screen at Ranworth, Norfolk.* Norwich, 1867.

GUNN, Rev. JOHN. *Rood Screen at Barton Turf, Norfolk.* Norwich, 1869.

BIRCH and JENNER. *Early Drawings of Illuminations in the British Museum.* London, 1879.

MICKLETHWAITE, J. T. *Statues in Henry the Seventh's Chapel, Westminster. Archæologia,* xlvii. 361.

CAHIER, CH. *Characteristiques des Saints.* 2 vols. Paris, 1867.

CALLOT, JAQUES. *Images de tous les Saints et Saintes de l'année.* Paris, 1636.

TWINING, LOUISA. *Symbols and Emblems of Early and Mediæval Christian Art.* London, 1885.

MOLANO. *De Historia SS. Imaginum et Picturarum.* Lovanii, 1771.

ALT, A. *Die Heiligenbilder.*

RADOWITZ. *Ikonographie der Heiligen.* Berlin, 1834.

ECCLESIASTICAL SYMBOLISM

DURANDUS' *Rationale.* First book, translated with introduction by Neale & Webb.

DIDRON'S *Christian Iconography.* Completed by Miss Margaret Stokes. Bohn's Library, 1886.

MALE, EMILE. *The Religious Art of the Thirteenth Century in France.* Translated by Dora Nussey. London, 1913.

PORTER, A. K. *Mediæval Architecture,* ii. 115-145.

J. ROMILLY ALLEN'S *Early Christian Symbolism in Great Britain and Ireland before the Thirteenth Century,* being the Rhind Lectures for 1885. Whiting, 1887.

POOLE'S *Appropriate Character of Church Architecture.*

HULME, EDWARD. *Symbolism in Christian Art.* London, 1892.

KALENDARS

MASKELL'S *Monumenta Ritualia Ecclesiæ Anglicanæ.* 2nd edition. 1882.

GELDART, E. *Manual of Church Decoration and Symbolism.* Oxford, 1899.

BLUNT'S *Annotated Prayer Book.* 1903.

NEWMAN'S *Lives of the English Saints.* First volume.

Miss ARNOLD-FORSTER prefixes to her first volume on *Dedications* a calendar (movable feasts excepted) showing the days allotted to those saints who have churches dedicated to them.

FORBES, BISHOP. *Kalendars of the Scottish Saints.* 1872.

MARTÈNE, EDMOND, and DURAND, URSIN. *Veterum Scriptorum et Monumentorum, historicorum, dogmaticorum, moralium amplissima collectio.* 9 vols. Paris, 1724-1733.

GUÉRANGER, DOM. *The Liturgical Year.* Translated by Shepherd. Dublin and London, 1867.

STANTON, RICHARD. *Menology of England and Wales.* The seventh appendix gives a list of 21 martyrologies consulted in the preparation of the work.

GASQUET and BISHOP. *Edward VI. and the Book of Common Prayer.* London, 1890.

PART I

DEDICATIONS OF ENGLISH CHURCHES

CHAPTER I

Dedication, Meaning of—Intercessory Power of the Saints—Dedications to the Holy Trinity—The Second Person in the Godhead—Holy Cross or Holy Rood—S. Sepulchre—The Third Person in the Godhead.

ALL over Christendom, in the Latin and in the Greek Church, every church and chapel is or was connected with the name of some saint or of some sacred place or event; with the name of the Blessed Virgin, S. Peter, S. Michael, the Holy Sepulchre, the Assumption of the Blessed Virgin, or the like. It must be borne in mind, however, that no church or chapel is immediately consecrated or dedicated to any saint or event, but solely to Almighty God. Churches, says Hooker,[1] were consecrated to none but the Lord only. The general name "church" doth sufficiently show this, for it doth signify nothing but the "Lord's House." But founders of churches, for distinction's sake, did each what liked him best, intending that the name of the saint to whom the church was dedicated should put the person who used or heard the name in mind of some memorable thing or person. And S. Augustine saith, "To the saints we appoint no churches, because they are not unto us as gods, but as memorials as unto dead men, whose spirits with God are still living." So also Bingham[2] writes that "the naming of a church by the name of a saint or martyr was far from dedicating it to that saint or martyr, though it served for a memorial of him among the living, and so far was an honour to his memory, though dedicated only

[1] *Ecclesiastical Polity*, v. 13.
[2] *Origines Ecclesiasticæ*, vol. ii. p. 529.

I

to God and His service." This being so, it is properly not right to refer to a church as being dedicated to such and such a saint or event ; it is a sort of convenient shorthand way of expressing that we mean that it is *dedicated to God in memory of such and such a saint or event.* It is in this sense, and with this reservation, that the term "dedication" is used throughout this volume.

A convincing proof of this, which does not seem to have been hitherto pointed out, is that many a town hall and hospital is known abroad as *Hotel Dieu* or *Maison Dieu* (a fine example of the latter is still in use at Dover), but neither at home nor abroad are any churches dedicated to the First Person of the Trinity. Had such a dedication been given, the meaning would have been that the church so dedicated was dedicated to God the Father in memory of God the Father.

As regards England, we are now able to get a comprehensive view of the whole subject of English dedications.[1] It is one of curious interest, throwing strange and often unexpected side-lights on the feelings and practices of English churchmen, whether in Celtic, Anglo-Saxon, or Post-Conquest days. The dedications of the churches of England have much to tell us of English Christian belief and feeling from the beginning of Church history up to the present day.

In the first place it may be noted that, as was to be expected, a considerable number of churches are dedicated to the Trinity in Unity or to the Second or Third Persons of the Godhead. And here, at the very outset, we come across something which was not to be expected. It is that the above three dedications are outnumbered, far and away, by others. Altogether the three yield no more than 450 Pre-Reformation examples: a small number compared with the 2,335 dedications to the Blessed Virgin, 1,255 to All Saints or All Hallows, 1,140 to S. Peter, 687 to S. Michael and All Angels, 637 to S. Andrew. The reason for this is probably to be found in the ever-growing tendency to attach great importance to the Intercessory Power of the Saints, to the belief in the efficacy of their mediation, which is already to be found in Christian doctrines and practice even as early as the fourth century.

---

[1] Thanks to Miss Frances Arnold-Forster, who in the third volume of her *Studies in Church Dedications*, has given first the number of dedications of churches and chapelries, ancient and modern, connected with each saint or sacred event ; secondly, an alphabetical list of all the English parishes with the dedications of their several churches ; and thirdly, an alphabetical list of the saints, followed by the names of the parishes in which their churches are found.

A. H.

Trinity Emblem.
From brass at Tideswell, Derbyshire.

HOLY TRINITY

Under this heading are found 297 ancient [1] dedications. Comparatively few churches were dedicated to the Holy Trinity or the Sacred Trinity before the closing years of the twelfth century. But S. Thomas of Canterbury had been consecrated Archbishop in 1170 on the first Sunday after Whitsuntide; he had celebrated his first mass in Prior Conrad's Trinity chapel, which was to be burnt down four years later; and it was to this Trinity chapel that the archbishop constantly resorted for private prayer. The Church of Rome had refused to institute a separate festival to the Holy Trinity, but Becket ordained that all churches in his province should henceforth observe the first Sunday after Whitsuntide as Trinity Sunday.[2] After the rebuilding cf Canterbury choir the relics of the archbishop had been transferred in 1220 from the crypt to the chapel at the back of the High Altar occupying the same relative position as his beloved Trinity chapel.[3] The great English martyr, therefore, whose influence was enormous throughout Christendom, was closely connected in the popular mind with the doctrine of the Trinity, and the result was naturally a great increase in the number of dedications of churches to the Holy Trinity. At a second period also this dedication was in special favour; viz., from the time of Henry VIII. to the end of the seventeenth century; this was due mainly to a reaction against the veneration of non-Biblical saints and of saints in general. It was Henry VIII. who introduced the Trinity into the dedications of the cathedrals of Ely and Winchester and of Trinity College, Cambridge. A third period is the first half of the nineteenth century, when the evangelical party in the Church selected this dedication for more than 230 churches.[4]

It is of interest that our mercantile marine, our harbours, anchorage grounds, lighthouses, lightships, and buoys are all under the care of a guild founded in 1515 by Sir Thomas Sport, who had been captain of the great galleon *Harry Grace à Dieu*,

[1] The term "ancient dedication" as used throughout this volume is *not* synonymous with "Pre-Reformation" dedication, as it includes all dedications of the sixteenth and seventeenth century.

[2] It was not till nearly 150 years later that the Roman Church universally followed the practice of the English Church in observing Trinity Sunday as settled by Becket. The Greek Church does not recognise this festival.

[3] The new chapel was called S. Thomas' chapel, but in modern times it has recovered its old style of Trinity chapel.

[4] Arnold-Forster, i. 27.

under the title of "the Master, Wardens and Assistants of the Guild or Fraternity of the Most Glorious and Undivided Trinity, and of S. Clement," the latter being more immediately connected with roads and anchorages by reason of the part played in his legend by an anchor.   Another contemporary use of this

A. Y. N.

From a brass to Lady Exeter (1474) in S. George's chapel, Windsor.

dedication may be cited.   When Columbus was on his third voyage to America, he saw riding across the sea what appeared to be three distinct mountains or islands; but as the vessel drew near, they merged into one another at the base, being a single immense mass of basalt.   This so struck him that he named the island Trinity Island, La Trinidad.   On his first voyage the first land he reached was christened by him Saviour Island, "San Salvador."[1]

THE SECOND PERSON IN THE GODHEAD
(THIRTY-EIGHT DEDICATIONS)

For the reason given above the direct dedications to Our Lord are few. "*Christ Church*" occurs twenty times. Canterbury cathedral has retained this dedication ever since it was appointed by Augustine in the seventh century. When Henry VIII. set to work to re-dedicate the cathedrals, his favourite names were "The Holy Trinity," "Christ Church" and "The Blessed Virgin Mary." It was he who introduced the name of Christ into the dedications of the cathedrals of Worcester, Rochester, Chester, Durham, and Oxford. In another form the dedication appears as *Jesus* chapel at Troutbeck, near Windermere, and at Southampton; and formerly as "The *Holy Jesus*" at Attercliffe, Yorkshire. Thirteen dedications are found to "*S. Saviour*" or "*Our Saviour*"; the best known is that of Southwark cathedral, which, till Henry VIII. suppressed the Augustinian house, was dedicated to S. Mary Overie, S. Mary over the river. In his presence in the Holy Host ("*Hostia*") at the Eucharist Our Lord is commemorated once in "S. Mary and *Corpus Christi*," Hatherley Down, Gloucestershire; and once in "S. Mary and the *Holy Host*," Cheveley, Cambridgeshire. Both Oxford and Cambridge have colleges dedicated to "Corpus Christi" as well as to "Jesus."

HOLY CROSS OR HOLY ROOD

Connected with these is a series of dedications bearing on incidents of the life of Our Lord. Of these the most numerous are the twenty-three dedications to the "*Holy Rood*," and the eighty-three to the "*Holy Cross.*" In our Church Calendar the 14th of September is marked as "Holy Cross Day"; in the Roman Calendar, more precisely as *Exaltatio Crucis*, the "Setting up of the Cross," by way of distinction from the 3rd of May, which is the day when the Cross was discovered, *Inventio Crucis*. The latter date commemorates the discovery at Jerusalem by the Emperor Constantine of three crosses, the former the dedication of a church built over the spot. In later days the Holy Cross was carried off by the Persian conqueror, Chosroes,

---

[1] Charles Browne, *Transactions of S. Paul's Ecclesiological Society*, i. 269.

but was at length recovered by Heraclius, who brought it back and set it up again on its old site in Jerusalem. On its original

Alabaster panel in S. Peter Mancroft, Norwich.

discovery a large slice from it was cut off by the Empress Helena and sent to Rome, where there was built to receive it the famous church of S. Croce in Gerusalemme. In America numerous places bear the name of Vera Cruz because their churches contain fragments of the True Cross; Santa Cruz owes its name to the fact that it was discovered on Holy Cross Day. Among noteworthy dedications are those of Holyrood abbey,[1] Scotland ; S. Cross, Winchester ; Holy Cross abbey at Shrewsbury; Holy Cross and S. Lawrence, Waltham, Essex; and S. Crux, a parish church in the city of York, now demolished.

S. SEPULCHRE

A remarkable group is that of the circular churches dedicated to S. Sepulchre or Holy Sepulchre at the Temple, London, Cambridge, Northampton, and Little Maplestead, Essex. The circular plan of these was an imitation of that of the church of the Holy Sepulchre at Jerusalem with which the Knights Templars and the Knights Hospitallers were closely connected. The demolished Cluniac priory of Thetford, Norfolk, had this dedication. Altogether there are 150 dedications connected directly, and 112 connected indirectly with Our Lord.

THE HOLY GHOST

Two dedications to S. Esperit survive in Warwickshire, Marton, and Wappenbury, and from their form may well have come down from Norman days. North of Basingstoke station may be seen the ruins of the chapel of the Holy Ghost built by Bishop Fox and Lord Sandys ; portions of its famous glass have been removed to the parish church.[2]

[1] Charles Browne, *Ibid.*, 272.
[2] Arnold-Forster, i. 18-36.

CHAPTER II

Memorial, Proprietary, and Personal
Dedications—S. Edward, K.M.—
Celtic Dedications

SETTING aside the above dedications
to the Second and Third Persons in
the Godhead we come to what are,
in a vast majority, dedications to the
saints. Of these three classes may
be distinguished. The first comprises the dedications of "*Memorial
Churches*"; the second what Bishop
Stubbs calls "*Proprietary Dedications*"; the third, which enormously
outnumbers the others, may be styled
"*Personal Dedications.*"

Some of the oldest, if not the
oldest of all, are dedications of those
churches which were built over the
actual tomb of a martyr to commemorate his faithful witness. From
the fourth century onwards such
memorial churches were built in every
land. As soon as the Peace of the
Church, 312 A.D., set the Church at
liberty, churches were built over the
tombs of the martyrs at Rome,
usually above ground, such as the
basilicas of S. Peter and S. Paul
extra muros, sometimes down in the
Catacombs, partially or wholly underground, such as the basilicas of S.
Lorenzo, S. Agnese, S. Clement, and
S. Petronilla. So we in England
built new churches or re-dedicated
old churches to be the memorials of
many a beloved saint, S. Alban, S.
Etheldreda, S. Guthlac, S. Ethelbert,

w. s. w.

S. Edward, K.M.
Westminster.

2

S. Frideswide, S. Cuthbert, S. Chad, S. Edmund, and many another. Perhaps the earliest memorial church is one at Carthage, which S. Augustine tells us was dedicated to S. Cyprian in the place where he suffered martyrdom in the year 258. An example nearer home is that of the boy-King Edward slain at eventide in 979 at the gate of Corfe Castle. He was buried at Wareham; afterwards his remains were transferred to Shaftesbury abbey, where the shrine was so famous that the town was long known as Edwardstow. In the church of Lady S. Mary, Wareham, a low vaulted chapel of curious construction is shown; it is known as S. Edward's Chapel, and is reputed to be a reproduction of the little wooden chapel in which the body of S. Edward, King and Martyr, was deposited after his murder.[1]

A second class comprises those churches which commemorated not the martyr or saint buried within their walls, but the founder of the church. Such a church was not dedicated to the founder by himself, but by his admirers or successors. In many cases we are certain that this was so; e.g., S. Cuthburga founded Wimborne minster and dedicated it to the Blessed Virgin; later on the dedication was changed to " S. Cuthburga." These *Proprietary Dedications* are especially characteristic of the Celtic Church.[2] Indeed, strictly speaking, there were no dedications at all in the Celtic Church. There was a ceremony of consecration—it was exceedingly elaborate— *e.g.*, at Lastingham, where it is described at length by Bede, but the church was not dedicated. All churches founded in any one of S. David's missionary tours were called " David's churches," those founded by S. Teilo were called " Teilo's churches," and so on; but they were not dedicated either to S. David or S. Teilo. Such of these proprietary dedications as survive are naturally of very ancient date. Historically too they

---

[1] On the west front of Wells cathedral he is represented holding in his hand the stirrup cup (broken) given him at the gate of Corfe Castle by his stepmother, on whom he tramples. In Henry the Seventh's chapel, Westminster, is a statue, unfortunately mutilated, of S. Edward, K.M. (9).

[2] The Celtic proprietary dedications stand quite apart from the usual personal dedications, and require detailed and lengthy treatment, for which there is no room in this volume. There are admirable treatises on the subject by Rice Rees, Borlase, Baring-Gould, and others, which are detailed in the Bibliography prefixed to this volume, and to these the reader is referred. It may be taken as generally true, that in this book, as in Miss Arnold-Forster's three volumes, the dedications dealt with do not refer to Wales.

T. P.

S. Edward, K.M.   S. Kenelm.

West Front of Wells Cathedral.

are very important; for by working out the groups of churches so named it may be possible to delimit the district within which the Celtic saint worked.[1]   As has been pointed out above, it is not unusual to find the founder's dedication set aside in favour of a re-dedication to himself.   The process was not always so drastic.   Sometimes the original dedication was retained, but the founder's name was added;   *e.g.*, Lichfield cathedral was dedicated by S. Chad to S. Mary;   Ripon cathedral by S. Wilfrid to S. Peter;   Minster in Sheppey to S. Mary;   but the dedications are now to SS. Mary and Chad, SS. Peter and Wilfrid, and SS. Mary and Sexburga.[2]

Both these classes were quite outnumbered by the *Personal Dedications*.   Of these we may distinguish two classes.   The first has already been dealt with;   it comprises all those churches which are dedicated to the Second Person or the Third Person in the Godhead or to the Holy Trinity: it is a small class. The second class comprises what we may style *Intercessory Dedications*;   that it includes more than ten thousand examples will give some idea of the proportions which the doctrine of intercessory mediation ultimately assumed in the mediæval Church.   At first it seemed to be thought that intercession, to be effectual, should be made at the tomb of the saint whose mediation was desired—the S. Peter, S. Paul, S. Apollinare, or the like—or at any rate within the walls of his memorial church. But only one church in all Christendom contained the body of a S. Peter, a S. Paul, or the like.   Even when the relics of the saints became more widely diffused, there was many a village church in Christendom without even the fragment of a relic of the saints whose aid and mediation it was desired to obtain. This necessitated an extension of the personal dedication.

---

[1] "There can be little doubt that the primitive churches were not dedicated at all in the modern sense ;   in other words, they were not put under the protection of any particular saint or patron.   The earliest churches were named after the person who built them, or from the locality in which they stood, or from some marked characteristic of the building.   If they bore the name of a saint or martyr it was because they were erected over his grave or contained his relics, and thus became in a sense his monument " (Precentor Venables in *Archæological Journal*, xxxviii. 366).

[2] "In most cases," says Mr Kerslake, "the proprietary dedication has been ousted altogether ;   in some it has been allowed to remain as part of a 'compound dedication';   *e.g.*, Crowland is dedicated no longer to the primitive local saint only, but to S. Mary, S. Bartholomew and S. Guthlac.   So also with the dedications of S. Peter and S. Etheldreda at Ely, S. Andrew and S. David at S. David's, S. Teilo and S. Peter at Llandaff."

S. Edmund.

From a painting on rood-screen in Norfolk.

S. Alban.

From the brass of Abbot Delamere, in S. Albans abbey.

S. Olave.

From a rood-screen in Norfolk.

J. H. P.

S. Anthony.

From an illuminated MS.

S. Denis.

From a painting on the rood-screen, Grafton Regis, Northants.

S. Stephen.

From painted glass, Nettlestead church, Kent.

All the mediæval churches of the Roman Rule were placed beneath the protection of some saint, even if the church contained no fragment of him. Of these intercessory dedications in England some 6000 are addressed to Biblical saints, the personages in the Old and New Testaments. Such dedications are obvious and natural ; and being obvious and natural are as a rule not of great interest ; it is when we reach the non-Biblical saints that the real interest of the study of dedications begins. For the present we will take the Biblical and non-Biblical saints together ; and we will arrange them, if we may so say, in order of merit, at any rate in the order of their respective popularity as shown in the dedications of English churches up to the end of the seventeenth century. The following are the respective numbers of English dedications up to that period.

In the following analysis of Miss Arnold-Forster's statistics the dedications include those both of churches and chapelries. Eighteenth and nineteenth century dedications are here, as far as possible, excluded ; they are included in Miss Arnold-Forster's tables ; hence her lists will be found to give larger totals than are set out here. A few eighteenth and nineteenth century examples may have crept in under the heading of compound or alternative dedications, or dedications of demolished churches, but they will not be numerous : nevertheless it should be remembered that the totals here given may be slightly overstated. And it must be borne in mind, that whatever pains be taken, results can only be approximately correct : there is a very large percentage of dedications of doubtful authenticity as well as many that are still unknown. A very large number of chapels were built in the fifteenth and sixteenth century at the request of hamlets far from a parish church, the rights of baptism and burial, however, being reserved to the mother church. At the Reformation the vast majority of these chapels perished, and even when they are known to have existed or exist still, it is seldom that the dedication can be ascertained. The dedications of chapels inside churches, e.g., of S. Erasmus in Westminster abbey, are *not* included in the statistics. Where there is a compound dedication, e.g., to SS. Peter and Paul, each saint is credited with one dedication. If there are two or more dedications, and it cannot be ascertained which is the correct one, each saint is credited with one ; e.g., if some accounts give S. Mary and others S. Sampson as the patron saint of a particular church, one dedication is credited to S. Mary and one to S. Sampson. Dedications are included of churches which have perished but of which documentary evidence exists. The

S. Erasmus.

From painted glass, San-
dringham church, Norfolk.

S. Augustine of Hippo.

From an illustrated MS.

S. Cornelius.

From a Flemish MS.

J. H. P.

S. Clement.

From the Lubeck *Passionale.*

S. Leonard.

From stained glass, San-
dringham church,
Norfolk.

S. Hubert.

From a painting by
Wilhem.

table below does not stop at the Reformation, but includes
dedications up to the end of the seventeenth century; very
few churches, however, were built between the Reformation and
the Restoration, and not many between 1660 and 1700. So
the results therefore may be taken as a view almost wholly
of Pre-Reformation dedications.

D. W.

S. John Evangelist.
Westminster.

CHAPTER III

LIST OF SAINTS, WITH NUMBER OF DEDICATIONS, ARRANGED IN ORDER OF POPULARITY

1.	The Blessed Virgin	2,335
2.	All Saints, 1,217 or All Hallows, 38	1,255
3.	S. Peter, 1,129 S. Peter *ad vincula*, 11	1,140
4.	S. Michael or S. Michael and All Angels - -	687
5.	S. Andrew - -	637
6.	S. John Baptist -	500
7.	S. Nicholas - -	437
8.	S. James the Elder	414
9.	S. Paul - -	326
10.	Holy Trinity -	297
11.	S. Margaret - -	261
12.	S. Lawrence - -	239
13.	S. Mary Magdalene	187
14.	S. John, Apostle and Evangelist -	181
15.	S. Leonard - -	177
16.	S. Martin - -	173
17.	S. Bartholomew -	165
18.	S. Giles - -	162
19.	S. Helena - -	135
20.	S. George - -	126
21.	Holy Cross or Holy Rood - -	106
22.	S. Thomas of Canterbury - -	80
23.	S. Cuthbert - -	72
24.	S. Oswald - -	67
25.	S. Botolph - -	64
26.	S. Catherine - -	62
27.	S. Edmund - -	61
28.	S. Swithin - -	58
29.	S. Wilfrid - -	48

30.	S. Stephen - -	46
31.	S. Thomas the Apostle - -	46
32.	S. Anne - -	41
33.	S. Clement - -	41
34.	S. Denys or Dionysus - - -	41
35.	Our Lord - -	38
36.	S. Chad - -	33
37.	S. Matthew - -	33
38.	S. Gregory - -	32
39.	S. Philip - -	31
40.	S. Augustine of Canterbury -	30
41.	S. Luke - -	28
42.	S. James the Less -	26
43.	S. David, Wales -	23
44.	S. Faith - -	23
45.	S. Benedict of Cassino - - -	20
46.	S. Dunstan - -	20
47.	S. Bridget or Bride	19
48.	S. Edward the Confessor - -	17
49.	S. Ethelbert - -	16
50.	S. Edith of Polesworth - -	15
51.	S. German - -	15
52.	S. Hilda - -	15
53.	S. Petrox - -	14
54.	S. Barnabas - -	13
55.	S. Olave or Olaf -	13
56.	S. Etheldreda -	12
57.	S. Werburga - -	12
58.	S. Alban - -	11
59.	S. Pancras of Taormina - -	10

3

S. Dorothea.

From a MS. in the
Bodleian Library.

S. Clare.

From the Spanish Gallery
in the Louvre.

S. Faith.

From a brass in S. Lawrence
church, Norwich.

J. H. P.

S. Frideswide.

From Cardinal Wolsey's *Evangelisterium* in the
library of Magdalen College, Oxford.

S. Martha.

From a painting at
Florence.

Nine Dedications

60. S. Christopher
61. S. Cyril
62. S. Guthlac
63. S. Jude

64. S. Kenelm
65. S. Kentigern or Mungo
66. S. Mildred
67. S. Teilo

Eight Dedications

68. S. Cadoc
69. S. Columba
70. S. Maurice

71. S. Patrick
72. S. Rumbald

Seven Dedications

73. S. John of Beverley

74. S. Julian Hospitaller

Six Dedications

75. S. Dubricius
76. S. Eadburga
77. S. Felix
78. S. Gabriel
79. S. Mark
80. S. Pancras of Rome

81. S. Remigius or Rémi
82. S. Samson of Dol
83. S. Vincent
84. S. Winifred
85. S. Anthony the Great
86. S. Sepulchre

Five Dedications

87. S. Agnes
88. S. Alphege
89. S. Blaise
90. King Charles Martyr
91. Holy Innocents
92. S. Julitta
93. S. Kebi

94. S. Leger
95. S. Milburga
96. S. Paulinus
97. S. Piran
98. S. Radegund
99. S. Ebba

Four Dedications

100. S. Agatha
101. S. Aldhelm
102. S. Alkmund
103. All Souls
104. S. Cecilia
105. S. Godwald
106. S. Hybald

107. S. Neot
108. S. Ninian
109. S. Nun or Nonna
110. S. Osyth or Sitha
111. S. Owen or Ouen
112. S. Rumon
113. Wynwalloe or Wonnow

S. Blaise.

From painted glass, Christ Church
cathedral, Oxford.

S. Agatha.

From painted glass, Winchester
cathedral.

J. H. P.

S. Lawrence.

From painted glass, Nettlestead
church, Kent.

S. Etheldreda.

From Porter's *Lives of the
Saints.*

Three Dedications

114. Holy Spirit or Holy Ghost
115. S. Bega or Bees
116. S. Constantine of Cornwall
117. S. Cosmas
118. S. Damian
119. S. Edith of Wilton
120. S. Erme
121. S. Eustachius
122. S. Hilary of Poitiers
123. Martyrs or Holy Martyrs
124. S. Ives
125. S. Magnus
126. S. Melan
127. S. Menaacus
128. S. Meugan
129. S. Nectan
130. S. Osmond
131. S. Quiricus or Cyril
132. S. Senan
133. S. Simphorian
134. S. Theobald
135. S. Wenn or Gwen
136. S. Wyston or Winston or Wistan

Two Dedications

137. S. Advent or Dwynwen
138. S. Aldate or Eldad
139. S. Alkelda
140. S. Aroan or Arvans
141. S. Basil
142. S. Bertoline or Bertram
143. S. Brandan or Brendon
144. S. Breock or Brioc
145. S. Candida or Whyte
146. S. Clare
147. S. Cleodicus or Clydog
148. S. Cornelius
149. S. Crida or Creed or Sancreed
150. S. Deiniol or Deinst
151. S. Eanswith
152. S. Egwin
153. S. Elphin or Elgin
154. S. Erth or Herygh or Urith
155. S. Everilda or Emeldis
156. S. Evilla or Eval or Noell or Uvell
157. S. Firmin
158. S. Frideswide
159. S. Genesius or Genewys or Gennys
160. S. Genevieve
161. S. Hippolytus
162. S. Hubert
163. S. Just
164. S. Lambert
165. S. Lucy
166. S. Mabena or Mabyn
167. S. Melorius or Melor
168. S. Mewan or Mevan
169. S. Paternus or Padarn
170. S. Sebastian
171. S. Sidwell or Sativola
172. S. Tesiliah or Tyssilio
173. S. Tewrdic or Tewdwr or Theodoric
174. S. Ursula
175. S. Vedast
176. S. Vigor
177. S. Wulfram

S. Barbara.

From a MS. in the Bodleian
Library.

S. Lucy.

From a painting in the Spanish
Gallery in the Louvre.

J. H. P.

S. Agnes.

From painted glass.

S. Catherine

From stained glass, West Wickham
church, Kent.

One Dedication

180. S. Acca
181. S. Adeline
182. S. Aidan
183. S. Aldwyn
184. S. Allen
185. S. Arilda
186. S. Aubyn or Albinus
187. S. Austell or Hawstyl
188. S. Barbara
189. S. Barrog
190. S. Bartholomew of Farne
191. S. Brannoc
192. S. Branwallader
193. S. Breaca
194. S. Brevita
195. S. Briavel
196. S. Britius or Brice
197. S. Bruard or Breward
198. S. Buriena
199. S. Cadwaladr
200. S. Calixtus
201. S. Carantoc or Cairnech
202. S. Cassyon
203. S. Clarus or Clair or Cleer
204. S. Clether
205. S. Collen
206. S. Congar
207. S. Corentin
208. S. Crewenne
209. S. Cuthburga
210. S. Cyprian
211. S. Day or Dye
212. S. Decuman
213. S. Dilpe
214. S. Dinabo
215. S. Dingat
216. S. Disen or Disibod
217. S. Dochoe
218. S. Dominic
219. S. Eadnor
220. S. Eata
221. S. Edwin, King

222. S. Edwould
223. S. Egelwine
224. S. Elidius
225. S. Eloy or Eligius
226. S. Enoder
227. S. Enodoc or Wenedocus
228. S. Erney
229. S. Ethelburga of Barking
230. S. Ethelwald or Adelwold
231. S. Fabian
232. S. Felicitas
233. S. Feock
234. S. Fimbarries or Finbar
235. Four Crowned Martyrs (Quattuor Coronati)
236. S. Francis of Assisi
237. S. Geraint or Gerrans
238. S. Germoe
239. S. Gluvius
240. S. Gomonda
241. S. Goran or Guron
242. S. Goven
243. S. Gwithian or Gothian
244. S. Hardulph
245. Holy Angels
246. S. Hugh of Lincoln
247. S. Hydroc
248. S. Illogan
249. S. Illtyd
250. S. Ive or Ivo
251. S. Jerome
252. S. John de Sepulchre
253. S. Joseph of Arimathea
254. S. Julian or Juliana
255. S. Kew
256. S. Keyna or Kayne or Ceinwen
257. S. Kingsmark or Cynfarch
258. S. Kuet or Knuet
259. Queen Kyneburga
260. Abbess Kyneburga

S. Giles.

From painted glass, Sandringham
church, Norfolk.

S. Wilfrid.

From *Masculi Encomia
Cœlituum.*

J. H. P.

S. Ambrose.

From Callot's *Images.*

S. Veronica.

From a MS. in the Bodleian Library.

261. S. Laud or Lo
262. S. Levan
263. S. Lioba
264. S. Lucian
265. S. Mapley
266. S. Marcellina
267. S. Marvenne or Mere-
    wenna
268. S. Materiana
269. S. Matthias
270. S. Mawes or Mauditus
271. Mawnanus or Mawnan
272. S. Maxentius
273. S. Medardus or Medard
274. S. Menefrida or Minver
275. S. Meran or Merryn
276. S. Meriadoc
277. S. Merther
278. S. Metherian
279. S. Mewbred
280. S. Modwen or Modwenna
281. S. Moran or Maruan
282. S. Morwenna
283. S. Onslow or Onolaus
284. S. Pandiana
285. S. Pega
286. S. Petronilla
287. S. Pinnock
288. S. Protus or Pratt
289. S. Probus
290. S. Protasius
291. S. Quintin or Quentin
292. S. Ricarius or Riquier
293. S. Richard of Chichester
    or de Wych

294. S. Robert of Knares-
    borough
295. S. Ruthin
296. S. Salvy
297. S. Samson of York
298. S. Sexburga
299. S. Silin
300. S. Silvester
301. S. Sithney
302. S. Stedian
303. S. Stithian
304. S. Tallan
305. S. Teath or Tetha
306. S. Teggvyddy or Tegg-
    wedd
307. S. Torney
308. S. Tudy
309. S. Twinnock
310. S. Uny or Ewny
311. S. Veep
312. S. Walstan of Bawburgh
313. S. Wandregisilus
314. S. Welvela
315. S. Wendreda
316. S. Wendron or Gwendron
317. S. Wennap
318. S. Weonard
319. S. William of Norwich
320. S. Winnow
321. S. Withburga
322. S. Wolfrida or Wilfreda
323. S. Wolstan or Wulstan
324. S. Woolos
325. S. Wynner or Gwinear or
    Fingar

What must strike every one in this analysis, especially in the lists of dedications which occur only once or twice, is the extraordinary number of saints whom nobody has ever heard of. These are nearly all from Celtic districts, especially from Cornwall, or from districts adjacent to Cornwall and Wales.[1] They go back to the early days of Christianity in this country ; nearly

---

[1] It may be repeated that the above list includes dedications in England including Cornwall, but not those in Wales.

4

S. Guthlac.

From a MS. in the
Cottonian Library.

S. Dunstan.

From painted glass in a window of the
Bodleian Library.

J. H. P.

S. Oswald.

From the Lubeck *Passionale*.

S. Nicholas.

From a MS. in the Bodleian
Library.

all of them did their work before Augustine from the South and Aidan from the North set forth to evangelise Anglo-Saxon England. The vast majority of these Celtic saints, as the table shows, have only one or two dedications to their credit. They perhaps were saints in the opinion of their own parish, and in the opinion of the next parish; but their reputation extended little further. The fact is, they were not saints at all at the outset; but merely missioners who first evangelised the village, or persons who built the first humble Christian church of wattle or wood. Time rolled on; in many cases the whole story of the foundation of the church had long been forgotten. Finally, on the analogy of churches dedicated to a S. Andrew, a S. Leonard, a S. Michael, it was concluded that the ancient missioner or church-builder whose name clung to his church was himself a saint also.

W. M. D.

The Virgin and Child.
S. Lawrence, Ludlow.

CHAPTER IV

List of Biblical Saints, with Number of Dedications, arranged in Order of Popularity—The Blessed Virgin—S. Peter—S. Michael—S. Andrew—S. John Baptist—S. James the Greater—S. Paul—S. Mary Magdalene—S. John the Evangelist—S. Stephen—S. Thomas the Apostle—S. Anne—S. James the Less—All Souls—All Saints—S. Petronilla.

[S. G.

The Annunciation.   Bench end at Warkworth.

WE may now take out the personages in the gospel story, and arrange them in the order of their popularity as shown by the dedications. A very remarkable order it is!

BIBLICAL SAINTS

1. The Blessed Virgin 2,335
2. S. Peter - - 1,140
3. S. Michael - - 687
4. S. Andrew - - 637
5. S. John Baptist - 500
6. S. James the Elder 414
7. S. Paul - - - 326
8. S. Mary Magdalene 187
9. S. John the Apostle 181
10. S. Bartholomew - 165
11. S. Stephen - - 46
12. S. Thomas the
Apostle - - 46
13. S. Anne - - 41
14. S. Matthew - - 33
15. S. Philip - - 31
16. S. Luke - - 28
17. S. James the Less - 26
18. S. Barnabas - - 13
19. S. Jude - - 9
20. S. Gabriel - - 6
21. S. Mark - - 6
22. The Holy Innocents 5
23. S. Joseph of Ari-
mathea 1
24. S. Matthias - - 1
25. S. Petronilla - - 1

F. H. C.

The Blessed Virgin
(2,335 Dedications)

The Annunciation.
Wells Cathedral.

The position of this first name explains itself. History is crowded with examples of woman's appeals for man. And to whom should God listen so readily as to Our Lady, His Mother on earth, whom mediæval art loved to represent as crowned by her Son, and seated beside Him on her throne, ever ready

The Annunciation.   Gresford, Denbigh.

and able to make intercession to Him for all who brought their
supplications to her? At first indeed this dedication is not
one of the most common. In Bede's list there are but three
dedications to Our Lady; those to SS. Peter and Paul out-
number all the rest put together. But in the twelfth century,
under the influence of S. Bernard and Pope Innocent the Third
(1198-1216), a great impulse of increased veneration for the
Blessed Virgin was felt through Western Christendom. At the
end of the twelfth and throughout the following century Lady
chapels were built, or were rebuilt on a larger scale, and hundreds
of parish churches set apart one of their altars to Our Lady.
From this time her dedications continually increased in number;
even Henry VIII. added to them, by re-dedicating to "Christ
and the Blessed Virgin Mary" the cathedrals of Chester, Durham,
and Rochester. Many were the forms in which love and
reverence for the Mother of God found expression.[1] Sometimes
the dedication was to "S. Mary" or to "S. Mary the Virgin,"
sometimes to the "Blessed Virgin" or the "Blessed Virgin
Mary"; twice to "Our Lady"; twice to "Our Lady of Pity";
once to "S. Mary of Charity"; once to "S. Mary de Grace";
once to "Lady S. Mary"; once to our "Lady of Sorrows";[2]
once to the "Mother of God." Sometimes there were several
churches in one town with this dedication; to distinguish these
we get such curious forms as "S. Mary the Great," "S. Mary
the More," or "S. Mary le More," "S. Mary Senior"; and again
"S. Mary the Less," and "S. Mary Junior."

To make up the total of 2,335, the dedications have to be
added which commemorate the festivals of the Blessed Virgin.
"Lady Day," March 25th, was observed as the festival of the
Annunciation as far back as the fifth century. It is the more
strange then that there is only one example of a dedication to
the "Annunciation." There is but one also to the "Purifica-
tion," one to the "Salutation," i.e., the "Visitation," and one
to the "Conception." There are twelve dedications to the
"Nativity," which was observed as a feast in the fifth century.
August the 15th, the feast of the Assumption, is still a great
harvest holiday on the Continent. It was believed that the

---

[1] In the scene of the Annunciation much prominence is usually given to
the archangel Gabriel, who frequently holds a scroll with the salutation *Ave
Maria, gratia plena, benedicta tu in mulieribus et benedictus fructus ventris
tui* (30). In the Wells Annunciation, the treatment of which recurs in
alabaster in the British Museum, Gabriel is a tiny angel (29). The lily is
nearly always present.

[2] Her symbol—a heart pierced with a sword—appears on a stall end in
Wensley church, Yorkshire.—F. E. H.

E. K. P.

Assumption of the Blessed Virgin.
Speke Chantry, Exeter Cathedral.

Blessed Virgin did not die a natural
death, but was "taken up" to heaven
by her Son. There seem to be thirteen
dedications to "The Assumption of the
Virgin Mary," or to "Our Lady of
Assumption," including Salisbury cathedral.[1]

S. Peter (1,140 Dedications)

The frequency of this dedication is
also natural. First, there was the great
Roman influence, asserting the supremacy of S. Peter among the apostles.
Secondly, there is the feeling that turned
the scale against the Celtic Church in
the Synod at Whitby, when the authority
of S. Columba paled before that of the
champion of the Roman party, the
Prince of the Apostles, to whom Our
Lord Himself promised the keys of
heaven. "If Peter is the doorkeeper,"
said King Oswy, "I will in all things
obey his decrees, lest when I come to
the gates of the kingdom of heaven,
there be none to open them." Dedications to S. Peter are both numerous
and ancient. York minster was dedicated to S. Peter early in the seventh
century; Peterborough abbey not long
after. Ely, Exeter, Gloucester, Peterborough, Ripon, Winchester, and York
cathedrals all have, or once had, dedications to S. Peter.[2] As for the abbey
of S. Peter, Westminster, when King
Sebert of Essex built the first church in
the seventh century on Thorney isle,
a fisherman on the Lambeth marsh late
one wintry eve saw—

"A strange wayfarer coming to his side
Who bade him loose his boat and fix his oar,
And row him straightway to the further
    shore."

S. Peter.
Ranworth Rood-screen.

---

[1] Arnold-Forster, 41-50.   [2] Ibid., 51-55.

H. P.

S. Peter.
West Front of Peterborough Cathedral.

The stranger lands where " The Minster's outlined mass rose dim from the morass."

> " Lo, on a sudden all the pile is bright ;
> Nave, choir, and transept glorified with light ;
> While tongues of fire on quoin and carving play,
> And heavenly odours fair
> Come streaming with the floods of glory in,
> And carols float along the happy air."

It was S. Peter come to consecrate his own church.

C. F. N.

S. Michael weighing Souls.
Wall painting at South Leigh, Oxon.

When the Empress Eudocia visited Jerusalem, she was presented with the two chains with which S. Peter was bound. One she sent to Constantinople, where a church was built for it ; the other to Rome, where there is still an important church, *S. Peter ad vincula*, on the same site. From this latter chain the pope at times took filings to be presented as relics ; they were usually enclosed in a golden key ; such was the origin of the prison church of S. Peter *ad vincula* in the Tower of London, where lie Anne Boleyn and many others.[1]   This dedication occurs in England about eleven times.   In the vaulted chancel of S. Peter-in-the-East, Oxford, the diagonal ribs are carved with a chain-pattern ; the original dedication therefore may have been " S. Peter *ad vincula.*"   The collect for Lammas Day, *i.e.*, " loaf-mass day," August 1st, in the Sarum Manual, " Benedictio novorum fructuum," runs, " O God, Who deliveredst blessed Peter the Apostle from his chains, and set him, untouched, at liberty ; deliver us, we beseech Thee, from the bonds of our sins, and mercifully protect us from all evil."

S. Michael (687 Dedications)

The great archangel is only mentioned in the Bible five times,[2] but dedications to him either as " S. Michael " or " S. Michael and All Angels," are extraordinarily common.   He was especially the protector of high places, as one sees at S. Michael's Mount, Cornwall, facing Mt. S. Michael, Normandy, S. Michael's chapel at Le Puy, perched on the stump of an old volcano, and Skelig Michel on the west coast of Ireland. On the summit of Brent Tor, in the middle of Dartmoor, is a church dedicated to S. Michael, where the custom used to be to commence service with the Absolution, the penance of climbing up so steep a hill being considered as equivalent to the recital of the Confession.[3]

This chapel in many churches was placed in a loft, *e.g.*, over a porch ; at Christ Church, Hampshire, it occupies the whole space between the vault and roof of the Lady chapel, where it retains the name of S. Michael's loft.   In the most common representation in which the saint tramples down a devil, or a devil in the shape of a dragon, the symbolism is that of the final victory of the principle of Good over that of Evil, which is to

[1] Charles Browne, *Transactions of St Paul's Ecclesiological Society*, 282.
[2] But there is a host of passages in which the commentators identified S. Michael with persons not mentioned by name in the Biblical narrative.
[3] Charles Browne, *Ibid.*, 279.

W. D.

S. Michael.
Ranworth Rood-screen.

be found everywhere in ancient Egyptian art, and indeed in all religious art.

The battling of S. Michael and the dragon is taken from Revelation xii. 7 :—

"And there was war in heaven : Michael and his angels fought against the dragon ; and the dragon fought and his angels, and prevailed not ; neither was their place found any more in heaven. And the great dragon was cast out, that old serpent called the Devil and Satan, which deceiveth the whole world : he was cast out into the earth, and his angels were cast out with him."

Secondly, S. Michael is the leader of the Church Militant in heaven, and so the protector and champion of the Church Militant on earth. Thirdly, he has succeeded to the functions of the pagan Hermes or Mercury, who is himself derivative from Egyptian art ; hence he is represented with a pair of scales, in which he is weighing the souls of the departed, and which often a little imp is trying to pull down ; e.g., on the grille of Henry the Seventh's monument at Westminster and in a wall painting at South Leigh, Oxfordshire (35).

What especially distinguishes him is a series of apparitions, the first at Colossæ in Phrygia ; this at once led to a special cult in the Eastern Church, and early in the fourth century the Emperor Constantine built and dedicated to him a magnificent church in Constantinople. In the West also there were famous apparitions of S. Michael. In the fifth century he appeared in a high place, viz., on the summit of Mount Gargano in Apulia, where he revealed a cave-church with three altars, and a spring of pure water which was sovran against diseases. In the next century there was a great plague in Rome, and S. Gregory, afterwards pope, for three days headed a procession through the streets, singing what were afterwards known as the Great Litanies. On the third day, when opposite the Mole or Mausoleum of Hadrian, Gregory beheld the archangel alight upon the Mole, sheathing a bloody sword, and the plague was stayed. In the ninth century a chapel dedicated to S. Michael was built on the Mole : *Ecclesia Sancti Angeli usque ad coelos*, and ever since the Mole of Hadrian has been known as the Castle of Sant' Angelo. In modern times a bronze statue has been placed on the summit of the castle, the work of a Flemish sculptor ; " not beyond criticism ; but with its vast wings poised in air, and seen against the deep blue sky of Rome or lighted up by a golden sunset, to me ever like what it was intended to represent—a

vision."[1] A fourth legend, which is but a variant of that of
Mount Gargano, describes an appearance of S. Michael to a
Bishop of Avranches, which led to the building of a church on
the lofty rock opposite Pontorson ; this church developed in the
twelfth century into one of the greatest Romanesque abbey
churches in Normandy. Dedications to S. Michael occur at all
periods, but many are of great antiquity ; it is remarkable also

D. W.

The Blessed Virgin and S. Michael.
Westminster.

that they are peculiarly common in Celtic districts and in the
North of England. No saint is more frequently depicted, for,
being a fighter, and clad in armour and vanquishing a dragon,
he was admirably adapted for pictorial representation, whether
in stained glass, where the coils of a great ruby dragon told
with great effect, or on bench ends, as at Haverfordwest, or
on misericords, as in Norwich cathedral. Moreover, the joint

[1] Mrs Jameson's *Sacred and Legendary Art*, i. 98. The apparitions of
S. Michael are given at length in the *Golden Legend*.

S. Andrew.
Ranworth Rood-screen.

dedication gave recognition to the deep-seated mediæval belief in the ministry of angels. On S. Michael's Day, 29th September, the English Church still prays God "mercifully to grant that, as Thy holy Angels always do Thee service in heaven, so by Thy appointment they may defend and succour us on earth." The angelic host, moreover, were peculiarly adaptable for pictorial treatment; angels and cherubim and seraphim in the windows abode in the trefoils and quatrefoils of the tracery bars, and perched on every hammer-beam of the roofs.[1] It is to be noted that S. Michael's Day is properly the 8th of May; Michaelmas Day, 29th September, is the anniversary of the church built in honour of S. Michael on Mount Gargano.[2]

S. Andrew (637 Dedications)

It is not easy to see why S. Andrew should be such a favourite, surpassing in popularity even S. James and S. John and S. Paul. Fuller says: "I read at the Transfiguration that Peter, James and John were admitted to behold Christ, but Andrew was excluded. So

[1] See illustrations of the roofs of Woolpit, Knapton, Fressingfield, East Stonham, etc., in the writer's *Introduction to English Church Architecture.*

[2] At South Leigh (35) on the right are seen little demons trying to weigh down the scales, and to plunge the souls of the wicked into hell mouth which yawns below. On the left a soul in the scales obtains the intercession and help of Our Lady, who holds a rosary in her left hand. At Ranworth, S. Michael with uplifted sword is about to slay the dragon on which he stands (37). S. Michael and the dragon are also represented on the rood-screen at Ashton, Devon (213).

again at the reviving of the daughter of the ruler of the synagogue these three were let in and Andrew shut out. Lastly, in the Agony in Gethsemane the aforesaid three were called to be witnesses thereof, and still Andrew left behind." On the other hand, S. Andrew was the Protoclete, the first called of the apostles. And two of the very earliest and most important churches in the history of Anglo-Saxon Christianity, Rochester cathedral and Hexham abbey, were and are still dedicated to S. Andrew. S. Augustine of Canterbury had come on his mission from the monastery of S. Andrew on the Cælian Hill at Rome, and he dedicated Rochester cathedral to S. Andrew. And when S. Wilfrid went to Rome, he prepared himself in " S. Andrew's oratory " for his mission to unify English Christianity; and when he built his church at Hexham, of which the crypt and the foundations of the apse still exist, he dedicated it to S. Andrew. Of Scotland S. Andrew is the patron saint, and thus his cross saltire finds its way into the Union Jack. As we shall see, the popularity of S. Andrew is mainly of literary origin, his mission labours having been written up in most amazing fashion.

S. John Baptist (500 Dedications)

John the Baptist was indeed "a burning and a shining light " to our forefathers; in popularity he surpassed all the apostles and evangelists except Peter and Andrew. The presumption therefore is that when a church is anciently dedicated to " S. John," it is the Baptist, not the apostle, who is to be credited with it. The chief festivals of S. John the Baptist are at midsummer, S. John's Eve and S. John's Day, which have superseded a primeval solar feast. But some villages still commemorate in their feast on 29th August the " Decollation of S. John Baptist." The Baptist was the patron of the Knights Hospitallers, whose function was to guard the Holy Sepulchre at Jerusalem, and to provide convoy and protection for pilgrims to and from the Holy Land. The plan of their church at Little Maplestead, Essex, with circular nave surrounded by an aisle, is a repeat of that of the mother church in Jerusalem, and the church is dedicated to S. John of Jerusalem. For scores of years the gateway of S. John, Clerkenwell, appeared on the outer cover of the *Gentleman's Magazine*; here are still the headquarters of the revived order of S. John of Jerusalem. It is very remarkable that the Baptist should have had so vast a popularity. Unlike S. Andrew, S. Nicholas, S. Margaret, and scores of others, his story had not been and could not be "written up"; all there was of it is told shortly but completely in the gospels, and received subsequently little literary embellishment. But this short gospel story was admirably adapted for pictorial embellishment (vi). There was the robe of camel hair— the baptism in the river—Herod's feast—the dance or rather tumbling—the decollation of the Baptist—the bringing of the head in a charger. Moreover, the Baptist had the merit of distinctiveness. To put a book in the hand of S. John

D. W.

The Baptist and S. John.

Westminster.

Evangelist told little; there was a crowd of saints who had written gospels, epistles, theological treatises. But the Baptist's vestment of camel's hair identified him at once to everybody. Again, the commemoration of his nativity on 24th June connected him with one of the very greatest festivals of the Pre-Christian world. And on the Christian side he was connected above all other saints with the great sacrament of Baptism, which in the mediæval world still vied to some extent with the sanctity of the Lord's Supper. And so he is represented hundreds and thousands of times in missals, wall paintings, mosaics, tapestry, bench ends, statuettes, stained glass; his image frequently appeared in Early Christian baptisteries, but, strange to say, very seldom indeed on mediæval fonts, even when, as in the Seven Sacrament fonts of East Anglia,[1] the font received most elaborate sculptural treatment. In the Italian Renaissance, on the other hand, the Baptist obtained charming recognition, as a small figure in white marble standing on the edge of the font. The Baptist is one of the very few who has two saint's days in the Calendar; his great festival, S. John's Day, preceded by S. John's Eve, being at midsummer on 24th June; while his death is commemorated on 29th August.

D. W.
S. James the Greater.
Westminster.

S. James the Greater (414 Dedications)

It was not the simplicity of the Bible story and of the words of Eusebius that gave S. James his great popularity, but the legendary stories, especially that of the battle when he rode with Christian warriors of Spain and wrought death and defeat on the Moors. So he became the patron saint of Spain, and the Spanish Canterbury bears his name, " Santiago," — Sant Iago, S. James. This church was dedicated under the title of S. James the Apostle, " San Giacomo Apostolo," which in time, being shortened to " Compostella," became so unintelligible that the Spanish term for S. James or Giacomo was added, giving the city its present reduplicated title of Santiago de Compostella.

The form "James" appears to be Celtic, and may have come to us through the Scotch kings, who were styled Hamish, i.e., James. The Syriac form, however, was Yacoub, and this was retained in the Latin and Greek forms of Jacobus, or Jacob. Here and there the ancient and correct form is retained in

---

[1] See the writer's Fonts and Font Covers for illustrations and descriptions of these, pp. 257-264.

D. W.

S. John Evangelist.   S. James the Greater.
Henry the Seventh's Chapel, Westminster.

dedications ; *e.g.*, in the twelfth-century church of SS. Philip and Jacob at Bristol.

S. James was *par excellence* the patron of pilgrims, and being usually represented in pilgrim dress, with a scalloped shell fastened to his hat, and a long staff and a wallet, has the merit of being easily recognisable. As all the world and his wife went pilgriming in the thirteenth, fourteenth and fifteenth centuries, representations of S. James and dedications in his honour continually increased in vogue. It is not possible to state with precision how many dedications he has ; for some may belong to S. James the Less, and vice versa.[1]

S. Paul (326 Dedications)

Most striking of all is the comparatively low position of S. Paul ; modern Christendom would perhaps put him at the top of the list. Even the figures given fail to represent the unpopularity of this dedication. For of the 326 dedications, no less than 283 are "double dedications," viz., to " S. Peter and S. Paul." If we deduct those dedications in which S. Paul is indebted for his position mainly to the popularity of S. Peter, the total is actually reduced to 43. And some, even of the 43, are suspect ; in some cases they are certainly dedications to S. Pol de Leon, or to Pawl Hen, or to Paulinus. Among the earliest are

[1] In a statue at Westminster S. James has a staff and wallet; on his hat is a scallop shell (44). There is a similar representation on the grille of Henry the Seventh's tomb (43).

S. Paul.
Ranworth Rood-screen.

D. W.

S. Martha or S. Elizabeth.   S. Mary Magdalene.
Henry the Seventh's Chapel, Westminster.

the dedications of S. Paul's cathedral, London, and that of
Jarrow. Benedic Biscop had dedicated Monkwearmouth to
S. Peter; so he dedicated Jarrow, which he built later, to S.
Paul. Similarly S. Peter's is the West Minster, and S. Paul's the
East Minster of London. The two saints are commemorated
together on 29th June, and both, if Eusebius' statements are
warranted, suffered martyrdom together on the same day.

D. W.

SS. Mary Magdalene and Barbara.

Westminster.

S. Paul is represented as tall, broad-shouldered, dignified, with a
bald forehead and a long beard, and holding point downward
before him the long sword by which he was decapitated.[1]

[1] On the Ranworth screen S. Paul is represented with the sword pointing
upward : usually it points downward. In Exeter cathedral, on the vault of
S. Paul's chapel and on the tomb of Bishop Marshall, S. Paul holds the
sword upwards by the point : this is said to represent "the sword of the
spirit which is the word of God" and not the sword of martyrdom
—E. K. P.

D. AND P.

Female Saint and S. Mary Magdalene.
West Front of Wells Cathedral.

S. Mary Magdalene (187 Dedications)

The life-story of S. Mary Magdalene has been enriched by confounding her first with Mary of Bethany, secondly with " the woman that was a sinner," thus making her to be a woman of evil life, an assertion for which there is not a grain of evidence. Nevertheless our Christian forefathers believed it, and practically everybody believes it nowadays. Not only were 187 churches and chapelries dedicated to her, but she has a college at Oxford and another at Cambridge. Probably some of her dedications have been shortened to " S. Mary," and have been transferred to Our Lady. S. Mary Magdalene is indebted almost wholly for her renown to the pathetic episode in the gospel wrongly attributed to her.[1] Whether attributed wrongly or not, no words or act of Christ touched our fathers more deeply than this instance of loving-kindness to a sinner. We shall hear it echoed in the forgiveness, though but for one day each year, of Judas Iscariot, and in the words of God to Satan pleading against the harshness of his penalty.[2] It was not till much later days that the celebrated legend grew up of the oarless boat that brought Lazarus and Martha and S. Mary Magdalene and the two Maries to Provence, where the fame of the two Maries has quite eclipsed that of the others.[3]

S. John, Apostle and Evangelist (181 Dedications)

We should have expected more than 181 dedications to one who was at once the " beloved disciple " and the most spiritual of the evangelists. Perhaps King John contributed to make the name less popular both as a Christian name (it was largely superseded by " William ") and as a dedication name. Beverley minster is dedicated to S. John; not to S. John of Beverley, as is often said, but to S. John Evangelist, a church of whom the archbishop found there when he retired to Beverley in the seventh century. Another John is S. John of Bridlington : to him also there may be dedications now appropriated to S. John Evangelist (199).

[1] In her statue, which is 6 feet 1½ inches high, on the west front of Wells cathedral, she holds a box of ointment in her hand, and wears a flat cap and chin band (48). At Westminster she is shown with flowing locks ; she is opening the lid of the box of precious ointment (46). On the tomb of Henry the Seventh she has flowing locks and holds the vase in her left hand (47). She is also represented, with S. Barbara, on a bench end at Coombe-in-Teignhead, Devon (118).

[2] Page 99.   [3] Page 145.

M. L.

S. John Evangelist.
All Saints', York.

S. John Evangelist is well commemorated in the Calendar,
for he has a red-letter day and a black-letter day. The latter
falls on 6th May under the name of "S. John *ante portam
Latinam*," and keeps alive the tradition found in Jerome and
Tertullian that on that day the saint was thrown into a cauldron
of boiling oil before the Latin gate at Rome and emerged

S. S.

S. John *ante port. Lat.*

Misericord in Lincoln Minster.

unharmed. In the east window of the south aisle of Lincoln
minster is a figure of S. John immersed by order of the Emperor
Domitian in a cauldron of oil, placed over a furnace, the flames
of which are fed by two figures, one on either side, by means
of poles.[1] On a misericord in Lincoln minster the saint
(mutilated) stands in a cauldron, round which are faggots which
have just been lighted ; a man on the left blows up the fire with

[1] Nelson's *Painted Glass*, 141,

M. L.

Mary Cleopas and her family.
Holy Trinity, Goodramgate, York.

W. S. W.

S. John Evangelist.

Westminster.

W. S. W.

S. Stephen.

Westminster.

a bellows.[1]   Few, if any, village feasts are kept on 6th May, but on that day is held the annual commemoration of benefactors at S. John's College, Cambridge.   Many a church now dedicated to the Evangelist, properly belongs to the Baptist ; *e.g.*, Ulpha chapel in Cumberland now bears the dedication of S. John Evangelist, but its fair is held on S. John Baptist's Day (Old Style).   The Evangelist, or, as he is sometimes termed, S. John the Divine, *i.e.*, the Theologian, had many claims to pre-eminence here and abroad.   There was a tradition that a priest of Diana challenged him to drink a draught of poison, but that when he made the sign of the cross over it, Satan rose from it in the form of a dragon and flew away.   Moreover, he was the patron of King Edward the Confessor, whose body, once venerated by the whole English race, reposes secure at Westminster behind the High Altar in the great shrine of marble and mosaic built for him by Henry III.[2]

S. Stephen (46 Dedications)

English dedications to S. Stephen do not appear till Norman days.   Perhaps the introduction of his name is due to the fact that William the Conqueror dedicated his own abbey church at Caen to S. Stephen.   The influence of this great church in its plan and architectural design was very great in the history of English church building ; and its dedication to S. Stephen would naturally have great weight.   The coronation of King Stephen took place on S. Stephen's Day ; and near the abbey of Westminster he built S. Stephen's chapel, greatly enlarged later by the Plantagenet kings ; part of its structure is incorporated in the present Houses of Parliament.[3]

[1] In the misericord at Lincoln the body of S. John has been broken away ; the man on the right has lighted a fire, which is beginning to curl up from the faggots ; the man on the left is using a bellows (51).   There is a fine etching of this subject by Albrecht Durer in the print room of the British Museum.

[2] On the Ranworth rood-screen (61) and in a statue at Westminster, S. John bears in his left hand a chalice and dragon ; with his right hand he has just made the sign of the cross (53).   On the grille in Henry the Seventh's chapel he bears the poisoned chalice (16).   The chalice and dragon with a palm appear on a shield in the Stanbury chantry chapel in Hereford cathedral (135).   In stained glass at York he is shown with the eagle, his evangelistic emblem (50).

[3] In glass at Nettlestead S. Stephen is shown in a dalmatic as a deacon, holding in one hand a closed book and in the other a stone.   At Ranworth, Norfolk, the stones are held in a napkin (55).   At Westminster the stones support an open book (53).

S. Stephen.

Ranworth Rood-screen.

Rood-screen, Ranworth, Norfolk.

S. Thomas the Apostle (46 Dedications)

Many of these dedications no doubt belonged originally to S. Thomas of Canterbury, whose name Henry VIII. ordered to be deleted from the service books in 1537. Here and there, however, the dedication is genuine, *e.g.*, S. Thomas Hospital, opposite the Houses of Parliament, replaces a hospital built in 1215 by Peter de Rupibus, Bishop of Winchester, and dedicated to "S. Thomas the Apostle." So also at Stanhope in Durham the dedication of S. Thomas must be to the apostle, for the fair is held on 21st December. S. Thomas is often represented as a carpenter or builder.

E. K. P.

S. Thomas.

West Front of Exeter Cathedral.

According to the apocryphal Acts of the Apostles, he was appointed to India by casting of lots. And when he came there, he was brought before King Gudnaphar (an actual personage, who was reigning near the Punjab, A.D. 46), who asked him, "What art thou skilled to make?" And Thomas replied, "In wood I make yokes and ploughs and ox-goads, and oars for barges and ferry-boats and masts for ships; and in hewn stone I make tomb-stones and monuments and palaces of kings." And the king said, "Build me a palace." And Thomas set forth on the sand the ground plan of a palace. There were doors to the east for light, and windows to the west for air; and he put the bakehouse to the south, and water-pipes to the north. And the king said, "Verily it is a good palace," and gave him money for the building, and went forth on a far journey. But when he returned, lo! there was no palace, for Thomas had spent the king's money on the poor. But the king was wroth and ordered Thomas to death on the next day. Now the king's brother had died. But in the night the soul was restored to his body, and he returned to the king, and told the things that had happened on his passing, and that he had seen heaven and the mansions thereof, and among them was a great and glorious palace, and that it had been built for the king by

8

S. Anne.
Westminster.

Thomas, his architect. So the king forgave Thomas and was baptized.[1]

The apocryphal Acts report that S. Thomas was stabbed to death at Mazdai in Persia. He is represented in Art holding a spear or an arrow, or, more frequently, with a carpenter's rule. S. Thomas is the patron saint of Portugal and of Parma.

S. Anne (41 Dedications)

It was from the apocryphal gospel of James that the names Joachim and Anne were obtained as the parents of the Blessed Virgin. S. Anne was exceedingly popular in later Gothic days; she is often depicted teaching Our Lady to read. After 1530 there passed a hundred and fifty years without any dedication to S. Anne. But in the later days of the seventeenth century many churches were dedicated to her, with one eye to the good mother of Our Lady and the other to " Good Queen Anne." For some reason S. Anne is a patron of wells, *e.g.*, at Buxton, Malvern, and Nottingham.[2]

S. James the Less
(26 Dedications)

The title of S. James the Less gives an impression of the

[1] In the west front of Exeter cathedral S. Thomas bears a model of his palace (57). On the Ranworth screen he carries the spear by which he was slain (56).

[2] Arnold-Forster, i. 99.

apostle which is the exact reverse of the truth: in reality
S. James was by far the more important, being a near relative,
ἀδελφός, of Our Lord, and president of the first General Council
of the Church. S. Philip and S. James the Less happen to
share one feast day between them. The latter had met
martyrdom in the East, and his relics were brought to
Constantinople and afterwards to Rome, where they were
placed in a reliquary which already contained some relics of

D. W.

SS. Christopher and Anne.

Westminster.

S. James the Less. A church was built to contain this reliquary,
and was dedicated to SS. Philip and James on the 1st of May,
A.D. 560, which ever since has been the joint festival of the two
saints in the Western Church.[1]   In the Eastern Church S. Philip's

---

[1] On the Ranworth screen S. Philip carries a basket of loaves (61).
On the rood-screen at Cawston, Norfolk, he holds a staff in one hand and
a closed book in the other (62). In the stall-panels at Blythburgh he holds
the Tau cross on which he was said to have been crucified (63).

S. James the Less.

Ranworth Rood-screen.

Day is 14th November, and S. James'
Day 10th April.[1]

All Souls (4 Dedications)

This dedication is of late date, being
due to a monk of Cluny, who in 998
visited Sicily and Mount Etna, and
being drowsy, fell asleep on the warm
mountain side, and there had a vision
wherein he saw the devil rebuking
his *aides-de-camp*, Belial, Mephistopheles,
Beelzebub, Asmodeus, and the rest, for
letting so many Christian souls escape
their clutches. They urged in reply
the great interference they experienced
from the new order of Cluniacs. These
things became common talk in Cluny
and throughout Christendom, and a
special day, the 2nd of November, was
appointed when prayers should be made
for the release of souls from purgatory;
an Act to that effect was passed by
the English Parliament. A college at
Oxford, dedicated to All Souls, was
founded by Archbishop Chichele, under
the influence of Henry VI., and the
fellows were enjoined by its statutes to
pray for the souls of those who had
fallen in the wars of Henry V.[2]

All Saints or All Hallows

The origin of this festival is a little
unusual. In the year 731 Pope Gregory
III. added a new chapel to Old S.
Peter's, Rome; and dedicated it to All
Saints. The dedication took place on
1st November, which has been set apart
for the commemoration of All Saints
ever since. The form All Hallows
is more common than All Saints in
ancient dedications.

[1] Charles Browne, *Ibid.*, 284.
[2] Charles Browne, *Ibid.*, 285.

Rood-screen, Ranworth, Norfolk.

W. D.

S. Philip.   S. Matthias.

Cawston Rood-screen.

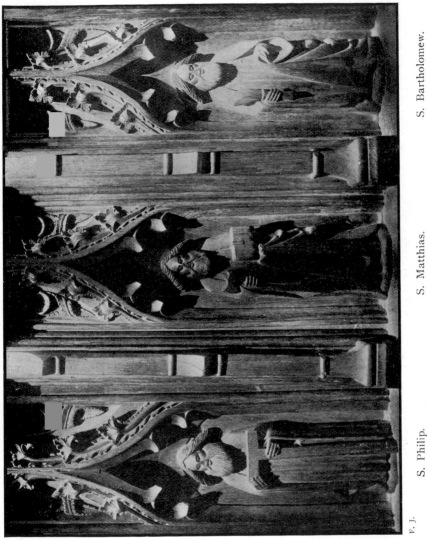

F. J.

S. Philip.

S. Matthias.
Blythburgh, Suffolk.

S. Bartholomew.

S. Petronilla

To her probably is dedicated Whipstead church, Suffolk. Her name was taken to mean " Peter's little daughter," and out of this "diseased etymology" there grew up curious and interesting legends, which are discussed at length in Bishop Lightfoot's *Clement of Rome,* vol. i., and in Miss Arnold-Forster's *Studies in Dedications,* i. 100, to which also the student is referred for an account of the other Biblical saints to whom churches are dedicated.

CHAPTER V

Reasons for Selection of a Patron Saint—S. Andrew—S. Pancras of Rome—
SS. George and Denys—Four Crowned Martyrs—Monastic Connections
—Benedictine Influence—Dedications to Missioners—S. German—
Private Reasons for Dedications—Cluster-Dedications—Mother Churches
in City of London.

ALTOGETHER there are some 370 saints to whom English
churches or chapelries are or have been dedicated. Of these
23 are mentioned in the Bible. This leaves a vast multitude
of non-Biblical saints. But from these we must separate,
as has been pointed out above, a very large number of saints,
especially in Wales and Cornwall, who were really not saints
at all. Even with this further deduction there was a great crowd
of non-Biblical saints for the mediæval Christian to choose
from. One would like to know what decided his choice. Some
of these saints seem to modern eyes to be honoured quite
beyond their merits, and others just as certainly not to have
won their just meed of praise. Why should such persons as
S. Nicholas, S. Margaret, S. Leonard, S. Giles be so high up the
tree? Why should S. Mark, an evangelist, and one whose
memorials are to be seen in every nook and corner of the
Venetian empire, have but a paltry half-dozen churches in
England, while S. Nicholas has 437? Why should S. Michael
have 687 dedications, while S. Gabriel, the angel of the
Annunciation, has but 6, and S. Raphael and S. Uriel none at
all? Nearly every name suggests a query and calls forth a
remonstrance. Probably we shall never get to the bottom of the
matter ; the mediæval mind is often very curious in its workings,
and now only too often incomprehensible.

But there are some reasons which may be detected for the
mediæval churchman's likes and dislikes. For instance, many
dedications are plainly due to knowledge of ecclesiastical procedure on the Continent, or to visits to holy places outside
England. We have seen that the churches at Rochester and
Hexham were not merely dedications to S. Andrew, but probably
also loving reminiscences of the monastery of S. Andrew at
Rome. But this monastery was built on land that had belonged

9

to the boy-saint, S. Pancras. So when S. Augustine dedicated to S. Pancras the very first English church he had consecrated —its foundations and some parts of the walls have lately been brought to light [1]—he doubtless had in his mind the monastery on the Cælian Hill which so long had been his happy home. Manchester cathedral is dedicated to "the Blessed Virgin Mary, SS. George and Denys." Randle Holme, a Lancashire antiquarian, who wrote in 1652, tells us that this is because the church was made collegiate in 1433 by Thomas de la Warre, who attached to it the names of the champions of England and France, because he was himself half an Englishman, half a Frenchman. Certainly no one would have dedicated the Canterbury church, now gone, to "the Four Crowned Martyrs," unless he had personal knowledge of some church at Rome dedicated to the "Quattuor Incoronati," four craftsmen who were beheaded by Diocletian because they would not sacrifice to Æsculapius.[2]

Geography also had something to say to the choice of a dedication. Thus S. Nicholas, being patron of ships and sailors, was of more avail in maritime countries and towns ; e.g., Brighton, Harwich, Liverpool, Lynn, Newcastle, Yarmouth ; the inland county of Derbyshire has not a single church, and only one chapel dedicated to him.[3] Again, it was common for churches and chapels on eminences to be dedicated to S. Michael, e.g., Abbotsbury, Dorset, and S. Michael's church on the Tor above Glastonbury, where on the tower—all that remains—is a statue of S. Michael with the scales, weighing souls.

Sometimes the association of a dedication is with a neighbouring monastery. Thus Glastonbury monks of the Benedictine abbey dedicated one of the parish churches of the town to S. Benedict, the founder of their order. And when the church of S. Mary, Spalding, passed into the possession of S. Nicholas's abbey at Angers, it was re-dedicated to "SS. Mary and Nicholas." Again, the parish church of Ashton-under-Hill in Gloucestershire is dedicated to S. Barbara ; it is her only church in England. This village is, however, connected ecclesiastically with the neighbouring village of Beckford, and in Beckford there used to be a cell of the Augustinian house of "SS. Martin and Barbara" in Normandy.

[1] See *Archæologia Cantiana*, vol. 25.

[2] There is still at Rome a large church so dedicated ; it comprises portions built in 626, three years after the Canterbury church was burnt down.

[3] At Condicote, Gloucester, the church is dedicated to S. Nicholas, and the villagers are known as "Condicote Sailors."—H. B. W.

In not a few instances we may trace the frequent occurrence of a dedication to services rendered to the Benedictines in the establishment of their order in England. In the seventh century an East Anglian abbot, who had been much on the Continent, introduced the new and rigid discipline of the Black Monks. It is certain that Ceolfrith, one of the disciples of S. Wilfrid, visited Botolph in 670 with the express purpose of being instructed in the Benedictine Rule. Dedications to S. Botolph number no less than 64. S. Oswald of Worcester, A.D. 992, was also devoted to the propagation of Benedictine influence; even more thoroughly than Dunstan, he carried into practice the substitution of monks for secular canons; the founding and oversight of monasteries were his special delight. In Dunstan, at once Archbishop of Canterbury and Prime Minister of England in the tenth century, the Benedictines had a most constant and powerful friend. All sorts of stories, among others that of the talking crucifix, were invented to show his indignation with the secular clergy, whose lives certainly at that time ill bore comparison with those who lived after the strict Benedictine Rule. Dunstan is commemorated with 20 dedications, chiefly in the South of England. In painted glass in the Bodleian, S. Dunstan with a pair of pincers has seized a devil who appears to be making off with a couple of chalices. The saint was an expert silversmith, and at the back are seen various vessels of silver and gold; much of the church plate in Glastonbury abbey was said to have been made by Dunstan (26). Gervase of Canterbury speaks of him as "Sicut David psalterium sumens, citharam percutiens, modificans organa, cimbala tangens. Præterea manu aptus ad omnia; facere potuit picturam, literas formare, scapello imprimere ex auro, argento, ære et ferro et quidlibet operari. Signa quoque et cimbala faciebat." (Twysden's *Scriptores*, x. p. 1646.)[1]

Not only in Celtic districts but elsewhere a dedication may commemorate the visit of some famous missioner, a S. Chad, a S. Aidan, or a S. German. The latter was consecrated, in 418, Bishop of Auxerre, where the campanile, choir, and crypts of the

---

[1] On the screen at Great Plumstead, Norfolk, he is seizing a dragon with a pair of pincers, which unfortunately are mutilated (68). A boss in the vault of Exeter cathedral shows S. Dunstan standing and playing a large harp. According to William of Malmesbury, "Most of all he delighted not only in the practice but the science of music and in the making of musical instruments." It is said of him that one day he hung his harp on the wall, while designing some embroidery, in which also he was an expert, and as he sang over his work, the harp of its own accord played an accompaniment (157).

great church of S. German still survive.   Later on he was sent by the Gallican Church more than once to aid the British Church in withstanding Pelagianism.   During one of these visits

Paintings of Saints, formerly in the rood-screen, now (1859,) preserved in the Church of Gt Plumstead.

S. Benedict.   S. Dunstan.

the British were threatened with an attack by heathen Saxons; but before German was ordained he had been a fine soldier and a "dux."   His tactics now were so successful that the British won the famous "Alleluia Victory."   There is no doubt as to the reality of these visits, and doubtless some of the fifteen

English dedications are attached to places visited by S. German ; at any rate that of S. German's in Cornwall, where the tradition is that he landed, and where both the town and the noble church preserve his name.

Saints, in the Church, G? Plumstead, drawn 1859.

S. Martin.   S. Giles.

In some cases the choice of dedication is due to some private reason, which as a rule is nowadays irrecoverably lost. But in some cases we know the reason for the choice ; *e.g.*, it was common for a man to put himself under the protection of the

saint on whose day he was born ; and if he liked to found later
a church, a chapel, a hospital, a college, to put that also under
the same patronage. King Henry VI. was born on S. Nicholas
Day, and dedicated his two foundations, King's College,
Cambridge, and Eton College, to SS. Mary and Nicholas'
Again, the lord of the manor of Rotherfield, Sussex, being
grievously sick, had gone to the monastery of S. Denis near
Paris, and had obtained relief. On his return in 792 he built a
church at Rotherfield and dedicated it to S. Denis. The well-
known antiquary, Browne Willis, in 1724 built a church at Fenny
Stratford ; he laid the foundation stone on S. Martin's Day, and
dedicated it to S. Martin, because his grandfather had died on
S. Martin's Day in S. Martin's Lane. In somewhat similar fashion
King Stephen dedicated the famous chapel which he built at
Westminster.

Sometimes there is a cluster of identical dedications confined
to one small area ; *e.g.*, to S. Denis and to S. Andrew near
Sleaford and Folkingham in Lincolnshire, and to S. Edith in
the Lincolnshire marsh, and S. Helen on the eastern slope of the
Lincolnshire Wolds. It may be that rebuildings or additions
took place simultaneously in these groups of churches, and that
the churches after the rebuilding were re-dedicated to the favourite
saint or the patron saint of the consecrating bishop.[1]

In a few examples, chiefly modern churches, the dedication
is due to the fact that the younger church has assumed the
dedication of the mother church with the aid of whose funds it
was erected. In the City of London this is specially provided
for by Act of Parliament ; hence such examples as S. Dionis or
Denis, Fulham ; S. Antholin, Nunhead.

Usually, however, churchmen had full liberty of choice as
regards dedications to non-Biblical personages; and though their
choice comes so often as a surprise to a modern churchman, it
by no means follows that it was without rhyme or reason.

[1] Borlase's *Age of the Saints*, 67.

W. M. D.

S. Dunstan.
Ludlow.

W. S. W.

S. Helena.
Westminster.

CHAPTER VI

Non-Biblical Saints—Saints of Royal Blood—S. Helena—Anglo-Saxon Saints—Danish Saints—Edward the Confessor—Anglo-Saxon Princesses—S. Hilda—Early Christianity of Wales—S. David—The Sons of Brychan.

NON-BIBLICAL SAINTS OF ROYAL BLOOD

LEAVING the saints connected with the Bible story, we turn to the far more numerous examples of later date. We will begin, as in duty bound, with saints of royal blood.[1]

It is astonishing what a swarm of kings and queens and princesses, with their sisters and their cousins and their aunts, attained to the honours of sainthood. The dedication lists begin nobly with an empress, S. Helena, the wife of the Roman emperor, Constantine.

S. HELENA OR HELEN

S. Helena has the large number of 135 dedications.[2] It is an honour she well deserved as a historical personage, but there can be little doubt that her position is rather due to the unhistoric legends that gathered round her. The genuine Helena is perfectly well known from the history of her contemporary, Eusebius, whose account we epitomise. According to S. Ambrose, who wrote but seventy years later, she was an innkeeper's daughter, and this was the general and received belief. One day Constantius, nephew of the reigning emperor, Claudius, met her, and in due course they were married. For twenty years they had a happy married life. Then for State reasons a separation took place, which lasted till Constantius' death fourteen years later. Their son was the great Constantine, the first Christian

---

[1] In Stanton's *Menology*, Appendix III., is a list of saints belonging to the reigning houses of the various kingdoms in England, from the time of S. Augustine.

[2] There is an excellent article on the Empress Helena by Bishop John Wordsworth in Smith and Wace's *Dictionary of Christian Biography*, *sub voce* ; see also Arnold-Forster, *Ibid.*, i. 181.

emperor. His love, respect, and honour of his mother were remarkable, both during the separation from Constantius and after he came to the imperial throne. In 312 Helena joined her son in allegiance to Christianity ; though not hitherto a worshipper of the True God, so good and sweet was her nature that "she seemed from her tender years to have been taught by the Saviour Himself." On his accession and all the days of her life Constantine ever sought fresh ways to do her honour. By all the legions and in all the provinces she was styled *Augusta* and *Imperatrix*, and gold coins were stamped bearing her image ; also he gave her authority to use the imperial treasures as she would. In old age she determined to "worship in the very footsteps of Christ." She was nearly eighty, but "had a youthful spirit," says Eusebius, "and the greatest healthiness both of body and mind." And so she set out for Jerusalem, where she felt that she ought to give thanks with supplications for her son so glorious, the emperor, and for his sons, the Cæsars, her grand-children. Constantine had put at her disposal the vast wealth of the Imperial Exchequer ; and though herself plainly clad and living with simplicity, she "heaped innumerable benefits and favours both on cities and churches and on every private person who approached her." While in the Holy Land, she founded the great church of the Nativity at Bethlehem, a still standing memorial of her munificence.[1] Some time later "she closed her life, the great Emperor being present with and standing by her, paying all imaginable respect and embracing her hands." So passed one of the most noble and gracious women that ever stepped across the scene of history. This is the true Helena.[2]

The other Helena is extremely unhistoric. The first thing told—which endeared her above everything else to all Christendom—was the part she took in the discovery of the Cross while she was in Jerusalem, and in the dispersion of precious fragments of it throughout Europe. But Eusebius, who was her contemporary, says not a word of this. It is inconceivable that, writing in such detail as he did of the empress, he should have omitted this momentous fact. The whole story of her connection

[1] It has been held that this church was not built till the time of Justinian, but later knowledge shows that it is substantially of the age of Constantine. See monograph on the church, published for the Byzantine Research Fund in 1910.

[2] In Henry the Seventh's chapel, S. Helena is reading an open book supported by a Tau cross (71). She also bears a cross in an alabaster table in the vestry of S. Peter Mancroft, Norwich (7).

D. AND P.

S. Ethelred.   S. Ethelbert.

West Front of Wells Cathedral.

with the *Inventio Crucis* grew up later, but not much later. It first appears in the historian Socrates a hundred years after her visit to the Holy Land—the divine vision which caused her to go on pilgrimage; the bringing to light of three crosses; the test which showed one only of the number to be endowed with miraculous powers of healing; the gift to Constantine of the two nails, and the strange use he made of them, converting them into helmet and bridle; and lastly, the ascription of the erection of the church of the Holy Sepulchre at Jerusalem to Helena, and not to Constantine, its real founder.

In addition to all this, an English myth grew up, and more than one. For these we are indebted to the chroniclers Geoffrey of Monmouth and Henry of Huntingdon, two of the worst liars in the Middle Ages. Starting with a vague tradition that the Emperor Constantine was born in Britain, they fill in all the detail. She was the daughter of

> " Old King Cole,
> That merry old soul,"

who reigned in Colchester. This the Colchester people devoutly believed, and in 1407 founded one of the most fashionable of the guilds of the Middle Ages, that of S. Helen, whose chapel was dedicated to the Holy Cross; later on, the guild was converted into the " Fraternity of S. Elene." But there was another tradition that the birth of her son Constantine took place in York; whether that was so or not, he spent a considerable time in that city. And so the great county became interested in his mother, Helena; and no less than 34 churches are dedicated to her in Yorkshire: one of them, indeed, S. Helen-on-the-Walls, York, claims to contain the grave of her husband, Constantius; in Yorkshire she stands sixth in order of popularity. She was very popular also in the neighbouring county of Lincolnshire, where she stands seventh, with 28 dedications. Other interesting churches dedicated to her are the nuns' churches of Elstow (Helen-stow), Bedford, and S. Helens, Bishopsgate, London, and the parish church of S. Elena, Thoroton, Notts.[1] In Lancashire, she gives her name to smoky "S. Helens." To gauge her true position we should add to her dedications those to " Holy Cross " or " Holy Rood."

At Ashton-under-Lyne, Lancashire, are eighteen panels of stained glass, *c.* 1480, which depict the life of S. Helena. The first depicts her birth, with the scroll, " *Hic nascitur Elena Coyle regis filia,*" " Here is born Helena, daughter of King Cole." At

---

[1] Arnold-Forster, *Ibid.*, i. 188.

Morley, Derbyshire, is another Holy Cross window in ten panels, brought from the refectory of Dale Abbey.[1]

From this fourth-century empress we pass to the Anglo-Saxon kings of the seventh and following centuries. In early Anglo-Saxon days political murders were so frequent that

C. G.   D. W.

S. Ethelbert.   S. Edmund.

Hereford Cathedral.   Westminster.

royal saints had not long to wait for martyrdom. There are dedications to Edwin, first Christian king of Northumberland (1), defeated and slain in 633; to Oswald (67), his successor, defeated and slain in 642; to Oswin (1), king of Northumbria, murdered in 650; to Ethelbert (16), king of East Anglia,

[1] Nelson's *Painted Glass*, 70, 131.

assassinated in 794 by Offa, king of the Mercians; Hereford cathedral is dedicated to Ethelbert;[1] to Alkmund (4), the boy-

J. H. P.

S. Edward the Confessor granting a Charter to a Monastery.
From painted glass in the Priory of Great Malvern.

[1] King Ethelbert was murdered, it is said, by King Offa at the instigation of the wife of the latter, Queen Cynethryth, on whom he is seen trampling in the west front of Wells cathedral (74). The small statue of S. Ethelbert shown on page 76 was dug up about the year 1700 at the entrance to the Lady chapel of Hereford cathedral.

king of Northumbria, murdered in 800 by Hardulph, as well as to Hardulph (1), his murderer ; to Edmund (61), king of East Anglia, murdered by the Danes in 870 ; Bury S. Edmund commemorates his name. To these add three boy-kings, all foully murdered ; Kenelm of Mercia (9), murdered at the instance of his sister in 819 ; Wyston or Winston of Mercia (3),

assassinated by order of his uncle in 849, and Edward, king of the West Saxons (5), murdered at Corfe Gate in 979. Next we have a Scandinavian king, Olaf or Olave (13), whose missionary message was the simple one, "Be baptized or be killed"; he fell in 1030. Then comes a somewhat unkingly king, Edward the Confessor (17), who died in his bed in 1066. Abnormal both in body and mind, he was almost an albino, and was subject to strange trances, and "saw visions," and was devoted to every observance of religion ; on the one hand he was looked at with superstitious reverence, on the other hand he was regarded with that curious mixture of feelings, more pity than contempt, that country people still have for an "innocent." He was, moreover, the last on the long roll of the old dynasty of Anglo-Saxon kings. For a long time he was practically the patron saint of England, till Edward III. converted S. Edward's chapel at Windsor into S. George's chapel, and formally constituted S. George England's patron saint.[1] Richard II. does not appear in dedications ; nor do Edward II. or Henry VI., though both were held in great reverence. It was not till 1649 that England provided itself with another kingly saint and the last, King Charles the Martyr.

D. W.
The Confessor.
Westminster.

[1] On a tile in the Westminster Chapter house the king is shown giving his ring to a beggar (173). He is represented on the grille of Henry the Seventh's chapel, but the ring is missing (78). Similar is the representation on the tomb of Henry the Seventh (117). In glass at Malvern he is giving a charter to a kneeling monk (77).

When from kings we turn to saintly queens and saintly princesses, they abound amazingly. Both in the Celtic and in the Anglo - Saxon Church this was so. Thus "in the East Anglian royal family there were three sainted sisters —S. Etheldreda of Ely, S. Sexburga, and S. Withburga.[1] These sisters again are connected with many another royal saint. The Northumbrian abbess Hilda is their maternal aunt; the Mercian saints, Werburgh and Milburgh, are their nieces; Etheldreda is allied by marriage with the Wessex princess, S. Cuthburga; while S. Sexburga's marriage with Ercombert, king of Kent, brings her into kinship with all the saints of the Kentish royal family."[2] And there are many others, some of high family, and some of royal blood, such as S. Frideswide,[3] S. Pega, S. Sidwell, S. Alkelda, S.

[1] On page 20 S. Etheldreda is represented as a crowned abbess. On the ground lie the crown and sceptre she resigned in order to take up conventual life.

[2] Arnold - Forster, *Ibid.*, ii. 351.

[3] In Oxford cathedral S. Frideswide is depicted in fourteenth-century glass, crowned, bearing a sceptre in her left hand and a closed book in her right (18).

S. Etheldreda.

Ranworth Rood-screen.

Eadburga of Pershore, S. Eanswith,[1] S. Edith of Polesworth, S. Wolfrida, and that charming girl, S. Edith of Wilton. Of royal ladies there are some twenty-five to whom Anglo-Saxon churches are dedicated; and of these three only have the title of martyr; S. Alkelda, S. Arilda, and S. Osyth. How then are their posthumous honours to be accounted for? It is not to be attributed to chivalry, for the glamour of chivalry had not yet come in with the Normans, with whom no form of obeisance to woman could be too reverential, while all the time she was to them but a pretty toy. There never was a time in the history of England when women were given such full scope for the power which many possess in an exceptional degree, of organisation and administration, as in Anglo-Saxon days. The Anglo-Saxon ladies were strenuous and capable both in Church and State; in the foundation of their institutions and in the government of them displaying judgment, tact, and ability. Of S. Hilda Bede says, " Such was her wisdom, that not only all common people in their necessities, but even sometimes kings and princes sought counsel of her." The monastery at Whitby was in fact the great theological college of all England; among Hilda's pupils were five bishops; one of them was S. John of Beverley. The Church acknowledged such good service by the highest honour it could confer. Then one must remember how new Christianity was in the seventh and eighth centuries; the story of the conversion of the English kingdoms was fresh in all minds and was on all lips; and to the personages in the story, the king who had brought Christianity into his realm, the queen who had converted a heathen husband, the princess who had founded the first convent, to all these the Anglo-Saxon world was full of gratitude and praise.

Earlier still, in the Celtic Church, royalty is equally conspicuous in the calendar of saints. There again few won their way to sainthood by the bloodstained path of martyrdom. After the departure of the last Roman soldier in 407, life in England had been one long horror up to the Settlement in the seventh or eighth century; every fragment of Roman civilisation, and practically every trace of the British Church, had been obliterated on English soil. In the words of the petition of the British Christians to Rome in 446 : " The barbarians drive us to the sea, the sea to the barbarians; we are massacred or we are

---

[1] On an ivory in the British Museum S. Eanswith is seen standing on a sturgeon. To the right are the Blessed Virgin and S. Peter. At Folkestone S. Eanswith is shown on the Corporation seal with two fishes on a half hoop; and on the Mayor's seal with a fish on each side of her.

drowned." Wales, on the other hand, was for the most part a
quiet and peaceful land in those days ; the last half of the fifth

C. L.

S. Eanswith. The Virgin and Child. S. Peter.

Ivory Panel in British Museum.

and the beginning of the sixth century, just when things were
about at their worst in England, was almost a Golden Age

11

Rood-screen, Ranworth, Norfolk.

there; and it was at this time that the greatest church work of Wales was done. Christianity was the settled religion of the country; organised in a very curious way, not at all after the episcopal fashion which ultimately prevailed in England, and which later was forced on Wales, but directed by the heads of monasteries. Now it is that S. David and his associates worked; some of them of noble or royal blood; also that extraordinary royal family in Brecknockshire, which goes by the name of the "Sons of Brychan," who, according to Welsh tradition, were forty-nine in number, while the Cornish lists reckon over seventy. To them are to be added eight minor royalties; and that by no means exhausts the list.[1]

[1] For the literature on Celtic Saints see the Bibliography prefixed to the volume.

CHAPTER VII

Dedications to Evangelists, Divines, and Theologians—SS. Ignatius and Polycarp—Dedications to Saints of Pious and Austere Life—S. Chad—S. Cuthbert—S. Botolph—S. Guthlac.

TURNING to more general considerations, we note in the dedications of English churches the comparative indifference shown to scriptural learning and theological literature. S. Paul gets little credit for his epistles. The apostle S. John, with Gospel and Apocalypse to his credit, is far below his namesake, the Baptist, in popularity. None of the evangelists, S. Matthew[1] (33 dedications), S. Mark (6 dedications), S. Luke (8 dedications), S. John (181 dedications), stand high on the list. As for the Fathers of the Church, the great Doctors and Theologians, who formulated, defended, and promulgated that body of doctrine which is the life-blood of the Church's teaching, to most of them those who dedicated the churches were indifferent. S. Ignatius had personal knowledge of the apostles, and passed the tradition on to S. Polycarp. The former suffered martyrdom at Rome, c. 110: " I am ground," he said, " by the teeth of wild beasts that I may be found pure bread of Christ." Polycarp also had known the aged apostle John, and was wont to describe his intercourse with the " beloved disciple " and with others who had seen Our Lord, and would repeat their words. He suffered martyrdom at the stake in 168. Yet we have no ancient church dedicated either to Ignatius or to Polycarp. Nor is there one to S. Cyprian of Carthage, to S. Chrysostom of Constantinople, or to the great S. Ambrose of Milan.[2] Those who built our churches cared little for those who wrote the Scriptures, and for

---

[1] The popularity of S. Matthew is probably largely due to the story of his imprisonment and rescue in the City of Dogs (page 154).

[2] On the rood-screen at Ashton, Devon, S. Ambrose is represented as a bishop with crozier and closed book (267). In another representation he is rebuking the emperor ; behind him is a hive, because as a child, bees, the symbol of eloquence, had settled on his lips, as on Plato's (24). In Henry the Seventh's chapel, S. Ambrose holds an open book in one hand, and in the other a broken scourge or " discipline " (85).

W. S. W.

W. S. W.

S. Ambrose.

S. Antony.

Westminster.

Westminster.

those who interpreted the Scriptures still less. The reason is not far to seek. Nowadays we print Bibles by the million; everybody can have a whole Bible for a few pence. But in the old days hardly anybody had a Bible, and practically nobody could read. Moreover, in the services it was not the custom to read great blocks of Scripture, any more than it is now in Catholic churches; it was only a few selected verses here and there that people were familiar with. And if the Bible was but an empty name to them, they were still less likely to have on their shelves the voluminous works of the Fathers.

Our forefathers had no particular respect for a man sitting at a desk; they liked to see him *doing* something; the strenuous, active life was their ideal, not the contemplative peacefulness of the scholar recluse. They liked to see their saint riding about slaying dragons and rescuing chained maidens, like S. George, or, clad in shining armour like S. James, charging down the Moors.

On the other hand, it is very clear that simple saintliness was held in the very highest regard. Holiness of life canonised many a good man and woman. Many a pretty story survives to tell us how affecting was the spectacle of a life of innocence and piety. When S. Chad was dying, one of his chaplains heard a sweet melody of singing, which descended from heaven into the saint's oratory, and filled the same for about half an hour, and then rose again to heaven. Nor could any life well be less eventful than that of S. John of Beverley—a life of study and teaching, of missioning and healing, and a final three years of prayer in his dear refuge at Beverley. Of Edward the Confessor, William of Malmesbury says, " He was a man devoted to God, and God directed his simplicity."

But the world liked outward and visible signs of the holy life; it looked for austerities, asceticism. The hermit and the anchorite were older personages than monk and nun, and kept firm hold of the popular imagination. All over Christendom and from the earliest times this was so. It is a far cry from England to the deserts of Egypt and Sinai, where S. Antony had his abode till his death in extreme old age in 356, unfriended save by a wild boar;[1] but the mediæval world did not forget him

---

[1] On the screen at Ashton, Devon, S. Antony holds a Tau staff, and probably had a bell; at his feet is a wild boar (141). In an illumination he is shown with book and bell, Tau crosses, and pig (13). He appears with rosary and pig on the tomb of Henry the Seventh at Westminster (153). In a statue in Henry the Seventh's chapel he has a rosary, sheath-knife, and Tau staff; in his right hand is a bell; below is a pig (85).

D. W.

S. Cuthbert.   S. Eloy.

Henry the Seventh's Chapel, Westminster.

T. P.

S. Oswald.

Wells Cathedral.

or S. Simeon Stylites, and many another who fought and subdued the temptations of the world, the flesh, and the devil. Another saint, with many churches, was S. Leonard (177 dedications), who from being courtier to King Clovis turned hermit. Another famous hermit and abbot was S. Giles (162 dedications), of very uncertain date but with many churches. S. Jerome was more respected as an anchorite than as a theologian. It is as a fierce, half-naked, old hermit, beating his breast with a stone, that he is most often represented in later Italian art.

Of S. Cuthbert (72 dedications) we have detailed accounts from his contemporary, Bede, in the seventh century. He was a shepherd lad, keeping his master's flocks in Lauderdale; athletic and brave, a good horseman and a good fighter. But one night when saying his prayers, he saw in the dark sky a track of light, down which descended holy angels, and presently returned bringing back from earth a resplendent soul. Next morning he heard that Aidan, Bishop of Lindisfarne, the Evangeliser of Northern England, had died in the night. So Cuthbert, then fifteen, joined the monks of Melrose. Then for many years he went forth as a missioner among the savage Border folk, traversing to and fro the wild country from Solway to Forth, passing

P. N.

S. Cuthbert.

weeks and even months away from Melrose, preaching, administering the sacraments, and practising extraordinary austerities; stone bathing-places, where, as was the wont with Celtic saints, he would lie all night in freezing water engaged in prayer, are still shown here and there in the countryside. Then for twelve years he was prior of Lindisfarne;

when at home observing the harshest discipline, three nights out of four singing the praises of God as he paced the aisles ; and again continuing his labours in Northumbria, preaching, healing the sick, confessing, and communicating. Then, when nearly forty, he left Lindisfarne for a rocky islet opposite Bamburgh, hollowing a cell out of the rock, and building round it a mound so high that he could see "nothing but Heaven to which he so earnestly aspired." To Farne came the faithful, humble and great, from all Northumbria to make confession and receive his blessing. For two years he was dragged away from his cell to be Bishop of Lindisfarne, missioning once more all over the countryside from Lindisfarne to Carlisle, preaching, confirming, confessing, healing the sick and halt, penetrating remote dales, crossing pathless fells, living in the open or under a shelter of branches of trees. After Christmas, 686, he returned to his beloved Farne, to make preparation for his passing, and two months later was buried at the foot of the cross which he had set up. "I would fain rest," he said, "where I have fought my little battle for the Lord, from whence I hope my merciful Judge will call me to a crown of righteousness. Bury me, wrapped in the linen which I have kept for my shroud out of love for the abbess Verca, the friend of God, who gave it me."[1]

At the south end of the choir transept of York minster is a vast window which retains 85 panels of ancient glass. In it are depicted—(1) His childhood, boyhood, and youth ; (2) his monastic life at Melrose, Ripon, and Lindisfarne ; (3) his retirement to Farne Island ; (4) his life as Bishop of Lindisfarne ; (5) his second retirement and death at Lindisfarne ; (6) his shrine and posthumous miracles.[2]

Then there was S. Botolph, who dwelt in a dismal hut amidst the swamps of the fenland rivers, and in the East of England has no less than 64 dedications, but only a single one in the West country ; he flourished in the seventh century, and is credited with being one of the pioneers in England of the Benedictine Rule, which, however, did not come into predominance till the time of Archbishop Dunstan three centuries later.

In the eighth century there was his successor, S. Guthlac,[3] with 9 dedications, who abode in the swamps of Crowland summer and winter, amid snow and mire, flood and ice, ague and

[1] Baring-Gould's *Lives of the Saints*, 20th March.

[2] Nelson's *Painted Glass*, 257.

[3] In the Harley Roll Y 6 in the British Museum are eighteen pictures of the life of S. Guthlac. In the illustration S. Guthlac is chastising a devil with a scourge or "discipline" (26).

rheumatism, wearing himself out with impossible fasts, till his
poor brain gave way, taking the will o' wisps of the marsh for
tapers of dancing witches, and "the myriad shriek of wheeling
waterfowl" for howls of witches and devils, who had great heads
and crooked nebs and fierce eyes, and cried hoarsely with their
voices, and came with immoderate noise and horror and tugged
him from his cot, and led him to the black fen and sunk him in
the muddy waters; after which they brought him into thick
beds of brambles that all his body was torn; and they beat him
with iron whips, and after that brought him on their creaking
wings athwart the cold regions of the air.[1] After his death
there rose above his bones, on piles driven into the mud, the
abbey church of Crowland, whereof the north aisle and western
steeple still survive, and which, with its dykes and parks and
vineyards and orchards and rich ploughlands, fed in time of
famine all the fenland folk, and whose tower was a sanctuary
for them that fled from slavery and wrong, for between "the
four rivers" of Crowland, S. Guthlac and his abbot were the only
lords. S. Guthlac's life is recorded by Felix of Crowland, a
contemporary. Many a saint, *e.g.*, S. Martin of Tours and
S. Cuthbert, though not a professed hermit, led lives of as
stern asceticism as any of them.

[1] Baring-Gould, 11th April, and Kingsley's *Hermits*.

CHAPTER VIII

Dedications to the Evangelisers of Western Europe, Scotland, Wales, and Ireland—S. Martin of Tours—S. German—S. Ninian—S. David—S. Patrick—S. Rémi—S. Bridget—S. Brandan—S. Wulfram—S. Boniface.

ESPECIALLY did the Church turn with grateful eyes to those who brought into the shadow of darkness the glad tidings of the gospel of peace. Among them was S. Martin of Tours (173 dedications), who in the last half of the fourth century did so much to Christianise the villagers of Western France, who remained sunk in heathendom long after the towns had accepted the new religion. The life of the saint was written about A.D. 392 by Sulpicius Severus, some years before S. Martin's death. He was a tribune or colonel in a Roman cavalry regiment quartered in Amiens in the year 332. It was a winter so exceedingly severe that men died of cold in the streets. One day S. Martin, riding out of the town, met a naked beggar, and with his sword divided his cloak in half, giving one half to the beggar.[1] That same night he saw in a dream the Lord Jesus, having on His shoulders the half of the cloak which had been bestowed on the beggar. Then said He, " Thus hath my servant Martin arrayed me, though yet unbaptized." In his twenty-third year he was baptized, and in 371 was elected Bishop of Tours. One day in his cathedral he saw a poor beggar—

> " Then Martin bade his archdeacon straightway
> That he should without delay clothe the poor man.
> But the archdeacon would not clothe the poor man ;
> And the poor man stole in to Martin,
> And bemoaned to him that he was very cold.
> Then Martin immediately unclothed himself
> Under his chasuble secretly, and put his own raiment
> On the poor man, and bade him go out.
> Then after a little space the archdeacon came,
> And said that it was time that he should go into church
> To say mass for the people and to do honour to God.
> Then Martin said to him that he could not go
> Into the church before the poor man was clothed.

[1] This is the scene portrayed in Vandyck's famous picture at Windsor.

D. W.

S. Martin.   S. Armel.

Henry the Seventh's Chapel, Westminster.

> Then the archdeacon, being angry, went
> And brought a garment impatiently to him,
> Mean and little, bought at little cost,
> And with great ire laid it at his feet and said:
> ' Here is the garment, but here is no poor man.'
> Then the holy man bade him wait outside somewhere,
> Desiring that he should not know that he was naked;
> Then he clothed himself with the mean garment,
> And went to church and at once said mass.
> At that very same mass three of the monks
> And one of the priests and one of the nuns saw
> Above Martin's head as it were a burning globe
> So that the flame drew the hair far up." [1]

The devil was scandalised at the indiscriminate lavishness of S. Martin's charity. But the saint replied, "O most miserable one! if thou also couldest repent, thou also shouldest find mercy through Jesus Christ." Innumerable are the stories told of S. Martin, and greatly to his credit. He was a furious rooter up of Paganism, its temples and its idols; nor was he to be deterred by impersonations of Jupiter, Minerva, Mercury, or even a Venus rising from the foam of the sea. But there is not room to allude to a tithe of the pleasant stories told about him, which made him, next to S. Nicholas, the best liked saint of Western Christendom. The west window of S. Martin's church, York, has a figure of him in the central light; there are also thirteen panels depicting incidents in his life; the window was begun in 1437. [2]

Nearly all the painted glass in S. Mary, Shrewsbury, is Flemish or German; some of it from the church of S. Jaques, Liège. At the feet of S. Martin are the three geese. It was customary to kill and eat a goose at Martinmas in memory of the geese which the saint scolded and banished because of the mischief they did (95).

There was S. German of Auxerre, who more than once in the early years of the fifth century ventured into Britain, leaving memorials of his successful campaign against the heresy of the British theologian, Pelagius, in the shape of 15 dedications.

---

[1] Ælfric's Homily, XXXI. 900.

[2] At Westminster a cripple holds up his bowl for alms to S. Martin, who is represented as a bishop (93). In another statue he wears the cloak which he divided with a beggar; underneath is armour to show that he had been a soldier; and he carries a mitre to show that he became a bishop. The omission of the horse and beggar is no doubt due to want of space (162). On the screen at Great Plumstead, Norfolk, he holds his crosier in his left hand, and an open book in his right (69).

W. M. D.

S. Martin.   The Blessed Virgin.   The Magi.

Gresford Church, Denbigh.

There is S. Ninian, with 4 dedications, the "Apostle of the Picts";[1] a wealthy British nobleman, who on his conversion went to Rome for theological training, and on his return built

A. J. N.

S. Ninian.
Prince Arthur's Chapel,
Worcester Cathedral.

what in those days was a great achievement—a church of stone; this he called Whitherne, "Casa Candida," perhaps because it was whitewashed, as was old York minster; this was in A.D. 432. This church he dedicated to S. Martin of Tours; this is the very first recorded church dedication in Britain. Ninian evangelised Galloway and the neighbouring districts. In Prince Arthur's chantry chapel in Worcester cathedral is a statuette holding a heavy chain. This representation also occurs in Mr Leighton's *Book of Hours* (see page 146), where the saint is in episcopal attire, and holds in one hand a crosier and in the other a heavy chain or perhaps fetters; he was Bishop of Whitherne. At the foot of the page is an "oratio deuotissima ad Sanctum Ninianum."

"Ave gemma confessorum
Ave dux et doctor morum
Niniane pontifex."

"Salve sanctitatis rosa
Mundi lampas luminosa
Cunctis eris opifex."

"Gaude pater pietatis
Summæ sidus honestatis
Regnans in galwedia," etc.

To the last half of the fifth and to the beginning of the

[1] For his life see Newman's *Lives of the English Saints.*

sixth century belongs a vast host of Celtic missioners, Irish, Welsh, Breton, Cornish; greatest of whom were S. David and S. Patrick, the Apostles and patron saints of Wales and Ireland. The fame of Remigius, the Apostle of the Franks— whose great abbey church of S. Rémi is one of the twin glories of Rheims—crossed the Channel, and is shown forth in 6 dedications. He it was who had baptized Clovis, king of the Franks, amid a magnificence of ceremonial long remembered in Eastern France; his life-story may be seen carved in stone on the tympanum of the doorway of the north transept of Rheims cathedral.

To the sixth century belong S. Bridget and S. Columba. Bridget was a delightful, impulsive, warm-hearted, thoughtless, hospitable Irish girl, but a bad housekeeper. Often when dinnertime arrived, Bridget had given away the milk and butter to passing tramps and the bacon to the dog.

On a time came two lepers unto Bridget to ask an alms. Nought was there in the kitchen but one single cow; Bridget gave it to the lepers. But one, who was a haughty leper, said, "Never am I to be slighted with a single cow." Then said Bridget to the other, who was a lowly leper, "Stay thou here to see whether God will put anything in the kitchen, and let the haughty leper fare forth with his cow." Then came a heathen having a cow for Bridget, and she gave it to the lowly leper. And the two lepers fared forth to the Barrow river, and the river rose up against them. Through Bridget's blessing the lowly leper escaped and his cow; but the haughty leper and his cow fell to the bottom of the river and were drowned.[1] Another day she came in wet through, and hung her wet cloak on a sunbeam, taking it for a clothesline; and the sunbeam did not move, but remained there, "as if on pot-hooks," till eventide, when Bridget released it, and it hasted away to catch up the sun.[2]

On another occasion, waiting for her father in his chariot, she gave away his sword; all she had to say in defence was that if beggars asked for her king and father, she would give him away also. Another day she came over the mountain, where there was a madman, and great fear seized the virgins who were with her. But quoth the madman: "I cannot be ungentle to thee, O nun, for thou art merciful to the poor and wretched. Reverence the Lord, O nun, and every one will reverence thee; love the Lord, and every one will love thee; fear the Lord, and every one will fear thee." Then the madman fared forth,

---

[1] Whitley Stokes, *Three Middle-Irish Homilies on the Lives of SS. Patrick, Brigit, and Columba.* Calcutta, 1877.

[2] The legend of the sunbeam is unfortunately rather common; at least nine saints hang their cloaks on a sunbeam; four their gloves; and one an axe.

and wrought no harm upon them.[1]   The chronicler shall be left to set forth the worth and passing of Bridget.   "There hath never been," he says, "any one more bashful or more modest than that holy virgin ; she never washed her hands or her face or her feet amongst men ; she never looked a man in the face ; she never spoke without a blush.   She was abstinent, innocent, generous, patient; she joyed in God's commandments ; she was steadfast, lowly, forgiving, charitable.   She was a consecrated vessel for keeping Christ's body ; she was a temple of God ; her heart and her mind were a throne of rest for the Holy Ghost.   Towards God she was simple ; towards the wretched compassionate : her miracles and wondrous deeds like the sand of the sea : her soul is like the sun in the heavenly city among quires of angels and archangels, in union with cherubim and seraphim, in union with all the Holy Trinity, Father and Son and Holy Ghost.   I, the writer, beseech the Lord's mercy through S. Brigit's intercession.   Amen."

In Ireland her churches are almost numberless ; in England she is remembered by 19 dedications, one of which is Wren's church of S. Bride, Fleet Street, London.   In memory of her, the "Fiery Dart," as she was called, the nuns of Kildare for 700 years kept ever burning a sacred fire.[2]   From Ireland too came S. Columba, from whose mission station at Iona went forth the evangelisers not only of Scotland, but of Northern England.   In Scotland he had some 50 dedications, in England 8.

S. Brandan [3] also was an Irishman ; two English churches are dedicated to him.   The stories about S. Brandan are only too good to be true.   S. Brandan voyaged forth for seven years to an isle of the West, another Avilion—

> "Where falls not hail nor rain nor any snow,
>   Nor ever wind blows loudly ; but it lies
> Deep-meadow'd, happy, fair with orchard lawns
>   And bowery hollows crown'd with summer sea."

"And it was a very fair land, standing thick with flowers ; and hard by a noble well stood a spreading tree, whose every bough was laden with fair white birds so that the leaves might scarce be seen ; and they sang so merrily that it was a heavenly noise to hear.   Then the saint bade tell wherefore they sang so merrily ; and one made answer :

---

[1] Whitley Stokes, *Ibid.*, 77.   The homily of S. Brigit is from a manuscript of the fifteenth century preserved in the library of the Royal Irish Academy, and evidently incorporates very ancient materials.

[2] She is not to be confounded with S. Bridget of Sweden, who founded the order of the Briggittines, and is represented with a pilgrim's wallet and staff.

[3] An English version in prose and verse of the legend of S. Brandan has been edited by Mr Thomas Wright for the Percy Society.

'Sometime we were angels in heaven ; but when Lucifer our master fell through pride, we fell with him ; but since our trespass is but little, our Lord hath set us here out of all pain, to serve Him, and to praise Him on this tree in the best manner that we can.' And yearly, at the Easter tide, S. Brandan and his companions returned to keep the holy season in the Paradise of Birds."[1]

It was on one of these voyages that S. Brandan met Judas Iscariot, who, for a brief space of respite from eternal woe, floats past on an iceberg. One act of kindness, Judas told S. Brandan, one only had he done in his lifetime ; and

> " That germ of kindness, in the womb
> Of mercy caught, did not expire ;
> Outlives my guilt, outlives my doom,
> And friends me in the pit of fire."

From every story of this far-away, mystical Irish saint there shines forth a real soul, one that ever preached a gospel of pity and forgiveness and long-suffering and love ; and that the Lord is full of compassion and mercy, and forgiveth sins, and saveth in time of affliction. Brandan and Bridget were lovely in their lives ; if anything, still more beautiful is the story of the great Columba ; here only a passing reference can be made to it. If Columba, Brandan, and Bridget are typical examples of what Christianity was in Ireland before the English missioners and soldiers arrived, Celtic Ireland must have been an Island of Saints. And indeed it was. Saints they had in such abundance that they were exported in large numbers for Continental use. Irish religion was a religion of simple piety and love.

Here is another story setting forth mercy and loving-kindness. " It is taken from some ascetical work, the title of which," says Count Joseph de Maistre, " I forget."

A saint, whose name I have also forgotten, had a vision in which he saw Satan standing before the throne of God. And the Evil one said, " Why hast thou damned me, who offended but once, and hast saved thousands who have offended many times against Thee ? " And God said, " Hast Thou asked for pardon once ? " For forgiveness is not denied but to them that ask not.[2]

> " The mercy of man is upon his neighbour,
> But the mercy of the Lord is upon all flesh ;
> Reproving, and chastening, and teaching,
> And bringing again, as a shepherd his flock."

[1] Arnold-Forster, *Ibid.*, ii. 37.
[2] Count Joseph de Maistre, *Lettres*, etc., i. 253, quoted in Delehaye, *Ibid.*, 231.

To the eighth century belongs the mission of S. Wulfram, Archbishop of Sens, to Friesland. It was S. Wulfram who was baptizing King Radbod, when the old king suddenly asked, " But what of my ancestors ? " " Those who died unbaptized are assuredly damned," was the stern reply. " Then," said King Radbod, stepping out of the water, " I cannot give up the companionship of my ancestors." S. Wulfram died *c.* 720 ; he has two dedications, Dorrington and Grantham. The next and the greatest evangelist of the century, and in Europe, was a wealthy young Devonshire man, Wilfred of Crediton, who gave up his monastic life at Nutshalling or Nursling, in Hampshire, and went as a missionary to Friesland, there continuing S. Wulfram's work. After work here, and in Bavaria and Saxony, he was raised to the rank of a missionary bishop, and started on a life-long campaign against the heathenism of Central Germany. His success was immense ; the whole country was evangelised ; schools and monasteries and churches arose on all sides ; he is the true Apostle of the Germans. In his later days he became Archbishop of Mayence ; was the friend of Kings Carloman and Pepin, and the leading churchman in Europe. When seventy-five years old he went forth once more on a mission to Friesland, and there was slain in 755 in a sudden attack of armed marauders. His name appears in six English dedications.

CHAPTER IX

Evangelisation of England—S. Gregory—S. Augustine of Canterbury—S. Paulinus—S. Aidan—S. Cuthbert—S. Chad—S. Felix—S. Kentigern —S. Birinus—S. Wilfrid—S. Aldhelm.

ALL the above famous missioners, S. Martin, S. German, S. Ninian, S. Rémi, and the Celtic saints, S. Patrick, S. Brandan, S. Columba, S. Bridget, and S. David, did their life-work mainly, if not wholly, outside England, and earlier than the seventh century. With that century begins and is carried far towards completion the great work of the Conversion of the Anglo-Saxon kingdoms to Christianity. This Conversion has its own bead-roll of honour, and scores of dedications survive to tell of the gratitude of the Church to the two famous missions, which, one from the South, the other from the North, revived the dying embers of British Christianity. In the South the impulse came direct from Rome, and from that greatest of the Popes of Rome, S. Gregory, to whom, in a life of terrible hard work and constant suffering, his mission to England was an especial delight. All know the story how, when a monk, he saw for sale in the market-place at Rome fair-haired boys from Yorkshire. " Non Angli sed angeli," he said, and heard how England was sunk again in heathenism ; and then and there organised a mission to England. But permission was refused, and the mission fell through. Gregory, however, did not forget the Yorkshire boys, and twenty years after sent forth a mission of his own, headed by S. Augustine. Pope Gregory then is really the Apostle, or at any rate, one of the two Apostles, of the English, as indeed Bede expressly acknowledges : " We may and ought to call him our Apostle, because he made our nation, till then given up to idols, the Church of Christ ; so that, though he is not an Apostle to others, yet he is so to us, for we are the seal of his Apostleship in the Lord." The success of the Roman mission in Kent and the conversion and baptism of King Ethelbert in 597 were a great joy to Gregory, and spite of his world-wide activities, he personally directed the English mission down to the smallest details. Augustine referred everything to him ; in fact the whole mission was governed from Rome rather than from

Canterbury, and Gregory, not Augustine, was its real head. Rightly and duly therefore is our Apostle, Pope Gregory the Great, commemorated in the dedications of 32 English churches.[1] S. Gregory died in 604, and his missioner, S. Augustine, in the following year ; he had worked at the mission seven years, and left his record behind in the foundation of the archbishopric of

J. H. P.

The Mass of S. Gregory.

From a M.S. in the Bodleian Library.

Canterbury and of the bishoprics of Rochester and London.

[1] The following are the emblems of the Crucifixion represented on the altar at the Mass of S. Gregory (102) :—

The Cross.	The Thirty Pieces of Silver.
The Three Nails.	The Hammer and Pincers.
The Spear.	The Ladder.
The Sponge.	The Sword.
The Pillar and Cord.	The Lantern.
The Two Scourges.	The Three Boxes of Spices for
The Three Dice.	Embalming.

A. W. S.

Gregory Mass.

Paignton, Devon.

S. Felix.

Ranworth Rood-screen.

At least 30 churches are dedicated to S. Augustine; his
noblest monument was the monastery at Canterbury, which he
dedicated to SS. Peter and Paul,
but which was re-dedicated in
commemoration of its founder
by S. Dunstan; the foundations
of the vast Norman church of S.
Augustine have recently been
disinterred. S. Paulinus was one
of a second mission sent by Pope
Gregory to help S. Augustine.
Eight years he laboured with
great success in the court of
Northumbria, penetrating from
this far down into the Midlands,
and baptizing vast multitudes in
the rivers of Yorkshire and the
Trent. Part of the Derwent is
still called the Jordan, in memory
of the many baptisms in its
waters of subjects of King Edwin
of Northumbria. With the fall
however of Edwin's kingdom
the mission collapsed, and S.
Paulinus spent his last years at
Rochester, of which he became
bishop. He died in 644: he had
worked at the evangelisation of
England for forty-three years.
He is commemorated by 5 dedications; but it is likely that
some of the churches which bear
the name of S. Paul really belong
to S. Paulinus.

The other mission did not
come from Rome at all, but
from the Celtic Church of the
North, whose headquarters were
at Iona and Lindisfarne. Till
recently the great work of S.
Aidan had received scanty recognition. Now Bishop Lightfoot has gone so far as to

assert that "Not Augustine but Aidan is the true Apostle of
England." Aidan died in 651 at the old royal Northumbrian
city of Bamburgh; whose parish church is the only one
dedicated in his honour. We may well believe that many a
church once commemorated his great work; but all that was
to the credit of the Celtic Church would be studiously ignored
when at the Synod of Whitby the Roman Church succeeded in

W. T. O.

S. Kentigern.

Glasgow Cathedral.

expelling Celtic Christianity from England. To Melrose and
Lindisfarne and Northumbria belong, as has been said above,
the labours of S. Cuthbert; he made a deep impression on his
times, and is greatly honoured in his own country. With him
are connected the original dedications of Durham cathedral,
where at length his body found rest and still remains, and of
Bolton and Worksop priories, both dedicated to SS. Mary and
Cuthbert. Dedications to S. Cuthbert are rare in Southern
England; that of the parish church of Wells is an exception.

14

Altogether he is commemorated in 72 churches. S. Chad was a mission-bishop, first at York, afterwards at Lichfield, where he died in 672; his dedications number 32. S. Felix was the Apostle of East Anglia; he died in 654; he has 6 dedications; his name is preserved in the S. Felix School, Southwold.[1] S. Birinus died in 650; his work was in Wessex. He was buried in Dorchester Priory church, Oxon., from which his relics were translated to Winchester cathedral. It was reported of S. Birinus that after celebrating mass before going on board ship, he left behind his corporal, which was the gift of Honorius. When he remembered it, the ship was already at sea, but Birinus threw himself overboard and made for shore, recovered the corporal, and returned over the water to the ship. This scene is represented in stained glass in Dorchester Abbey church.

An earlier evangelist, who deserves mention, though his work was on Scottish soil, was S. Kentigern or Mungo; his mother was S. Enoch; both their names survive at Glas-

S. A.

S. Wilfrid.

Ripon.

[1] On the Ranworth screen the orphrey of the chasuble and apparel are of fleur-de-lis pattern, which has been thought to indicate a bishop of French origin, probably S. Felix, Apostle of the East Angles.—H. A. W.

gow, the former in S. Mungo's cathedral, the latter in a railway station.[1]

The following century, the eighth, saw the death of one of the greatest and most strenuous of the seventh-century churchmen of England, S. Wilfrid ; he was sufficiently remarkable as a missioner and a bishop, but still more so, perhaps, for the persistence and success with which he worked for the triumph of the Roman Church and the downfall of the Celtic mission in England. His was an extraordinarily active and troubled life ; at one time an archbishop, at another an exile, at another a simple missioner to the starving fishermen of Wessex ; again and again travelling to Rome on appeal from the English Church, gathering together all Roman fashions of ritual and architecture, and the Benedictine ways of the Roman monastery, bringing them back and introducing them into the churches which he built. The very stones and mortar put together by S. Wilfrid still survive in the crypts of Ripon and Hexham, orientated in Italian fashion to the west. Altogether he has 48 dedications ; Ripon minster, where he lies buried, was re-dedicated to SS. Peter and Wilfrid.[2] A famous scholar and missioner in the West country was S. Aldhelm or Mallem (*i.e.*, " My Aldhelm") of Malmesbury ; a notable ascetic was he ; winter and summer nightly he said his psalter standing up to his neck in a pool of water. He wrote songs and ballads too ; and if the village folk would not listen to a sermon, he would sing them his poetry. His great memorial is the monastery of S. Aldhelm (the nave of its twelfth-century church still stands) and the town itself, Malmesbury, *i.e.*, Mealdelmesburgh. He died *c.* 720 ; four churches are dedicated to him.[3] And so ends with the eighth

[1] The illustration shows a shield carved recently and placed in the roof of the choir of Glasgow cathedral (105). In his early days his companions killed a tame robin, which was a favourite with their master, S. Serf, and threw the blame on Kentigern. But Kentigern breathed upon it and it returned to life. On another occasion they put out all the lights which it was Kentigern's duty to attend to. But he went out—it was winter—and brought in a frozen branch, which, when he breathed upon it, burst into flame. *See also* page 322.

[2] The small figure illustrated was found buried under the Dean's stall in 1863, and is probably S. Wilfrid (106). In an old print he is shown baptizing the heathen ; in the foreground are fragments of temples and idols he has thrown down (24).

[3] His pastoral staff was reputed to have budded with ash-leaves during the course of a long sermon at Bishopstrow, Wiltshire, where the church is dedicated to him : other symbols of his miracles are the beam, the book and the boy.—G. F. B.

century the story of the great missionary movements of the
Dark Ages of mediæval England. Henceforth the work was
to hold what had been won—work in the main of organisation
and consolidation, which found scope for the services of many
great men ; in the ninth century S. Swithun of Winchester
(58 dedications), in the tenth century S. Dunstan (20 dedications),
in the eleventh century S. Wolstan or Wolfstan of Worcester (1
dedication) and S. Osmond of Salisbury (3 dedications), to whom
we owe the " Use of Sarum." The remaining great churchmen
whose names appear in dedications are, in the twelfth century
S. Thomas of Canterbury (46 dedications), and in the thirteenth
century S. Hugh of Lincoln (1 dedication) and S. Richard of
Chichester (1 dedication).

CHAPTER X

Chronological List of Martyrs—S. Candida—S. Agnes—SS. Cosmas and
Damian—S. Vincent—S. Blaise—S. Cyr—S. Margaret—S. Constantine
—S. Leger—S. Winifred—S. Oswald—S. Osyth—S. Edmund—S.
Alphege—S. Thomas of Canterbury—King Charles the Martyr—
Distribution and Dispersion of Relics of Martyrs—S. Bartholomew.

A VERY important set of dedications consists of those which
commemorate the "white-robed army of Martyrs." The choice
of martyrs' names, however, seems singularly capricious. Hardly
any two men rendered greater services than those great Fathers
of the Church, Ignatius and Polycarp, and both suffered
martyrdom ; yet we have not a single ancient dedication to
either. Setting aside the martyrdoms of Biblical personages,
the long list contains, in the first century, the names of SS.
Gervase and Protasius of Milan (1 dedication), and of S. Pancras,
Bishop of Taormina (10 dedications), reputed to have been sent
on mission to Sicily by S. Peter himself.

To the second century belong S. Clement (41 dedications),
who at any rate in legend suffered martyrdom ; S. Eustachius
(3 dedications), the Roman officer to whom appeared a stag
with a dazzling cross in its antlers, bidding him follow Christ ;[1]
S. Hermes or Erme (3 dedications), who may have been a
prefect at Rome ; S. Cecilia (4 dedications), whose blood-stained
body was recovered in the Catacombs by Pope Paschal I. in
817 ; and S. Symphorian of Autun (3 dedications), who like

---

[1] The illustration, which is from the west front of Wells cathedral, shows
S. Eustace carrying two boys across a river ; both children are mutilated ;
originally each had a hand on the father's shoulder. But in the *Golden
Legend* the story goes that S. Eustace (whose legend is largely a version
of that of Job), after losing all his property and his friends and his wife, fled
from his enemies with his two boys. But coming to a torrent, he found it
raging so furiously that he could not carry both across at once. So he left
one behind, and then crossed with the other, whom a wolf carried away.
Then he returned for the first child, but found that he had been carried off
by a lion. In later days the boys met and recognised one another and their
mother, and happiness returned to Eustace for a brief space (110).

D. AND P.

Female Saint.   S. Eustace.

West Front of Wells Cathedral.

Eustachius, scorned to redeem his life by sacrifice to the gods of Rome.

In the third century there are S. Hippolytus of Rome (2 dedications) who was torn asunder by wild horses, unless indeed the story be derived from a "diseased etymology" of his name; S. Fabian, Bishop of Rome (1 dedication); S. Agatha of Sicily, who has 4 dedications, including that of the ruined Premonstratensian abbey near Richmond, Yorkshire;[1] a great Father of the

H. G.

S. Agatha.

From stained glass at Manor Farm, Beauvale, Notts.

Church, S. Cyprian of Carthage (1 dedication); S. Lawrence, who has the astonishing number of 237 dedications;[2] S. Denis (41 dedications), patron saint of France, "Bishop of the Parisians," who ended this present life under the sword, and carried his severed head to Mont-Martre. S. Maurice (8 dedications), whose name survives in the little town of S. Moritz,

---

[1] In glass at Winchester S. Agatha holds a nipple in a pair of pincers (20): in glass at Beauvale Manor farm she holds a breast (111).

[2] In glass at Nettlestead S. Lawrence wears the dalmatic of a deacon, and bears a closed book and the model of a gridiron (20).

S. Lawrence.

Ranworth Rood-screen.

A. H.

S. Pancras of Rome.

From brass of the Prior of S. Pancras' Abbey, Lewes, at Cowfold, Sussex.

the place where occurred the decimation of the Theban legion ; S. Sebastian, with but two dedications in England, for his fame[1] was eclipsed by the similar martyrdom of Edmund, king of East Anglia ; S. George, the patron saint of England, with 126 dedications ; S. Lucian (1 dedication), Bishop of Beauvais ; and perhaps the most remarkable of all, S. Christopher, with 9 dedications.

To the fourth century, during the Diocletian persecution in 303 and 304, belongs S. Pancras of Rome (6 dedications), executed with the sword at the age of fourteen ; his church, of which important remains have been brought to light in the grounds of S. Augustine's College, Canterbury, was the first in England dedicated by S. Augustine, who had been a monk in the monastery of S. Andrew, Rome, founded by S. Gregory, and built on land which had belonged to the Pancras family. Another victim was S. Candida (2 dedications), who is probably commemorated in the church of S. Candida and the Holy Cross at Whitchurch, near Lyme Regis, near which was formerly a well bearing her name. Not far away are Whitestaunton, White Cross, White Lackington, White Town, all probably connected with S. Whyte or Candida. A better known virgin martyr is S. Agnes of Rome (5 dedications), who suffered martyrdom by fire ; she was but thirteen years old.

> "Agnes," says Ælfiic,[2] "in her thirteenth year lost mortality,
> And found eternal life, for that she loved Christ."

To her suitor, the son of the prefect of Rome, when he brought her precious gems and worldly ornaments, she made answer :—

> "Depart from me, I have another lover,
> Who hath granted me for a pledge the ring of His Faith,
> And hath set His token upon my face
> That I should love none other beside Him.
> He hath shewed me also His incomparable treasures,
> Which He hath promised me if I follow Him.

---

[1] In Henry the Seventh's chapel S. Sebastian is represented naked and tied to a tree : on each side is an archer with a cross-bow (160). The picture galleries of Italy are crowded with representations of the martyrdom of S. Sebastian.

[2] Homily VII. 25, from Ælfric's *Lives of Saints*, edited for the Early English Text Society by Professor Skeat, 1881 ; two more series of his Homilies were edited by Thorpe in 1844-1846. Ælfric wrote his Homilies between 993 and 997 ; he was first a monk at S. Swithun's, Winchester, and afterwards Prior of Eynsham.

I may not to His dishonour choose another
And forsake Him who hath espoused me by His love.
To Him alone ever I keep my troth ;
To Him I commit myself with all devotion."

Gent. Mag. Dec.r 1821. Pl.II. p. 497

S. Faith.   Westminster.

" I bless thee," she said, as the flames encompassed her, "O Father
of my Lord Jesus Christ, who permittest me unfearing through the

flames to come to Thee. Lo! what I believed, that I see; what I hoped for, that I hold: what I desired, that I embrace. Thee I confess with my lips; thee with my heart I altogether desire. One and true God, I come to Thee."

A. W. S.

SS. Cosmas and Damian.

Wolborough Screen, Devon.

The basilica of S. Agnese at Rome is her great memorial.[1] The

[1] In glass in the possession of Dr Philip Nelson a lamb is seen springing up at the feet of S. Agnes (180). In the other illustration (22) she is reading a book, and at her feet sits a lamb.

Diocletian persecution numbered many victims outside Rome. S. Faith of Agen (23 dedications) is said to have suffered by fire. To her was dedicated the crypt of Old S. Paul's. At the east end of the revestry of Westminster abbey is a thirteenth-century painting of S. Faith. Beneath is the Crucifixion. On the left

D. W.

The Confessor and S. Vincent.

Westminster.

is a Benedictine monk—perhaps the painter of the picture—from whose lips issues the couplet—

> "*Me quem culpa gravis premit, erige, Virgo salutis ;*
> *Fac mihi placatum Christum, deleasque reatum.*"

"Raise me, Maid and Saviour, weighed down by the load of my sin; reconcile Christ to me, and wash away mine iniquity " (115). The martyr carries a metal bedstead, as also in the brass of Prior Langley in S. Lawrence's church, Norwich (18); and in stained glass in Winchester cathedral. Martyrdom was the fate also of the two Arabs, Cosmas and Damian (3 dedications), who are said to have practised medicine in Cilicia.¹ The legend of these two saints is of ancient origin, and at quite an early date they were represented as the successors of the Dioscuri;

E. W. A.

S. Catherine.   S. Mary Magdalene.

Bench Ends at Coombe-in-Teignhead.

and the honours paid to them at certain of their shrines undoubtedly betray points of contact with pre-existing forms

¹ On the Wolborough screen Cosmas has in his right hand a pestle or ladle, and in his left a mortar or jar ; Damian holds up a glass phial (116).

of worship.[1]   The Spanish deacon, S. Vincent (6 dedications), was roasted over a slow fire till pain brought on unconsciousness, when he was removed to a soft bed, reserved for further torture ; but in his stupor he sank and died.   Cape S. Vincent is one of his many memorials.[2]   The persecution even reached the distant Britons; and S. Alban (11 dedications) was executed at Verulamium, because, though a Pagan, he had sheltered a Christian priest.[3]   S. German of Auxerre, with many other bishops and clergy, c. 430, is said to have worshipped at the shrine of England's Protomartyr.   S. Catherine of Alexandria (62 dedications) is said to have been saved for a time by the breaking of the toothed wheel to which she was bound, but was afterwards scourged and beheaded ; angels bore her body to Mount Sinai, where in the ninth century it was discovered amid great rejoicings. Another victim was Julian the Hospitaller (7 dedications), an Egyptian physician : S. Julian's hospital or "God's House" at Southampton preserves his name.   S. Blaise (5 dedications) was Bishop of Sebaste in Cappadocia or Lesser Armenia ; he was carded with iron combs and beheaded, c. 316.   His most important church in England was that of the Benedictine

K. M. C.

S. Blaise.

Rood-screen, S. Mary Steps, Exeter.

[1] Delehaye, *Ibid.*, 191.

[2] S. Vincent, as one of the patron saints of Henry the Seventh, is represented on his tomb (117).

[3] On a brass at S. Albans the saint is shown with a cross as missioner or preacher, and with the sword by which he was decapitated (13).

priory at Boxgrove, dedicated to SS. Mary and Blaise.[1]
Because of the manner of his torture he became the patron
saint of all wool-combers, and till 1825 " Bishop Blaize
Festival" was a high day at Bradford with processions and
pageants; and a child of five was chosen to recite the bishop's
story in verses, which began thus :—

" Hail to the day whose kind, auspicious rays,
  Deigned first to smile on famous Bishop Blaize." [2]

H. G.

S. Lucy.

From stained glass at Manor Farm, Notts.

[1] In glass at Oxford, S. Blaise is represented as a bishop, holding in his
hand a wool-comb (20). On the rood-screen of S. Mary Steps, Exeter,
S. Blaise is represented with a comb in the right hand, and in the left what
looks like a club. The panel, however, has been clumsily repainted, and the
club is probably a taper with beams radiating from it. The story is that on
his way to prison he extracted a fish bone from a child's throat. In the
evening the mother brought to the prison food and a taper, and the saint
promised that all who offered once a year a taper in memory of him should
have relief from throat trouble (119).

[2] Arnold-Forster, *Ibid.*, i. 494.

D. W.

S. Winifred.   S. Margaret.

Henry the Seventh's Chapel, Westminster.

16

S. Cyriac or S. Cyr of Iconium (9 dedications) was three years old when his mother, Julitta, was put on the rack for her faith by the heathen governor. The little child tried to run to his mother, crying, "I am a Christian too," when he was seized and flung against the marble steps and killed. The mother was then beheaded. S. Lucy of Syracuse (2 dedications) plucked out her eyes rather than marry a pagan.[1] To this period, perhaps, belongs the story of S. Barbara (1 dedication), who may have lived in Egypt; and of S. Margaret of Antioch in Pisidia (261 dedications), a very apocryphal martyr, but a very great favourite in dedications, largely, perhaps, because of the last words she uttered before her execution.

"Hearken to my prayer, O God, and grant to every man who shall write my life and relate my works or shall hear or read them that his name be written in the book of eternal life ; and whosoever shall build a church in my name, do not bring him to thy remembrance to punish him for his wrongdoings."

But in 312 A.D. came the Peace of the Church, and axe and sword and fire, scaffold and cross, gridiron and rack and wheel, ceased for a time to provide their quota of Christian martyrs. For two whole centuries, except in the Celtic Church, no names of martyrs survive in our list of dedications. The most remarkable is that of Constantine or Cystennyn, a king of Cornwall in the sixth century. In a letter written in 547, Gildas tells of his perjuries and dissoluteness, even of sacrilegious murder of two youths in the very church itself. But a great grief fell upon him in the death of his wife, and he was henceforth a changed man. He gave up his royal state and retired to an Irish monastery, where he lived unknown, grinding corn in a quern for the monks, till one day one of his brethren heard him say, with a laugh, to himself, "Can this be King Constantine of Cornwall, who wore helm and bore shield, drudging at a handmill?" His identity discovered, he was placed among the students, and afterwards went as a missionary into Scotland. There he laboured under the great Columba, and there in Cantire he met a martyr's death. To Constantine three if not more English churches are dedicated, and the Cornish parish of Constantine bears his name.

To the seventh century belongs S. Leodegarius, Bishop of Autun (5 dedications), whose remains now rest at Poitiers. When Autun was besieged, he defended it as long as defence was possible, and then ransomed the lives of all at the price of

---

[1] In a painting in the Louvre, S. Lucy holds the palm of martyrdom and carries her eyes in a dish (22, 120).

his own.   He was blinded and tortured and mutilated in every
limb ; but at last recovered articulate speech.   The letter which

E. W. A.
        S. Leger.   S. Apollonia.

Rood-screen at Ashton, Devon.

he wrote to his mother after the loss of his eyes and the slashing
of his lips is still extant.   Two years later he was conducted
forth into the forest.   For long the executioners wandered about,

seeking a fitting place, till the bishop said, "It is useless, my children, to tire yourself further; do quickly that for which you have come forth." Then he knelt down and received the death blow. Ashby S. Leger preserves his name, and its church is dedicated to SS. Mary and Leodegare.[1] Six churches are attributed, more or less doubtfully, to the Welsh virgin, S. Winifred or Gwenfrewi, who is supposed to have lived in the seventh century, but whose legendary life is five centuries later. At any rate her name is preserved in the spring which bursts up in Holywell, Flintshire. A spring of such volume and force was doubtless an object of worship long before Christian days. Above ground is a fifteenth-century chapel of the Church of England; the undercroft forms another chapel, leased to the Roman Catholic Church. Pilgrims still resort to it in great numbers; and crutches, spinal jackets and the like, hung on the walls round the pool in which the sick are immersed, bear evidence to the recoveries that have taken place. It is perhaps because of her connection with this famous spring that her name is attached to two other springs, Holywell, Oxford, and Woolston, Salop.[2]

To the same century belong two Christian kings of Northumbria, each slain by Penda, the heathen king of Mercia ; viz., S. Edwin and S. Oswald.[3] S. Edwin (1 dedication) was the first Christian king of Northumbria ; it was his queen, Ethelburga, who brought with her from Kent S. Paulinus as her chaplain. In 627 King Edwin was baptized in the church of S. Peter, York, the first York minster. In 636 he was defeated and slain by Penda. His successor, King Oswald (67 dedications), was one of the greatest and best of all the kings we have had in England, to be ranked with the French S. Louis and our

[1] On the screen at Ashton, Devon, S. Leger bears the auger with which his eyes were bored out (123).

[2] In the illustration there are at the feet of S. Winifred what looks like a beheading block and a severed head (121).

[3] S. Oswald is often represented with a raven which he used as a messenger to obtain the conversion and hand of a pagan princess. In the Lubeck *Passionale* he is receiving a letter from her and sending her a ring (26). Or he holds in his hand a dish, as on the west front of Wells cathedral. He was seated at dinner one day with S. Aidan, and there was outside a great crowd of poor folk begging for food. So the king sent them the food on his silver dish, and brake the dish and distributed the fragments to them. Wherefore, said S. Aidan, the right hand that brake the dish should be blessed. And after the king's death his right hand was found to be incorrupt, and was preserved in Peterborough abbey as one of its holiest treasures (88).

W. M. D.

S. Lambert.

S. Mary's, Shrewsbury.

own Alfred.   He fell in 642.   His skull was preserved at Lindisfarne ; and when the body of S. Cuthbert set out on its long wanderings Durhamward, it was placed in his coffin, where it was seen in 1829 and 1899.   S. Oswald's fame spread far ; he

K. M. C.

S. Sidwell.

S. Sidwell's Church, Exeter.

is mentioned in Swiss and German liturgies, and he is the patron saint of Zug.   Queen Osyth or Sitha (4 dedications) ran away from an apostate husband and became a nun at Chick or S. Osyth in Essex.   Danish pirates sailed up the Coln and slew her ; the place where she fell is still called the " Nun's Well."

When her head was struck from her body, there gushed forth a spring of pure water; and she walked to her grave—as she is shown on the Convent seal—carrying her head in her hand.

To the eighth century belongs King Ethelbert of East Anglia (16 dedications), murdered by Offa, king of the Mercians; also S. Lambert, Bishop of Maestricht, slain in 709,[1] to whom there are two dedications; and S. Sidwell or Sativola, martyred in 740 on the site of S. Sidwell church, Exeter, which therefore is a memorial church. The church of Laneast, Cornwall, is dedicated to SS. Welvela and Sativola. By far the most notable martyr in this century was that greatest of the men of Devon and most famous of missionary bishops, S. Boniface, slain in 755 (6 dedications).

In the ninth century almost all the English martyrs are of royal blood. They include young King Kenelm of Mercia (9 dedications); Wyston or Winston, another child-king of Mercia (3 dedications); Alkmund, a young king of Northumbria (4 dedications). Then we come to the terrible times which were to open out in England for nearly a century and a half another broad road to martyrdom: these were the days of the piratical forays of the heathen Vikings. Then it was, from the end of the ninth century, that the Irish built their Round Towers, each to be a strong place of refuge for the congregation of the church hard

J. F. E.

S. Edmund's Head.
Ely Cathedral.

by; then it was in England that yet another roll of saints and martyrs was added to the lists of those to whom England should dedicate her churches. They comprise S. Edmund, king of East Anglia (61 dedications); S. Alkelda (2 dedications); S. Alphege (5 dedications); and two more martyrs, Scandinavians both, King Olaf (13 dedications) and Earl Magnus (3 dedications).[2]

---

[1] The window at S. Mary's, Shrewsbury, contains foreign glass, probably Flemish. The saint's name appears at the back. Below is the donor of the glass (125).

[2] S. Magnus was beheaded in an invasion of the pagan Northmen.

As the number of his dedications shows, few things appealed more to churchmen and Englishmen than the martyrdom of S. Edmund, the beloved king of East Anglia, where one-third of his dedications occur. Tradition of long date connects his martyrdom with the village of Hoxne, Suffolk, where still Goldbrook stream is shown, beneath the bridge of which he hid, a bridge which no wedding party will cross—and the field where till 1848 stood a very ancient oak, twenty feet in girth, to which it was said he was bound as a target to the Danish arrows. When the tree fell, there was found "the point of an arrow, partly corroded, projecting from the inside of the hollow part of the trunk, about four and a half or five feet from the ground, which part had warted nearly two feet through the inside of the tree, and was perfectly decayed about the arrow, and was covered a little more than a foot thick with sound wood, the annual ring or layer showing the growth of more than 1,000 years, as near as can be made out."[1] After a time the king was unloosed from the tree and beheaded. In many places in East Anglia, *e.g.*, on the parapet of the beautiful porch of Pulham S. Mary the Virgin, a wolf is shown guarding his head.[2]

Here is a tenth-century version of the story. After the retreat of the Danes there was great search for the head of the king, and at last they came to the place—

> " Where lay a grey wolf who guarded the head,
> And with his two feet had embraced the head
> Greedy and hungry, and for God's care durst not
> Taste the head, but kept it against other beasts.
> Then they were astonished at the wolf's guardianship,
> And carried the holy head home with them.
> But the wolf followed forth with the head
> Until they came to the town as if he were tame,
> And then turned back again unto the wood."[3]

In stained glass, in a window of the Lady chapel of Bristol cathedral, S. Edmund is depicted nude, tied to a tree ; in his body are arrows shot by two archers ; also a white wolf guards

---

[1] *Bury Post*, Oct. 11th, 1848.

[2] On the Norfolk rood-screen S. Edmund holds in his hand two arrows (13). On a stone seat in Ely cathedral the wolf is shown guarding the king's head (127). The statuette on the grille of Henry the Seventh's tomb at Westminster is shown with a crown in Hollar's drawing. It probably held an arrow or arrows (76). In a stone statue in the same chapel, S. Edmund holds in one hand the orb of sovereignty ; in the other probably was an arrow (158).

[3] Ælfric's *Homilies*.

a head. Of the vast abbey of S. Edmund at Bury, Suffolk, where his remains were finally enshrined, little but the gateways remain.

To the tenth century belong young King Edward the Martyr, referred to above, and a princess of somewhat doubtful authenticity, Alkelda, with 2 dedications: she is said to have been strangled by the Danes.

To the eleventh century belongs S. Alphege, Archbishop of Canterbury, with 5 dedications, including that of S. Alphege, Greenwich, which is a Memorial church erected on the site of his murder. From the 8th to the 29th of September 1011, Canterbury had been besieged by the Danes. It was defended by the archbishop till it was taken by treachery. S. Alphege refused to allow himself to be ransomed ; and after being dragged about for seven months, was slain with stones and arrows in a drunken orgy of the Danes.[1] His bones lay for ten years in S. Paul's, London, till they were translated "with much state and bliss and songs of praise" to Canterbury cathedral by King Canute, himself a Dane. In Norway, King Olaf or Olave the Stout was so stern a proselytiser that the country rose against him, and he was slain near Trondhjem in 1030 ; whereupon he became Olave the Saint : he has 13 dedications in England. S. Olaf is represented in the east window of the south aisle of Holy Trinity church, York, as a saintly personage, with moustache and beard, carrying in his left hand three stones ; the story is that finding that a maidservant had been forced to bake instead of saying her prayers, he turned three of the loaves into stones.[2]

To the twelfth century belongs another Northman, S. Magnus, Jarl of Orkney, with 3 dedications. On his way from Mass he was arrested and beheaded in 1107 ; people say that a flower may always be found in bloom where he fell. On either side of London Bridge a church commemorates a Northman, the London church of S. Magnus facing the Southwark church of S. Olave. Both these commemorate martyrdoms which took place far away. But England was to have one more famous martyr, the most famous of all, S. Thomas of Canterbury, whose murder in 1170 sent a wave of horror through Christendom.

Here is the story of the martyrdom in Caxton's translation :—" Then one of the knights smote him on the head as he kneeled before the

[1] S. Alphege is probably one of a group of saints represented on an ivory in the British Museum.
[2] In the illustration S. Olave or Holofius carries a spear and loaves (13). For the shape of the loaves cf. S. Sitha (217).

A. H.

S. Thomas of Canterbury.

From Prior Nelonde's brass at Cowfold, Sussex.

altar.   And one, Sir Edward Gryme, that was his crossbearer, put forth
his arm with the cross to bear off the stroke, and the stroke smote the
cross in sunder and his arm almost off, wherefore he fled for fear, and
so did all the monks that were at that time at Compline.   And then
smote each at him, that they smote off a great piece of the skull of his

A. G.

Murder of Becket.

Alabaster Table.

head[1] that his brain fell on the pavement.   And so they slew and
martyred him; and were so cruel that one of them brake the point of

[1] He is therefore sometimes represented bearing in his hand the *corona* or
upper portion of his skull; *e.g.*, in one of the statues of the west front of
Wells cathedral (132).   In a window at the east end of the south aisle of
Lincoln nave S. Thomas of Canterbury is represented carrying in his hands
the severed crown (*corona*) of his skull, escorted to heaven by three angels,
two in front, while a third urges him forward (Nelson's *Painted Glass*, 141)

T. P.

S. Thomas of Canterbury and Warrior.

West Front of Wells Cathedral.

his sword against the pavement; and thus this holy and blessed Archbishop saint Thomas suffered death in his own church."

There is hardly a country in Europe but has churches dedicated to S. Thomas of Canterbury. In England 80 dedications
have been traced. But in 1537 Henry VIII. blotted out Becket's
name from the service-books, and most of the saint's churches
no doubt either changed their dedications, or, lopping off the
last two words, left the dedication apparently to S. Thomas the
apostle. A curious history attaches to the little cruciform
Norman church high up on the downs between Guildford and

E. K. P.

Murder of Becket.

Boss in Exeter Cathedral.

Dorking, on the way by which the pilgrims went to Canterbury. Originally it was the church of the " Holy Martyrs ";
then, no doubt after the murder of Becket, it was re-dedicated to
" S. Thomas of Canterbury and All Holy Martyrs "; then when
the former part of the second dedication had to be dropped, it
became " Martyrs' church "; finally this was corrupted into
" S. Martha's church " on S. Martha's Hill ; a dedication otherwise
quite unknown in England.[1] And so we come to the last solemn
scene of all, the end of the sad, eventful story of the martyrs,
the death at Whitehall in 1649 of King Charles,

[1] Charles Browne, *Ibid.*, 293.

"Who nothing common did or mean
Upon that memorable scene,
But bowed his comely head
Down, as upon a bed."

Churches are dedicated to Charles, King and Martyr, at Falmouth and Plymouth, Peak Forest, Derbyshire, Newtown, Salop, and Tunbridge Wells.

D. W.

S. Bartholomew.

Westminster.

A special reason which kept the name of a martyr in repute was the survival and the wideness of diffusion and the reputation of his relics. Of the non-Biblical saints in our lists of dedications, only two go back to the first century of our era. One is the double dedication of SS. Gervase and Protasius. They are supposed to be the proto-martyrs of Milan, and to have been executed in the time of Nero. The preservation of their names for 1,900 years is wholly due to the discovery by S. Ambrose in the fourth century of the bodies of two men of wondrous size, which were believed to be those of the twin brothers. As far as dedications go, they are honoured more than Ambrose; for Little Plumstead, Essex, is dedicated to them, while to Ambrose we have no certain dedication at all. So also the name of S. Clement is held in the greater honour because of the strange story of his shrine and relics. It may well be that the name of England's proto-martyr, S. Alban, would have altogether perished, had not Offa, king of the Mercians, warned by a dream, searched for his grave on the hillside of S. Albans, from which he translated the relics with all pomp and magnificence to the abbey church which he built to guard them.

A good many dedications to foreign saints are undoubtedly due to the fact that one or more English churches had obtained portions of their relics. Thus in the year 665 Pope Vitalian sent some of the relics of S. Pancras of Rome to King Oswy of Northumbria. The puzzle is that of the eight dedications to

S. Pancras of Rome, one is in Kent, three in Sussex, three in London ; only one, at Wroot, Lincolnshire, is within what were Oswy's dominions. The same explanation may apply to several cases in which there are but one or two dedications to some Gallican or Italian or Spanish saint ; *e.g.*, to S. Medard at Little Bytham, Lincolnshire ; to S. Firmin at North Crawley, Bucks., and Thurlby, Lincolnshire ; to S. Sebastian at Great Gonerby, Lincolnshire, and Wokingham, Berkshire.

Of the apostles the premier places are taken by S. Peter, S. Andrew, S. James the Greater, S. John, and S. Bartholomew,

W. P. Y.

S. John Divine. S. Bartholomew.

Stanbury Chantry, Hereford Cathedral.

with 1,140, 637, 414, 181, and 165 dedications respectively. Next comes S. Thomas with 46 dedications, some of them dubious. Why was that "somewhat obscure" apostle, Bartholomew, so much in favour ? It is not that his legendary history is specially striking. The reason is probably to be found in the many strange tales that were told of the miraculous preservation of his remains, as well in their wide diffusion. In the Middle Ages half the leading cities of the Continent appear to have boasted of some relic of this apostle. Nor was England omitted in the distribution. An arm was taken to Canterbury by Anselm ; it is possible that this relic may have influenced the dedication of several English churches.[1] His great memorial is the church of

[1] Arnold-Forster, *Ibid.*, i. 82.

S. Bartholomew, Smithfield, begun in 1123, of which the chancel and transept still remain. It was founded by Raherus or Rayer, "a pleasant-witted gentleman," says Strype, "and therefore in his time called the king's minstrel."

Being at Rome on pilgrimage, he fell ill of malarial fever, and vowed to found a hospital "for the recreacion of poure men" if he recovered. Then he was carried up in a vision by a great beast having four feet and two wings, to a very lofty place, whence he saw the horror of the bottomless pit. From this he was saved by a majestic personage who said unto him "I am Bartholomew, the Apostle of Jesus Christ, that come to succour thee in thy anguish, and to open to thee the secret mysteries of heaven. Know me truly by the will and commandment of the High Trinity to have chosen a place in the suburbs of London at Smithfield, where in my name thou shalt found a church; and it shall be the house of God; there shall be the tabernacle of the Lamb, the temple of the Holy Ghost. This spiritual house Almighty God shall inhabit and hallow it and glorify it; and his eyes shall be open and his ears intending on this house night and day, that the asker in it shall receive, the seeker shall find, and the ringer or knocker shall enter. Wherefore doubt thee not, in God having trust; do thou make nothing of the costs of this building, only give thy diligence, and my part shall be to provide things necessary, and to build and end this work, and with evident tokens and signs to protect and defend continually under the shadow of my wings this work by me accept." With these words the vision " disparyschydde."

Rayer, returning to London, got the sanction and help of his master, King Henry I., and began the work, which was soon aided by miraculous agency, for a marvellous light shone on the building as it arose; the blind who visited it received their sight, cripples were healed, and the hiding-place of a choir-book hidden by a Jew was miraculously revealed. Rahere died in 1144, leaving the church in the charge of thirteen Austin Canons, increased by his successor to thirty-five.[1] S. Bartholomew is recorded to have been flayed alive, and is represented with a flaying knife in his hand, and sometimes with his skin over his arm, as on the bronze grille round the tomb of King Henry VII. in Westminster abbey.

[1] At Blythburgh S. Bartholomew holds a flaying knife (63); this also appears with his name in the Stanbury chantry, Hereford cathedral (135). On the grille in Henry the Seventh's chapel, Westminster, his skin, including the skull, is thrown over the left arm (134).

137

CHAPTER XI

Saints without Dedication—S. William of York—S. Dorothy—
S. Ursula—Les Saintes Maries.

SUCH then is the story, told as briefly as may be, of the long
roll of the saints whose names and whose merits and whose
services the English Church has delighted to commemorate in
the dedications of her churches. It is a list which gives furiously
to think. Some personages appear whom perhaps it is a
little difficult to recognise as saints. It was not primarily for
religion that Archbishop Alphege, Kings Edwin and Oswald of
Northumberland, and many another Anglo-Saxon king gave up
his life. Many a high-born Saxon lady earned canonisation by
precisely such services as those rendered by the founders of
Cheltenham College, and Girton, Newnham, and Somerville.
Equally strange are the omissions. No English church is
dedicated to the "Apostles" as a whole; though Justinian's
church of the Apostles was as famous in Christendom as S.
Sophia, and was indeed the prototype of S. Mark's, Venice.
Of the apostles, S. Simon and S. Jude have no individual
dedications, but are nine times commemorated together.[1] S.
Matthias has one doubtful dedication.[2] There are many dedications to S. Anne, the apocryphal mother of the Blessed Virgin,
but none to the mother of S. John Baptist, the cousin of the
Blessed Virgin.[3] Yet "Elizabeth" is one of the most popular
Christian names in England, reminding one, as it does, not only
of the S. Elizabeth of S. Luke's gospel, but of good S. Elizabeth
of Hungary and of the greatest of our English queens. We have
no ancient dedication to S. Mary of Bethany, but that is because
she was identified with S. Mary Magdalene. Cleopas' walk to
Emmaus with the risen Lord on he first Easter Sunday
is forgotten; as also are Silas, fellow-sufferer with S. Paul at

[1] On the Ranworth screen, S. Simon, having been a fisherman, carries a
fish (56); while S. Jude carries a boat (82).
[2] On the stall panels at Blythburgh, S. Matthias holds the axe by which
he was slain (63). So also on page 261.
[3] S. Elizabeth is depicted in Morley church, Derbyshire, with a blue
cloak over a white robe, and holding a book in her right hand.

18

S. William of York.

York Minster.

Philippi, and Timothy and Titus and Philemon. So it is with the Fathers of the Church; we have no ancient dedication to S. Ignatius of Antioch, or to S. Polycarp of Smyrna, or to S. Athanasius of Alexandria, or to S. Chrysostom of Constantinople. Of the agents of the Conversion of Anglo-Saxon England, Birinus was forgotten, except so far as he once shared a compound dedication of Winchester cathedral. As to the founders of the great Religious orders, there is no recognition of the Cluniac S. Berno, of the Carthusian S. Bruno, of the Cistercians, Stephen Harding and S. Bernard; nor of the Black Friar, S. Dominic.[1] Saddest of all is the omission of Bede, to whose lifelong scholarly labours we owe such knowledge of early Church history as is to be found nowhere else in Europe. Without commemoration in dedications, but not uncommon on roods, screens, and stained glass, is S. William, Archbishop of York, after whose death in 1154 thirty-six miracles were

[1] S. Dominic, in a print in the British Museum, has a star over his head, a church in his left hand, and in his right a closed book, plant and crucifix.

M. L.

S. William of York.

All Saints', York.

reported to have been wrought at his tomb, a list whereof
formerly hung in the vestry of the minster: he was canonised

E. W. A.

S. Dorothy.   S. Clement.

Rood-screen at Ashton, Devon.

in 1227. The great window in the north-east transept of York
minster contains 105 panels of ancient glass, depicting the
donors of the window, scenes from the life of S. William, the

miracles performed after his death, incidents connected with his translation, and miracles of his lifetime.[1]

E. W. A.

S. Antony of Egypt.   S. Ursula.

Rood-screen, Ashton, Devon.

A very favourite saint, not commemorated by any dedication,

[1] The glass in the minster (138) is more than a century older than that of All Saints', North Street, York (139).

S. Ursula.

Wooden statuette.

is S. Dorothy. She is said to have been a high-born maiden of Cæsarea ; and having become a Christian during the Diocletian persecution, was ordered by the prefect to sacrifice to the gods. On her refusal she was put to the rack ; and two of her old playmates, who had been Christians and had apostatized through fear, were called in to persuade her to follow their example. But Dorothy succeeded in bringing them back to the Christian faith, and they were at once hurried off to martyrdom. Dorothy was reserved for further suffering ; and when her life was visibly sinking under the torments, she also was led to the block. The prefect urged her even then to recant and ask forgiveness of the gods ; but she answered that she would ask forgiveness for himself in the land whither she was going, "a land of perpetual light and joy, and spring and sunshine, and fadeless flowers and delicious fruits." Theophilus, a notary, standing by, asked her jestingly to send him some of the flowers and fruit of which she spoke. This she promised to do, and was presently beheaded.

And not long after there appeared to Theophilus a beautiful boy with three roses and three apples, and saying, " These my sister Dorothea sends from Paradise," immediately vanished. Theophilus became a Christian, and he too soon after suffered martyrdom.[1]

S. Ursula too is without a dedication in any English church ; which is the more surprising as she was fabled to be a British princess, to whom there were 11,000 virgins for handmaids. With these she sailed over the sea in a day, the ship having so good a wind, and came to a port of Gaul, and thence by some roundabout route to Rome, where she talked over the Pope Cyriacus and the Bishop of Ravenna and other bishops, and was joined by Prince Conan and a British king, whom some style her husband, Ethereus.[2] With these companions, some of whom are shown in the illustration on page 306, Ursula and her companions set out to Cologne, which was besieged by the Huns. Whom when the Huns saw, they ran upon them with a great cry, and all the virgins they beheaded save the blessed Ursula, whom their prince shot at with an arrow so that she died. Ursula and her virgins are buried at Cologne in a great church dedicated to her. With arrow and numerous virgins she is depicted in fifteenth-century glass at Hault-Hucknall, Derbyshire. At Morley, Derbyshire, she is represented in stained glass, ascending up to heaven with eleven virgin martyrs in a sheet.[3]

The Church of England is poorer also for the loss of a Bearded Lady. S. Wilgeforte or Uncumber actually went to the length of praying for a beard in order to ward off suitors, which it did effectually ; her statue in Henry the Seventh's chapel, Westminster, represents her with a woman's long hair, but a bushy beard. According to Sir Thomas More she was in great favour with housewives, because "for a peck of oats she would not fail to uncumber them of their husbands."

We may add the names of two saintly personages who have no dedications in England, but are held in great honour in Provence, viz., two Maries ; not Our Lady or S. Mary Magdalene

---

[1] On the rood-screen at Ashton, Devon, S. Dorothy carries in one hand a basket of fruit and in the other the palm of martyrdom (140). In glass in the possession of Dr Philip Nelson, S. Dorothy bears a flower in her left hand and a basket of fruit in her right (180).

[2] There are varying histories of her journey, all alike unveracious. According to one version her husband was Ethereus, a British king ; and among her companions was Pantulus, Bishop of Basle ; Jaques, Bishop of Liège ; Sulpicius, Bishop of Ravenna ; and Cyriacus, who is fabled to have resigned the papal throne to go with her. See the *Golden Legend.*

[3] Nelson's *Painted Glass*, 70.

D. W.

S. Barbara.   S. Uncumber.

Henry the Seventh's Chapel, Westminster.

or Mary of Bethany, but Marie Salomé and Marie Jacobé, as they are styled in French.

The story goes that some three and thirty years after the Ascension there was a great persecution in Judæa, and S. Mary Magdalene, Lazarus, and Martha, Mary, the mother of the Apostles James and John, and Mary, the mother of James the Less, and others, were arrested and put on board a ship without oars or mast or rudder, and set adrift. After many days they were thrown ashore in the swamps of the Rhone. Here a spring of pure water bubbled up in answer to their prayers, and an altar was set up, fragments of which are said still to remain. S. Mary Magdalene and Lazarus evangelised Marseilles, and Martha Tarascon;[1] but the two Maries stayed behind, and in due course died, and were buried near the spring and altar, and over their grave arose a church, which in 1144 was rebuilt, strong and new and fortified against the raids of the Saracens; this is the existing church, in which still flows the precious spring. In the sixth century mention is made in a will of the church of the two *Sanctæ Mariæ de nave*; and the ancient armorial bearings of the place show a ship containing the two Maries together with their servant, and the legend *Navis in Pelago*. In 1448 good King René of Provence got permission to excavate, and found buried two bodies, one on each side of the altar, and also four skulls arranged in a square exactly in accordance with the story preserved by Gervais of Tilbury, a chronicler of the preceding century. In December the relics were solemnly transferred to three coffers in the presence of a cardinal, an archbishop, twelve bishops, and four abbots, and the coffers were placed in a strong chest, locked and sealed; and above the chancel was built a strong room of stone for its safe custody. Above the chancel arch is an opening through which every year on the 24th of May the chest is passed, and slowly lowered by a capstan to the floor of the nave, where it remains for twenty-four hours. All the district attends the ceremony, for on it depend good harvest and good fishing, and many cures are wrought of the afflicted.[2]

[1] In a painting at Florence, S. Martha is shown exorcising the dragon of Tarascon with holy water. A huge canvas model of the dragon is still preserved at Tarascon (18, 46).

[2] *Sacristy*, iii. 188.

CHAPTER XII

Dramatic Stories—S. Margaret of Antioch—S. Barbara—S. George—S. Clement—S. Andrew—S. Maurice and the Theban Legion—S. Lawrence —S. Anthony the Great—S. Erasmus—S. Sebastian—S. Cecily—S. Catherine—S. Christopher and the Child—S. Rumbald—S. Nicholas— S. Leonard—S. Benedict—Julian the Hospitaller—S. Elizabeth of Hungary—S. Roche—S. Giles—SS. Cosmas and Damian—S. Hubert— S. Eustace—S. Francis.

IF now we turn to those who were actually admitted to the roll of honour, the reason for their presence is sometimes far to seek. Perhaps we do not always remember that the old Church folk were very human people; more human, less sophisticated than ourselves. The Bible stories and the Legends of the Saints meant to them all that Mudie's Library or the *Times* Book Club means to us. Just like ourselves nowadays, they preferred a good story to a bad one, an interesting story to a dull one, one with plot and incident and adventure to a story of ordinary people behaving in a commonplace manner; they liked flesh and blood personages better than abstractions; they liked local colour and abundance of detail and characterisation; they liked "strong" situations; they liked a story with plenty of fighting and adventure in it, if possible there should be dragons;[1] they

[1] Saints famous for conquest of dragons were SS. Michael, Pol de Leon, George, Martha, Margaret, and Armel. In a *Book of Hours* conjectured to have been executed in the time of Henry VII. for his son, afterwards king, and now in the possession of Mr Leighton, 40 Brewer Street, W., is a representation of S. Armigile, to which these words are affixed : " Whooso deuotely say this prayor followyng in the worship of allmyghti god and saynt Armyle they shalbe relesyd of all maner of sickenesse and soris."
" Sancte die preciose
Aduacote gloriose
Confessor Armigile."
The whole prayer is given in full from the *Horae*, No. 51, in Dr Montague James' Catalogue of Fitzwilliam MSS. In the above MS. S. Armyle is depicted in full armour, over which is a blue cloak ; he is bearded and has the tonsure ; in his right he holds a red book, in his left a crosier ; under his feet is the dragon of the river Seich which he slew. In a statue at

liked the dramatic and
picturesque; they liked incidents that gripped the
imagination; they liked the
ghostly and supernatural;
they wanted miracles and
plenty of them, and the
more out of the ordinary
the miracles, the more im-
pressive they were; they
greatly liked stories about
relics; they appreciated
Virtue and the Triumph of
Virginity as much as a
Drury Lane gallery; and
just as much they loved to
hear of the simple affec-
tions of daily life, of mother
and child, husband and wife,
brother and sister; they
loved stories about children
and about lovers of chil-
dren; and very much also
stories about kindness to
poor folk, and the sick, and
the lepers, and the captives;
and as much as anything,
being country folk, they
liked stories about animals.
As the stories were passed
on from one generation to
another, they were ampli-
fied and improved; ulti-
mately a fine old crusted
legend was evolved. The
story of the stoning of
S. Stephen in the Acts is

Westminster he is leading off a
dragon which he had bound
round the neck with his stole
(93). On an alabaster plaque
in the possession of Stonyhurst
College S. Armel wears plate
armour under a chasuble, and
with his stole holds a dragon.

S. Margaret of Antioch.

Ranworth Rood-screen.

dramatic enough ; and gained him 46 dedications ; he might have had more, but, being in the Bible, the story did not admit of amplification and embroidery. On the other hand, no mention is made in the Bible of the latter days of S. Mary Magdalene ; and so she could be provided by mediæval admirers with a set of legends as to her doings in Provence, and obtained 187 dedications. So with S. Andrew ; it is not to the Scriptural but to the legendary story that he owes in the main his 637 dedications.[1] The apostle S. Thomas stands fairly well in the list because of his adventures, not as an apostle, but as carpenter and builder in a missionary tour in India. S. Margaret of Antioch is a somewhat apocryphal saint, and 261 dedications seem rather more than she deserves. But listen to her story :—

"Then there suddenly appeared to her in the corner of the prison a marvellous dragon ; from his nostrils proceeded smoke and fire, and he uttered a strong, rough voice, and fire from his mouth gave light to all the prison. And the dragon came at her with his mouth wide open, and swallowed her. But the sign of the cross which she put upon her grew in the mouth of the dragon, and became greater and greater *until it cleaved him into two pieces.*"

Of this there was an improved version, which makes out that Margaret did not make the sign of the cross till she had been swallowed and was inside the dragon ; and she is often shown just emerging from the ruptured beast.[2] From this an important corollary was drawn, viz., that as Margaret had escaped from the dragon's belly, she was the proper saint to be invoked by women in the pangs of childbirth. This doubtless contributed greatly to her popularity. Of the legend of S. Barbara one version is told at length in the *Golden Legend.*

Her father was building a cistern or piscina with a tower, and in his absence she caused three windows to be substituted for two. And when he returned, he demanded why three. And S. Barbara answered, "These three windows betoken clearly the Father, the Son, and the Holy Ghost, on whom we ought to believe and worship." Then he incontinent drew his sword to have slain her, but she was borne away to a mountain. Here her father found her, and took her by the hair,

[1] One should take into account, however, the fact that both Pope Gregory, and S. Augustine, and S. Paulinus, and S. Wilfrid were all in one way or other connected with the Benedictine monastery of S. Andrew on the Cælian Hill at Rome.

[2] On Ranworth screen (147) and in an alabaster tablet in the vestry of S. Peter Mancroft, Norwich (7), S. Margaret is seen thrusting her cross-staff into the mouth of a dragon. At Westminster (121) the cross at the top of her staff has been broken off. On an ivory in the British Museum she is seen emerging from the middle of a dragon's back.

and drew her back to the town and delivered her to the judge. Next day and many days she was beaten and tortured ; at last her father slew her with his own hand. Whereon fire from heaven descended on him, and consumed him in such wise that there could not be found any ashes of all his whole body.

Hence she is represented as the protectress from thunderbolts and lightning, and, by an extension, from explosions by cannon or musketry, and may be seen depicted in company with armour and field-pieces. In Italian men-of-war it is common to call the stoke-hole *The Santa Barbara*. Six churches in Norfolk contain ancient glass in which she is depicted. She appears near a tower or carrying a tower on four Norfolk rood-screens ; sometimes she holds the palm of victory ; or, in Germany, she holds a feather, because the rods with which she was beaten were turned into feathers.[1]

The legend of S. George,

[1] At Westminster S. Barbara carries her tower in her left hand, and an open book in her right (144). She also carries a tower in an alabaster tablet in the vestry of S. Peter Mancroft, Norwich (7). In an illumination S. Barbara is shown crowned, with palm and tower, and trampling on her father (22).

S. Barbara.

Rood-screen, Ranworth.

W. D.

S. George.

Ranworth Rood-screen.

the dragon, and the rescued princess looks like a derivative from the Greek story of Perseus and Andromache:[1] and itself has had many imitators, such as the tale of Moor of Moorhall, "who slew the dragon of Wantley," and that of the Knight of Lambton, "John that slew the Worme." S. George is said to have been a tribune in Cappadocia; and coming to Libya, he found a town, Silene, assailed by a pestilential dragon, to whom the townsfolk paid quit-money till they had spent on it all their beasts, and their sheep, and their sons, and their daughters; last of all the lot fell upon the king's daughter. But as she wended out of the city, S. George came forth and said, " Fear nothing ; in the name of Jesus Christ I will be of aid." And the dragon arose from out the water. But S. George made the sign of the cross, and with his lance pierced through the dragon and cast it to the ground, and bade the princess put her girdle round the monster. Which done, the dragon followed like a dog. And when they had brought it into the town, the folk feared and marvelled, and S. George struck off the dragon's head.[2]

S. George was identified by the historian Gibbon with a rascally army contractor of Cappadocia; but it is pretty certain that the saint is of earlier date than the contractor. The popularity of S. George in England was of comparatively late date. Historical reason is given for it. It is said that he appeared at the head of a large army, carrying a red cross banner, to help Godfrey de Bouillon against the Saracens at the siege of Antioch,—

D. W.

S. George.
Westminster.

[1] See E. S. Hartland, *The Legend of Perseus*, vol. iii. 38. London, 1896.

[2] At Ranworth S. George with uplifted sword is about to slay the dragon on which he stands. (150). On the grille in Henry the Seventh's chapel, Westminster, he has helmet, shield, sword, and plate armour (151). On the tomb he is shown as a Roman soldier with banner and sword (broken) ; below is the dragon (153).

" A bloodie Crosse he bore,
The deare remembraunce of his dying Lord."

Moreover, King Richard Cœur de Lion had a vision, bidding him to take for his battle-cry next day, " *S. George for England.*" This he did, and won the day ; and S. George became the patron saint of Richard and his family and his soldiers. Under Edward III. he became the patron of the Order of the Garter, for the knights of which a magnificent chapel, dedicated to S. George, was built at Windsor by Edward IV. and Henry VII. It was under the flag of S. George—a red cross on a white field —that Nelson won the battle of the Nile. And the Union Jack (which, by the way, we owe to Oliver Cromwell) consists of a combination of S. George's red cross, the cross saltire of S. Andrew of Scotland, and the white cross of S. Patrick of Ireland.[1]

This is what the clerks used to sing according to Sarum use on S. George's Day, till the Missals and Breviaries were reformed by Pope Clement VII. and the reference to the dragon cut out.[2]

O Georgi martyr inclyte
Te decet laus et gloria,
Predotatum militia ;
Per quem puella regia,
Existens in tristitia,
Coram dracone pessimo
Salvata est.   Ex animo
Te rogamus corde intimo
Ut cunctis cum fidelibus
Coeli jungamur civibus
Nostris ablatis sordibus ;
Et simul cum lætitia
Tecum simus in gloria ;
Nostraque reddant labia
Laudes Christo cum gratia :
Cui sit honos in secula.

Henceforth, as Spenser says, S. George was to be saint of England.

" Thou, among those saints which thou doest see,
Shalt be a saint, and thine own nation's friend
And patron ; thou Saint George shalt callèd be,
Saint George of merry England, the sign of victory."

[1] Charles Browne, *Ibid.*, 287.
[2] Baring-Gould's *Curious Myths of the Middle Ages*, 296.

At S. Neots, Cornwall, is the whole life of S. George in twelve panels of stained glass, beneath each of which is a Latin scroll. (1) S. George fights against the Gauls. (2) He is captured by them and slain at the shrine of the Blessed Virgin ; who (3) brings him to life from the grave, and (4) arms him. (5) He rescues Princess Clcodolinda and slays the dragon. (6) He is arrested for treason and brought before the king. (7) His body

D. W.

SS. George and Antony. Westminster.

is torn with rakes. (8) On hands and knees he is ridden by the emperor's son. (9) He is heavily weighted and hung up by the wrists. (10) He is set in boiling lead. (11) He is dragged by a wild horse. (12) He is beheaded.[1]

Of the Fathers of the Church, S. Clement of Rome is the most popular : not that he was regarded as a theologian superior to Augustine,[2] or Jerome, or Chrysostom, or Athanasius, but

---

[1] Nelson's *Painted Glass*, 63.
[2] In an illumination S. Augustine holds in his hand a heart (15). On the Ashton screen he holds a book (267).

20

simply that there were better stories in circulation about him. S. Clement is made to go on mission to the Crimea ; there, by orders of Trajan, he is thrown into the sea with an anchor round his neck ; every year on the day of his martyrdom the sea recedes two miles, and there appears a stone shrine "not made by mortal hands." On the weathercock of S. Clement Danes in the Strand is an anchor.[1]

The vast popularity of S. Andrew—he stands fifth on the list of dedications—is mainly due to the *History of the Mar Matthew and Mar Andrew, the blessed Apostles, when they converted the City of Dogs, the inhabitants of which were cannibals.* The author of this "history" was Leucius Charinus ; and though this outrageous legend was declared heretical by Pope Gelasius so early as the fifth century, it had gripped Christendom, and in England alone S. Andrew obtained 637 dedications. The story goes that after the gift of tongues at the feast of Pentecost, the apostles drew lots to decide the places to which each should go on mission. It fell to the lot of S. Matthew that he should go on mission to Wrondon, or the City of Dogs, whither he departed. There he was cast into prison and sentenced to be executed at the expiration of thirty days. During his imprisonment the Lord Christ appeared to him, and promised to send S. Andrew to his succour. Twenty-seven days afterwards Our Lord called S. Andrew and his companions and took him away in a ship, the crew whereof consisted of Christ Himself and two angels. In the course of the voyage the apostle and his companions sink into a deep sleep, and in a vision the Garden of Paradise appears to them. They land at Wrondon and proceed to the prison, where the jailers fall dead. S. Matthew[2] and the other prisoners are liberated, and are incontinently translated to a mountain where S. Peter awaits them. Meanwhile in the city the escape of the prisoners is discovered, and lots are cast to find the guilty person, who is to be eaten for food. But instead of the victim his son and daughter are substituted, and are led off to the place of execution. Here, however, S. Andrew meets them, and by exercise of prayer prevents the sacrifice. The apostle is then denounced by the

---

[1] On the rood-screen at Ashton, Devon, S. Clement wears the papal triple tiara, and holds a double cross and anchor in one hand and in the other a closed book (140). In the Lubeck *Passionale* S. Clement has the papal triple tiara and double cross ; and holds in his left hand an anchor (15).

[2] In the statue at Westminster S. Matthew wears spectacles ; an angel holds up his gospel in one hand and an inkhorn in the other (155). On the Ranworth screen S. Matthew holds the sword by which he was slain (82).

devil, and is arrested and
put to the torture. There-
upon he lifts his eyes to
heaven and sees "large trees
which had grown up and
borne fruit," which are pieces
of flesh torn from his body.
The same night his wounds
are healed ; the city is inun-
dated. S. Andrew, however,
escapes; the flood ceases, and
the dead are restored to life ;
but the father of the two
victims and the executioner
are swallowed up alive. These
doings convert the citizens,
and they build a church.
The visit of S. Matthew and
S. Andrew to Wrondon is
depicted in ten panels of
stained glass in a window
at Greystoke, Cumberland,
which is dated 1520.[1]

Many of the legends, no
doubt, owed their popularity
to the fact that there was
something in them that made
its appeal at once, and, once
heard, was always remem-
bered. A famous legend is
that of the legion or brigade
of Christian soldiers under
the command of Mauritius,
which in the third century
refused either to join in
Pagan sacrifices or to be
led against the Christians of
Gaul. The legion was de-
cimated a first time, and yet
again. A third time Mauritius
was ordered by the Emperor

[1] See Nelson's *Painted Glass*,
67, from which the legend is
quoted.

W. S. W.

S. Matthew.
Westminster.

Maximin to obey, and a third time he refused. " O Cæsar," said he, " we are thy soldiers, but we are also soldiers of Jesus Christ. We are ready to follow thee against barbarians, but we will die rather than fight against our brethren." Whereupon a general massacre of the whole legion took place. This legend is so ancient and is so widely distributed that it doubtless has a historic basis. Another favourite story in England was that of the yoke of oxen that dragged the Holy Cross all the way from the West of England, but no further than Waltham in Essex would they go ; and thus resulted the great abbey church of Holy Cross, of which the twelfth-century nave still survives. Such are the stories of S. Denis [1] and S. Osyth, carrying their heads in their hands ; that of the stag and crucifix which appeared to S. Eustachius, and again to S. Hubert.[2]

More especially was this so if the saint was associated in legend with some special emblem. Each time folk saw a carpenter's rule they were reminded of the apostle S. Thomas ; a flight of arrows reminded them of S. Sebastian, and of Edmund, king and martyr ; a comb reminded them of S. Blaise ; a wheel, of S. Catherine ; a gridiron, of S. Lawrence,[3] or S. Vincent ; a pig, of S. Anthony ; a goose, of SS. Martin and Werburga ; a swan, of S. Hugh ; a horse shoe, of S. Eloy.[4] Each one of these provided a " *memoria technica*," keeping the story from being forgotten.

Some of the stories were decidedly humorous—the humour, perhaps, of the type of the farmers' " ordinary " ; such as that masterpiece of mediæval wit, the temptation of S. Dunstan by the devil in the form of a beautiful girl, whom the saint put to flight by seizing him by the nose with red-hot pincers.

---

[1] On the rood-screen at Kenn, Devon, S. Hubert is shown as a hunter (177). In a wooden statuette in the possession of Dr Philip Nelson, he has become a mitred abbot and is vested in a cope fastened with a large morse or brooch (178). In a painting by Wilhem, S. Hubert holds a model of a stag on a closed book (15).

[2] On a rood-screen at Grafton Regis, S. Denis is shown bearing his head in his hands (13).

[3] In the east window of Ludlow, Salop, which is dedicated to S. Lawrence, is glass (*c.* 1445) illustrating the life of S. Lawrence, the patron saint of the church. There are twenty-seven panels in three tiers. For full account of these see Nelson's *Painted Glass*, 176.

[4] In a boss of the vaulted porch of Ugborough church, Devon, S. Eloy is represented hammering a horse shoe on an anvil. At Westminster he holds a horse shoe in his right hand (87). In German glass at Stoke Pogis he is in plate armour, with a lion at his feet and a sword in his right hand ; in his left he holds a hammer and an anvil.

Here is a slightly different version of the legend :—

"The Divell appearing to him on a time in the likenesse of a yong and beautifull woman tempting him to uncleanesse, he tooke up a paire of pinchers that then lay by him, and caught the foule beaste by the upper lippe, and soe holding him fast and leading him up and downe his chamber, after divers interrogatories drave him away."

Very famous too were the temptations of S. Anthony, a hermit in the Egyptian desert in the fourth century, in whose cell the demons spread a table covered with delicious viands, and hovered round in the shape of lovely women, who with softest

E. K. P.

S. Dunstan.

Boss in Exeter Cathedral.

blandishments allured him to sin. Well-known pictures of the scene were executed by Salvator Rosa, Ribera, Annibal Caracci, and Tenicrs, who painted it twelve times. Gluttony is one of the vices which S. Anthony subdued by abstinence and austerities ; it may be symbolised by a black pig at his feet. The monks of the order of S. Anthony kept droves of pigs, which were regarded as sacred, and were allowed to feed where they would. On this they grew fat ; hence the proverb of the fatness of a "Tantony pig."

Another item that greatly affected the popularity of a saint was the frequency of the evil against which the saint was specific. Most of us, one time or other, have toothache ; hence the some-

D. W.

S. Erasmus.   S. Edmund, K.M.
Henry the Seventh's Chapel, Westminster.

what obscure saint, Apollonia, was in great request.[1] A more serious pest, the plague, raged horribly in the Middle Ages; hence the popularity of S. Roch, pointing to the plague-spot on

A. G.

S. Erasmus.

Alabaster panel in Society of Antiquaries.

his thigh. Mortal danger at childbirth sent every mother to intercession of S. Margaret. Life assurance for one day was the bid for popularity made by S. Christopher. And so with others.

[1] On the screen at Ashton, Devon, she holds a tooth in a pair of pincers (123).

Some again owed their popularity in part to the fact that they lent themselves readily to representation in art.

S. Erasmus was in great vogue in England in late days. His image is known to have been present in at least eleven churches in the mediæval diocese of Rochester. He appears in

F. B.

S. Sebastian.   Westminster.

stained glass in Lullingstone church, Kent; and a small chapel is dedicated to him in Westminster abbey. He is a somewhat apocryphal saint; but the gory subject of his martyrdom made him a favourite in stained glass, wherein his bowels are shown being drawn out by a windlass, or coiled round it.[1]

---

[1] In glass at Sandringham, S. Erasmus is shown as a bishop in eucharistic vestments; he holds a windlass; the bowels are not shown (15). Sometimes the martyr is prostrate, and the windlass is horizontal above. In the

S. Sebastian has but two dedications; but the manner of his martyrdom made him a good subject for the painter.

Here is Ælfric's description of the martyrdom of S. Sebastian :—[1]

> "Then the soldiers led away the servant of Christ,
> And set him for a mark, even as Diocletian commanded,
> And fastened their arrows into him before and behind,
> As thickly on every side as a hedgehog's bristles,
> And so left him alone, lying for dead."

In the martyrdom of S. Sebastian the saint is usually shown naked, shot at by two or three archers, sometimes with crossbows: whereas S. Edmund is generally represented in royal dress, and archers may be shown, as at Ely, or the king may merely hold an arrow or sheaf of arrows.

Other subjects "telling" in wall painting, carving, stained glass, and rood-screens were S. Michael weighing souls (35), S. Christopher and the Child (168), and Cecily playing on a harp or an organ, or what in a Devon screen looks like a lute.[2] On the other hand, the story of S. Lucy was ineffective owing to the minute size in the representation of the eyes on a platter which she bore in her hand. Those subjects which were seen most frequently in church windows, over doorways, and on walls naturally were best remembered.

But the most important factor yet remains. This was the influence of literature. We must not imagine that the old folks had no literature. There were plenty of religious biographies, and marvellous stories of all birds and beasts and fishes. And just as now an interesting biography popularises its hero, while a dull one sinks him in oblivion, so it was then. The more romantic the biography, and the better written, the more popular the saint. Hence, among other things, the enormous popularity of S. Martin of Tours; though he is not an Englishman, he has 173 dedications in England. His biography was written in his lifetime, and in a short time Rome and Egypt and Carthage

---

alabaster plaque illustrated, a judge or notary holds a scroll, and Diocletian, holding a falchion, sits cross-legged on a seat, with one foot on the saint. Round the feet of the latter is a rope which is hauled taut by a man below (159). Very similar tablets are to be seen in Norwich castle museum, and in the Ashmolean Museum, Oxford (158).

[1] Homily V., 424.

[2] In stained glass at Combs, Suffolk, S. Cecilia is about to be placed in a cauldron of boiling oil, her persecutor, Almachius, standing near ; in another fragment she is chained to the city gate, and is about to be slain by a soldier with a sword (Nelson's *Painted Glass*, 191).

W. S. W.

S. Martin.

Westminster.

were full of it; the book-
sellers at Rome were at their
wits' end to meet the de-
mand; S. Martin was mobbed
at Tours by tourists; and the
happy biographer had to
bring out a sequel with more
miracles than ever. Few
saints had so many stories,
and such good ones, told of
them as had S. Martin. S.
Nicholas runs him hard. If
anyone will turn to William
Caxton's translation of the
Golden Legend, he will have a
full afternoon's reading, and
a pleasant one, over the lives
of these two saints. Such
books were to the mediæval
clerk what the *Gentlemen of
France* and *Treasure Island*
are to us. This more than
anything else is the root and
origin of the popularity of
many of the saints. While
alive they were—at any rate
some of them—inconspicuous
persons; *e.g.*, Bishop Blaise,
Bishop Nicholas, Bishop
Erasmus; they became con-
spicuous and famous because
they fell into the hands of a
first-rate novelist. It may be
urged that the common folk,
being illiterate, could not
have been influenced by literature. But this is to ignore
two considerations. The first
thing is that such important
things as church dedications
were not settled by the common folk, but by learned
clerks, who could all more
or less read Latin. The
second is that the clerks

made for the use of the people selections, *Legenda*, from the legends of the saints, which were read aloud to the people on the feast day of each saint; and it by no means follows that the *Legenda* were always read to them in Latin; there were numerous translations in the vernaculars.

As with SS. Martin and Nicholas, so the story of S.

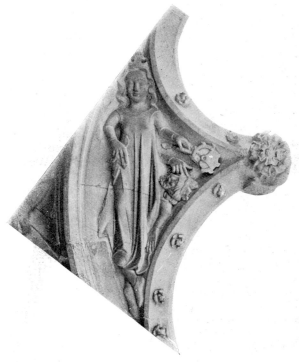

W. E. W.

S. Catherine of Alexandria.

Percy Tomb, Beverley Minster.

Catherine of Alexandria was polished by generations of Greek romancers; hence she has 62 dedications. Unfortunately, she is reputed to have died in 307, and the first mention of her in history or legend does not occur till five centuries later. The legend appears to be a compound of the stories of two saints, one of Alexandria, the other of Mount Sinai. Alexandria was famous for learned women, such as Hypatia; among them was the Princess Catherine, who was as beautiful and pious as she

W. M. D.

S. Catherine of Alexandria.

Ludlow.

was learned. She spurned all marriage except with the Spouse of the Church, and defended her principles against all the philosophers of the day with the wicked Roman emperor acting as assessor. So eloquent and so interminable was her discourse that the exasperated emperor ordered her to execution, bound to spiked wheels which should tear her flesh to pieces. The wheels, however, broke, and she was put to the sword.[1] (Hence she is represented sometimes with a sword in her hand, sometimes with a wheel at her feet, and trampling on Maxentius, as in her statue in Henry the Seventh's chapel, Westminster.[2])

[1] Execution by the sword here, as often, seems an anticlimax. Thus S. Clement of Ancyra, after enduring tortures which were prolonged over twenty-eight years, and which it would take a whole page to enumerate, after all had his head struck off by the sword. Decapitation by the sword was the normal punishment, and it is likely enough that in the legend of many a martyr all the previous tortures enumerated by the chronicler are but customary rhetorical embellishments.

[2] In a cusp of the Percy tomb in Beverley minster (163) and in glass at West Wickham, Kent, S. Catherine is crowned and tramples on the Emperor Maximin : by her side is a spiked wheel, and she bears the sword of martyrdom (22). She is seen also in a bench end at Coombe-in-Teignhead with crown, sword and wheel (118). In the tracing from glass in Castle Howard, which was made by Mr William Fowler of Winterton and for which the writer is indebted to his son, Rev. J. T. Fowler, D.C.L., the executioner holds S. Catherine by the hair

W. F.

Execution of S. Catherine.
Stained glass at Castle Howard.

Then angels took up the dead body and bore it over the desert and over the Red Sea to the summit of Mount Sinai, where was founded the famous convent of S. Catherine, in which was found the Sinaitic codex of the New Testament. Because of her scholastic victory over Maxentius and his heathen philosophers she is patron saint of schools. S. Catherine has 62 dedications, and has imprinted her name on S. Catherine Downs and S.

J. H. P.

S. Christopher.

From a MS. in the Bodleian Library.

Catherine's Point, in the Isle of Wight, a S. Catherine's Hill near Winchester, and another near Christchurch, Hants. The "Cat and Wheel" is a public-house sign. In the nave of York minster the first window from the east end of the north aisle contains representations of the martyrdom of S. Catherine ; the glass is c. 1306. (1) She appears before the Emperor Maximin, who is

with his right hand ; in his left is a sword. Below kneel the donors of the glass (165). In the Ludlow window S. Catherine has sword and wheel (164). In the group at Norwich she has sword only (7).

seated on a throne, with a devil perched on his shoulder. (2) She argues with the philosophers. (3) Being confuted, they are executed by Maximin's order. (4) She is visited in prison by the Empress Porphyry, whom she converts. (5) She is bound to spiked wheels, which are shattered by two angels, armed with swords. (6) She is beheaded and angels bear her soul to heaven. Other scenes are depicted in the tracery of the window.[1]

One of the most popular collections of stories was the thirteenth - century *Golden Legend*, which contained among others the story of S. Christopher, who was reputed to have suffered martyrdom in the third century.

The whole story may well have grown out of the etymology of the Greek word "Christopher," which signifies "Christ-bearer." In the old days hermits often stationed themselves by the banks of rivers, hoping to find favour with heaven by guiding travellers across perilous fords. One day there came to one of these hermits a big heathen giant, who wanted to be useful somehow, but did not know how. The hermit set him to help travellers across the river; and this he did for many years, supporting his steps by a knotted bough plucked from a tree. But one dark and stormy night he heard cries, and there was a little child begging to be put across. So he put the child on his shoulder and strode into the river. The wind blew and the rain fell, and the stream beat against him, and the child grew heavier and heavier, so that the giant could hardly keep his footing, and the weight on his shoulders was almost more than he could bear. And he looked up at the child, and the child said to him, "Heavy is the burden because thou carriest Him who bears the sins of the world." And then the giant knew that it was the Child Jesus. And when they came to the other bank, he fell down and did homage, and took Him for his master all the days of his life.[2]

It was believed that whosoever saw S. Christopher and the Child, on that day should be neither sick nor sorry, nor on that day meet death. There was not a church in England but had an image[3] of S. Christopher or else a wall painting. The usual entrance to a parish church was by the south door; facing this on the north wall of the nave, was commonly a gigantic representation of S. Christopher and the Child. We have nine ancient

---

[1] Nelson's *Painted Glass*, 246.

[2] In an illumination fish are shown swimming in the river, and a hermit with a lantern on the further bank points out the ford ; above is his cell (166). It was said also that the staff by which S. Christopher supported his steps broke forth into leafage, as is shown in stained glass at All Saints', North Street, York (168).

[3] One remains at Terrington S. Clement's, Norfolk, and is illustrated in the writer's *Introduction to English Church Architecture*, p. 49.

M. L.

S. Christopher and the Child.
All Saints', York.

churches and chapels, and seven ancient bells dedicated to S. Christopher. At Shapwick, Dorset, is a bell with the inscription :—

ILLO NEMPE DIE NULLO LANGUORE GRAVETUR

CRISTOFORI SANCTI CAMPANAM QUICUMQUE TUETUR

i.e., " Whoever looks on S. Christopher's bell, on that day shall be neither sick nor sorry." This is taken from an old Latin hymn, which, however, reads **SPECIEM**, " face," for which **CAMPANAM** has been substituted to the ruin of metre and sense.[1] Another version reads :—

ILLO NEMPE DIE MORTE MALA NON MORIERIS

CRISTOFORI SANCTI SPECIEM QUICUMQUE TUERIS

i.e., " If thou, whoever thou art, lookest on S. Christopher's face, On that day thou shall not die an evil death."

Another version is in the form of a pentameter :—

CRISTOFORUM VIDEAS POSTEA TUTUS ERIS

i.e., " Behold Christopher ; then shalt thou be safe."

Doubtless many another saint, *e.g.*, S. Perpetua, equally deserved honour ; just as—

" Vixere fortes ante Agamemnona
    Multi ; sed omnes illacrimabiles
        Urguentur ignotique longa
            Nocte, carent quia vate sacro."

Many a story is in praise of virginity, and in deprecation of the married state. For centuries the Church had the greatest difficulty in enforcing celibacy on the clergy ; and regarded with favour every story of virginal purity. Sometimes the maiden flies from the passion of a wicked man, as do S. Frideswide of Oxford, S. Agatha of Sicily, S. Winifred of Holywell. Sometimes the suitor is unexceptionable in birth and morals ; which make his repulse all the more creditable to the maid ; *e.g.*, S. Lucy of Syracuse, S. Margaret of Antioch, and S. Agnes of Rome ; sometimes the story of the maid, *e.g.*, of S. Catherine, is a protest against marriage with anybody, good or bad. If married already, then the saint runs away from her husband with the general approval of everybody, *e.g.*, S. Etheldreda of Ely and S. Osyth. If she does not run away, then husband and wife live in virginal continence, like Valerian and Cecilia. S. Bridget of Ireland was so beautiful that all men desired her, and

---

[1] Walters' *Church Bells of England*, p. 288.

22

she prayed that her beauty might pass from her. So a distemper fell upon her, and she lost an eye and became unsightly. But when she received the veil, the lost eye and her former beauty returned to her.

Other tales tell of the good mother teaching her little girl, as S. Anne taught Our Lady ; or of that Christian mother of Autun who cried out from the city wall to her son, S. Symphorian, as he was being led away to execution, " Fear not the death which leads to certain life." Mothers liked stories about good little children, and were not likely to allow to pass out of remembrance S. Pancras of Rome,[1] and three-year-old S. Cyril, and S. Kenelm singing the Te Deum till the murderer's blow struck off his head.[2] Precocious saintliness made the closest appeal of all. There are 8 dedications to S. Rumbald, who as soon as he was born said three times in a firm voice, " I am a Christian." Then he demanded baptism ; and being baptized, preached a sermon, and in due course of nature died three days after. In no one was piety more precocious than in S. Nicholas. The very first day he was born, he stood up in his bath and gave thanks that it had pleased God to bring him into the world. Moreover, from the first he observed the fasts of the Church, only taking the breast once on Wednesdays and Saturdays. And folks loved not only children but lovers of children. When the annual whipping-day came round, the boys of the King's School, Canterbury, resorted for aid to the tomb of S. Dunstan in the cathedral, and he kindly sent a deep sleep upon the masters.[3]

But the patron saint of children was and is S. Nicholas. He was born at Panthera, a city of Lycia in Asia Minor, in the third century, the son of rich Christian parents.

---

[1] Of S. Pancras it was said by Gregory of Turone, Doctor, that if there be a man that make a false oath in the place of S. Pancras' sepulchre, he shall be travailed with an evil spirit and out of his mind, or he shall fall on the pavement all dead. On the brass at Cowfold S. Pancras is shown trampling on a Saracen (113).

[2] In the west front of Wells cathedral, S. Kenelm is represented as young and beardless, and tramples on a woman prostrate over a book. He had been left in charge of his sister, Quendrida, who had him murdered. At his funeral she was reading the Psalter backward as a charm, when her eyes dropped out and stained the book with blood at the words, " This is the evil of them that defame to the Lord, who speak evil against my soul." The bloodstains, says William of Malmesbury, are still to be seen on the Psalter. —W. R. L. (11).

[3] Arnold-Forster, i. 329.

While still young, he inherited great wealth from his parents. Now it happened that in that city there was a nobleman with three daughters, so poor that he was about to send them forth to earn their bread by

J. H. P.

S. Dunstan at the feet of Christ.

Facsimile from an Anglo-Saxon manuscript in the Bodleian Library, said to have been drawn by the hand of the saint himself.

a life of shame. But one night Nicholas threw a purse of gold through the window, and with this dowry the poor nobleman married the

W. S. W.

S. Nicholas.
Westminster.

eldest daughter. A second night
Nicholas threw through a purse
of gold, and with this the second
daughter was dowried and married. So also with the third
daughter. S. Nicholas is represented with the three purses on
the font in Winchester cathedral.[1]

Again, during a great famine
at Myra, three children were kid-
napped and set before the guests
as meat. One of the guests was
S. Nicholas himself, who hurried
to the cellar and found in the
pickling cask the dismembered
limbs of three children. He
made the sign of the cross, and
the three boys stepped out of
the cask hale and whole. This
scene also is depicted on the
font in Winchester cathedral.

Also there was a rich man
who vowed a great cup to the
altar of S. Nicholas in gratitude
for the birth of a son and heir.
But the cup was so beautiful
that he gave a smaller one, and
kept the big gold cup for himself. One day later, journeying
with his son, he bade him fill
the big cup with water. But the
boy, overbalancing, fell in and
was drowned. Then the father
returned and gave to the altar a
silver cup, but it fell off, and this
happened a second and a third
time. And while all were amazed,
the rich man's son appeared
himself, safe and sound, for good
S. Nicholas had saved him. And
the father gave both cups to
the altar, and returned home
with his son. This scene is
represented on the font at Ledel-
ghem.

[1] Illustrated in the writer's *Fonts
and Font Covers*, 169.

He is also the patron saint of wolves and Russians. From sunset on the sixth of December, S. Nicholas' Day, to sunrise next morning, the wolves will not touch even chicken ; they spend the night in meditation, and will not hurt you even if you step upon their tails. And he is the protector of sailors, and is the patron of many a church by the sea, *e.g.*, at Brighton and Great Yarmouth.

Many stories are told of his powers over the sea. One day certain mariners in the Ægean called on his intercession to save them from the stormy sea, and S. Nicholas appeared and calmed the sea, and with lighted taper in hand, steered the ship to port. No wonder that Nicholas, Archbishop of Myra, has 437 dedications.[1]

Another virtue, appreciated far more then than now, simply because nowadays we have seldom opportunity to exhibit it, was kindness to captives. The petition in the Litany that it may please God to "show pity upon all prisoners and captives," means little to us, but it had a terrible meaning in the Middle Ages, when the Vikings and the Saracens and the galleys of Algiers were at sea, and every jail was a deadly pesthouse. S. Cyprian of Carthage, to aid a fund for the ransom of captives

The Confessor. Westminster.

in the hands of the Berbers, sold all that he had, even his beautiful gardens, though his friends bought them in and restored them to him. But the great patron of prisoners and captives

---

[1] In Henry the Seventh's chapel, S. Nicholas is a short stout bishop holding a boy in a basket (172). In an illumination he is shown as a bishop in the act of benediction ; near are three boys in a tub (26). In a lancet window beneath the "Bishop's Eye" in Lincoln minster, the second window from the east, is a ship at sea beneath clouds. In the ship are two sailors, one of whom holds an oar and a vase of oil ; on the shore stands S. Nicholas in vestments and mitre ; in one hand he holds his crosier, while with the other he draws the ship to land by a rope attached to its sail (Nelson's *Painted Glass*, 139).

was the hermit, S. Leonard, the Howard of the sixth century. To him prayed the captives and the captives' friends; and in many a church of S. Leonard fetters hung up in grateful remembrance of release by his intercessionary power. He has 177 dedications in this country.[1]

One must recollect, too, that there was no system of relief organised by poor laws, and that generosity to poor folk was far more incumbent than it is now, and held a much higher position among the social virtues. S. Benedict's directions were, " All the guests who come to us shall be received as the Lord Himself, for one day He will say, ' I was a stranger and ye took me in.' And *when the guests are poor, Christ is more especially received in their persons.*"[2] The story of S. Martin of Tours dividing his cloak with the beggar is one which the mediæval world was not likely to let die. There was the famous story, too, of the Confessor and the ring and S. John Evangelist.

One day the Confessor was returning from mass in the Abbey, when in a certain street of Westminster a beggar asked for alms, and the king drew the ring from his finger and gave it to him. Four and twenty years after two pilgrims in India, from Ludlow, met " an old man, white and hoary and joyously like unto a clerk," also in pilgrim's dress ; who, when he found that they were Englishmen, admonished them that they should journey to King Edward, and should take the ring and say from me to him, ' This is the ring that thou didst give me in a certain street in Westminster, and I am John Evangelist. Six months from this day shalt thou quit the world and shalt abide with me for ever." And the two pilgrims went to their own country, and expounded these things to King Edward in his palace of Havering-atte-Bower, and gave the ring to him. And the king set forth to order his passing.

Evidence for these things is that in the great collegiate church of Ludlow, founded by the Confessor, the stained glass in the chapel of S. John Evangelist depicts the story of the Ring. Also the name of " Havering" is held to be a corruption of " Have a ring."

Nor did people forget that Our Lord went about healing the sick, and was at least as ready to relieve their bodies as their souls. Of all his pastoral duties, what S. John of Beverley liked best was to nurse and tend the sick. Julian the Hospitaller and his wife Basilissa, on their wedding night, consecrated their lives to the service of God and man ; their house they turned into a

[1] In stained glass at Sandringham, S. Leonard has fetters and an open book (15).

[2] On the rood-screen at Great Plumstead, Norfolk, S. Benedict has his crosier in his left hand and a scroll in his right (68).

hospital, and all their wedded life they spent in ministering to the sick and the lepers, till came the martyr's crown. It is told of S. Elizabeth of Hungary that she laid in her bed a foul leper whom no one would tend any longer. The indignant duke, her husband, tore off the bedclothes, when "at that instant God Almighty opened the eyes of his soul, and instead of the leper he saw on the bed the figure of Christ Crucified." Another day when he met her, she had a heavy basket of food she was carrying to the poor. She was ashamed when he asked her what she was carrying; but when he insisted on looking in, there was nothing inside but red and white roses.

A very popular saint was S. Roch.

This is William Caxton's version of his story, translated from the *Golden Legend.* "Now this Roch was ever in great study how he might in the name of Jhesu and His passion deliver mortal men from the hurt of pestilence. And so a whole year he visited the houses of poor men at Placentia, and they that had most need, to them he did most help, and was always in thospytal. And anon he was himself sore taken with the pestilence under his both arms. And he went forth from the city into a certain wood. And there he was an hungered, and every day a hound brought him bread from his master's board. Then said the master, 'Since this hound without reason bringeth him bread, I sooner ought to do it which am a Christian man.' And long he and Roch lived in the woods; and the wild beasts which wandered in the woods, what

W. S. W.

S. Roch.

Westminster.

hurt, swelling, or sickness they had, they ran anon to S. Roch, and when they were healed, they would incline their heads reverently and go away."[1]

The martyrs Cosmas and Damian were especially popular physicians because they worked without fee or reward, and tended the dumb beasts as well as their fellow-men. They are patron saints of Bean and Challock, Kent, and Keymer, Sussex, and, originally, of Stretford, Hereford.

Again our forefathers were but few of them town folk, and if they were, the town was small and the country near, and they liked stories about country life and the animals they saw in the farmyard and the woods. And there were many stories, especially of the hermits and of their power over the wild creatures, who from constant familiarity with their gentle ways had lost all shyness and fear. It was perhaps natural that they should ; but it was believed by the country folk that the friendship of the creatures was of supernatural character. This the hermits believed themselves. One day a visitor found S. Guthlac of Crowland discoursing with two swallows, perched fearlessly on his shoulders, and "lifting up their song rejoicing." "Hast thou never heard, brother," said Guthlac, "that he who hath led his life after God's will, the wild beasts and the wild birds have become the more intimate with him?" S. Blaise fled from persecution to the woods and caves, and won the love of all the wild creatures and brought them submissive to his will.

S. Giles (162 dedications) is a hermit of most uncertain date ; he lived in the forests of the delta of the Rhone either in the sixth or the eighth century. One day a royal hunt wounded a hind, which fled to its friend, S. Giles, and put its head on his knee for protection. Another version, which is followed on a misericord in Ely cathedral, makes the arrow miss the hind and hit the hermit. On the misericord the hermit is seen with an arrow sticking in his leg ; he is telling his beads ; and the hind is trustingly laying its head on his knee. S. Giles was lame ever after, and so became the patron saint of all cripples and, by extension, of all beggars. It was common for blacksmiths to set up their smithies outside the gates of the mediæval cities, ready to attend to the shoes of travellers' horses and mules. It would be convenient for the travellers to hear an early Mass while their beasts were being shod ; so near the smithy was built a church, *e.g.*, S. Giles, Oxford, at the junction of the Wood-

---

[1] In Henry the Seventh's chapel, S. Roch has a pilgrim's staff and wallet, a rosary and cross keys on his hat ; he points to a plague-spot on his thigh (175).

stock and Banbury roads; S. Giles, Cambridge, where three roads meet; S. Giles, Norwich; S. Giles, Northampton; S. Giles, Cripplegate, London.[1]

The most important memorials of S. Giles are the nave of the abbey church of S. Gilles, Provence, world-famous for the sculpture of its Romanesque façade, and the picturesque cathedral of S. Giles, Edinburgh.

S⁺ HUBERT. (KENN)

B. AND C.

A great favourite abroad was the story of S. Hubert (2 dedications), especially in the Ardennes district, where his great abbey church still stands. He was a mighty hunter, not even sparing stag and boar on Good Friday. One day he came upon a stag bearing in its antlers a great crucifix, from which there was a voice bidding him turn to the Lord. The conversion of the sinful noble was instantaneous. He resigned his pleasures and his sports, and became a priest and afterwards a bishop; he died in 727. S. Eustace (3 dedications) was a wealthy officer in the Roman army, and was martyred about 118 A.D. Many centuries afterwards a romance was fabricated about him, almost identical with the story of S. Hubert. S. Eustace and S. Hubert are the patron saints of huntsmen.

When S. David of Wales was a little boy, learning the Psalms and Lessons and the Mass, "a golden-beaked pigeon used to play about his lips, teaching him and singing the hymns of God." Then there is the story of the big swan which was so fond of S. Hugh of Lincoln, and followed him about everywhere when he was at Stow Park. From the minute description given of the bird, it seems to have been a wild swan or hooper.[2]

---

[1] On the screen at Great Plumstead, Norfolk, an arrow is shown piercing the saint's leg, while a hart springs up at his feet (69). In glass at Sandringham he holds an abbot's crosier, and a hart springs up at his feet (24).

[2] Sir Charles Anderson writes that he has seen a gander, which followed a Lincolnshire farmer every day when he went shepherding, waddling along with great air of satisfaction, and fondling his legs with neck and bill when he stopped (178).

23

P. N.

A. G.

S. Hubert.

S. Hugh.

Wooden statuette.

S. Mary's Spire, Oxford.

There were the wild geese which were devastating Weedon, and which S. Werburga drove into a stable; next morning they came running up to her, begging to be let out. S. Samson of Dol could not scare the sparrows from his master's corn, so he drove them "like a flock of sheep" into the barn, where "they sang mournfully and repented for the damage done to the corn." S. Neot kept the crows out of the corn by the simple expedient of building a mound round them. Throughout Europe all sorts of privileges were given to S. Anthony's pigs, "Tantony pigs." When S. Kentigern was seeking where to build a monastery, a wild boar trotted through the forest before him, and stopped when the fitting site was reached. S. Cuthbert, not to distress his hostess, S. Ebba of Coldingham, had partaken of her hospitality; but in penance secretly walked up to his neck in the sea. At dawn he was there still, "praising God." When he came out, "two otters left the sea, and lying down before him on the sand breathed upon his feet and wiped them with their hair."[1] And every one knows how Francis of Assisi loved flowers and birds and every living thing. We will conclude with a quotation from the *Little Flowers of S. Francis of Assisi*;[2] is he not our namesake?

" What time Saint Francis abode in the city of Agobio there appeared in the country an exceeding great wolf, terrible and fierce, which not only devoured the flocks but also men, insomuch that all folk stood in great fear. For the which matter, Saint Francis, having compassion on the people, wished to go forth unto that wolf, albeit the townsfolk all gave counsel against it; and making the sign of the most holy cross he went forth, putting his trust in God. And lo! the said wolf made at Saint Francis with open mouth; and Saint Francis made over him the sign of the most holy cross. Whereas Saint Francis made the sign of the cross, right so the terrible wolf shut his jaws and stayed his running, and came gently as a lamb and lay him down at the feet of Saint Francis. Thereat Saint Francis thus bespake him : ' Brother wolf, much harm hast thou wrought in these parts and done grievous ill, spoiling and slaying the creatures of God; and hast dared also to slay men made in the image of God; for which cause thou art deserving of the gibbet as a thief and a most base murderer, and all men cry out and murmur against thee. But I would fain, brother wolf, make peace between thee and these, so that thou mayest no more offend them, and they

---

[1] At Westminster S. Cuthbert holds a sceptre in his right hand, and the head of S. Oswald in his left (87). There is a similar statue in Prince Arthur's chantry chapel in Worcester cathedral. At the bottom of a statuette of S. Cuthbert in the possession of Dr Philip Nelson, an otter is seen drying the left foot of the saint.

[2] Newly translated out of the Italian by T. W. Arnold. Dent, 1907.

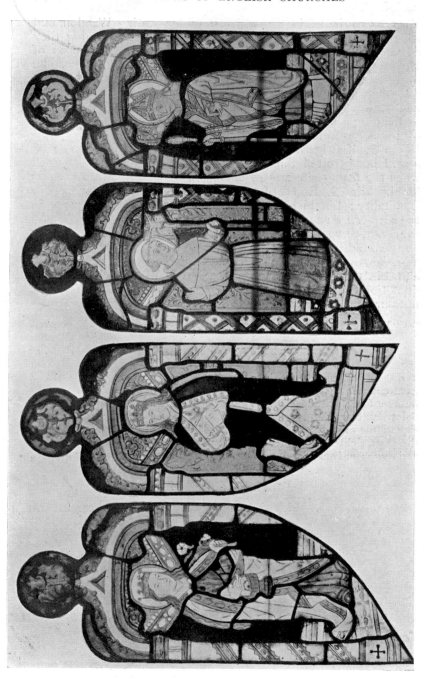

S. Francis.

S. Agnes.

S. Dorothy.

P. N.

may forgive thee for all thy past offences, and neither men nor dogs pursue thee any more.' At these words the wolf with movements of body, tail and eyes, and by the bending of his head, gave sign of assent of his will to abide thereby. Then spake Saint Francis again : ' Brother wolf, sith it pleaseth thee to make this peace, I promise thee that I will see to it that the folk of this place give thee food alway so long as thou shalt live, so that thou suffer not hunger any more ; for I wot well that through hunger hast thou wrought this ill. But sith I win for thee this grace, I will, brother wolf, that thou promise me to do none hurt to any more, be he man or beast ; dost promise me this ? ' And the wolf by bowing of his head gave clear token that he promised. Then quoth Saint Francis : ' Brother wolf, I will that thou plight me troth for this promise.' And Saint Francis stretching forth his hand to take plight of his troth, the wolf lifted up his right paw before him and laid it gently on the hand of Saint Francis. Then quoth Saint Francis : ' Brother wolf, I bid thee in the name of Jesu Christ come now with me, and let us go stablish this peace.' And the wolf set forth with him, in fashion as a gentle lamb, whereat the townsfolk made marvel ; and all the people, men-folk and women-folk, great and small, young and old, gat them to the market place to see the wolf. And the folk being gathered together, Saint Francis rose up to preach, avizing them how far more parlous is the flame of hell, the which must vex the damned eternally, than is the fury of the wolf that can but slay the body : how much then should they fear the jaws of hell that be afeard of the jaws of one so small a beast ? And done the preaching, said : ' Dost thou promise, brother wolf, to keep firm the pact of peace, that thou offend not man nor beast nor any creature ? ' Then the wolf, lifting up his right paw, laid it in the hand of Saint Francis. Therewith this act, and the others set forth above, wrought such great joy and marvel in all the people, that they lift up their voices blessing God, that had sent Saint Francis to them, who by his merits had set them free from the jaws of the cruel beast. And thereafter this same wolf lived two years in Agobio, and went like a tame beast in and out the houses, without doing hurt to any, or any doing hurt to him, and was courteously nourished by the people ; and as he passed, never did any dog bark behind him. At length, after two years' space, brother wolf died of old age ; whereat the townsfolk sorely grieved, sith marking him pass so gently through the city, they minded them the better of the virtues and the sanctity of Saint Francis."

One more story of S. Francis. "Once on a day it befell that a certain young man took turtle doves to market, and Saint Francis who had tender pity for gentle creatures, met him and said unto him : ' I pray thee give them me, that gentle birds, upon which the Scripture likeneth chaste and humble souls, may not fall into the hands of men that would kill them.' And the young man gave them to Saint Francis, who, taking them in his bosom, spoke tenderly to them : ' O my sisters, simple-minded turtle doves, why have ye let yourselves be caught ? Now would I fain deliver you and make you nests, that ye may be fruitful and multiply according to the commandments of your Creator.'

And Saint Francis made nests for them all ; and they, abiding therein, did lay eggs and hatch them ; and so tame were they, that they dwelt with Saint Francis and his brothers as though they had been fowls that had always fed from their hands, and never did they go away until Saint Francis with his blessing gave them leave to go. And it came to pass that the young man also became a brother and lived in the Order in great sanctity."

STIGMATA OF S! FRANCIS   (BRADNINCH)

B. AND C.

Of S. Francis it is recorded that on the fifteenth day of September 1224 there appeared to him the vision of a fiery seraph, between whose wings was the figure of a man crucified, which was his gracious and tender Master, Jesus Christ the Lord. And on the body of S. Francis there was imprinted the image of a crucifix as it were a seal on soft wax. And the marks of nails appeared on the palms of his hands and the upper part of the insteps of his feet. And in his side there was a wound, which for the two more years he lived at times threw forth blood. These marks were the famous *Stigmata*. S. Francis died in 1226 ; the Franciscans, or Grey Friars or "Little Brothers," only arrived in England two years before. Our ancient churches had got their dedications long before this ; but of the churches built by the Franciscans themselves, two at any rate were dedicated to S. Francis ; one a great church at Norwich, and the other the splendid London church in Newgate Street, afterwards dedicated to Christ by Henry VIII., whose site was formerly occupied by Christ's Hospital and now by the General Post Office and Christ church, Newgate Street (180). The *stigmata* are shown on rood-screens at Hempstead and Stalham, Norfolk, and Bradninch, Devon.

CHAPTER XIII

Criteria of the Credibility of the Legends—Martyrdoms of Perpetua
and Procopius.

IT may now perhaps be asked—some will have asked long
before this—" How much are we to believe of all this? Is it
all true? Or is it all false?" To neither question can a direct
affirmative be given. It would be ridiculous to credit all the
wild stories that are told of S. Margaret, S. Barbara, S. Catherine,
S. Ursula, and scores of others. But it would be equally foolish
to be so sceptical as to believe that there is no historical basis
for any of the legends of the saints. In many of the narratives,
in their main points, there is a substratum of truth. Bede, for
instance, wrote much about matters of his own time or of the
times immediately preceding his own, and much of it bears the
impress of a careful, painstaking, scholarly mind. So with the
plain and simple narrative of the Martyrdom of S. Perpetua of
Carthage—a narrative wholly free from late embellishment—
which is perhaps the reason why no English church is dedicated
to her.[1] " It bears every mark of authenticity"; it is allowed on
all hands that the narrative, minus its rhetorical embellishments,
is the genuine work of contemporaries.

It is recorded of S. Perpetua that, while in prison, she saw in a
dream a golden ladder which reached from earth to heaven; but so
narrow that only one could mount at once. To the two sides of which
ladder were fastened swords and hooks and knives, to the intent that if
any went up carelessly he was in danger of having his flesh torn. And
at the foot of the ladder there was an enormous dragon who terrified
those who would mount. But Perpetua said, " In the name of the
Lord Jesus Christ he shall not hurt me." Then the dragon, as if afraid,
lifted away his head, and Perpetua mounted to the top, and there she
saw a garden, and in the midst thereof a tall man dressed like a
shepherd, milking his sheep, and around were many thousand persons
clad in white. Then Perpetua knew that the day of her martyrdom
was at hand; and soon afterwards, with S. Felicitas, she was sent to
the amphitheatre of Carthage to be exposed to wild beasts on the festival

[1] See *The Passion of S. Perpetua*, edited by Very Rev. J. A. Robinson,
D.D., Dean of Wells, 1891.

of Cæsar Geta. Both were tossed and gored by a wild cow, and then were sent away to be despatched at the end of the show by the 'confectores.'

The plain unvarnished account of the martyrdom of Cyprian also carries conviction of authenticity with it. So also for the legend of Procopius there is a definite and reliable historical basis ; for two versions remain of the account of his contemporary, Eusebius, who was Bishop of Cæsarea in Palestine. He relates that Procopius held the rank of exorcist, and was reader and interpreter in Syriac. He was good and gentle, fasting much and living a hard life. "Entering Cæsarea one day, he was taken before the governor Flavian, and ordered to sacrifice to the gods. But he proclaimed that there are not several gods, but One God, the creator and author of all things. Neither would he sacrifice to the emperors. ' Listen,' he said, ' to Homer ' :

"'Οὐκ ἀγαθὸν πολυκοιρανίη · εἷς κοίρανος ἔστω, εἷς βασιλεύς.'

Whereupon he was led off to the place of execution, and they cut off his head. This was in the first year of our persecution (that of Diocletian, c. 302), and took place at Cæsarea." This simple and dignified account was expanded and embellished later into two legends of extraordinary complexity and length, filled with detail entirely mythical.

A very great deal of detail, too, is true, if not of the saint of whom it is told, yet surely and certainly of very many others. It cannot be proved now that S. Catherine suffered on the wheel, but it is known that a Christian slave-woman, Charitana, was broken on the wheel in the Diocletian persecution. It cannot be proved that S. Agatha and S. Lucy and S. Agnes preferred a Christian death to a Pagan marriage ; but it is surely and certainly true that this brought many another Christian maiden to her death. And so with other stories of Christian heroism and piety. There is danger in believing too little as well as in believing too much. We may be sure that for every name we know of a Roman officer who refused sacrifice to the gods of Rome, of every maiden who guarded virginity with death, indeed for every name of a martyr that we know, there are ten, it may be a hundred, names which we do not know and never shall know; "which have no memorial, who are perished as though they had never been, and are become as though they had never been born."

In his *Introduction to Hagiography*, translated by Mrs V. M. Crawford under the title *Legends of the Saints*, Père Delehaye proposes a classification of the Acts of the Martyrs and of hagiographic documents in general, which has already met with considerable acceptance, notably from Professor

Harnack. Following this in the main, eight categories may be formulated :—

I. The first comprises *official* reports of the interrogatories of martyrs before Roman proconsuls. These are of the highest value. But even these require critical examination, *e.g.*, the most perfect model of Proconsular Acts, the *Passio Cypriani*, is in reality a composite record, consisting of three separate documents ; first, the official text of an early examination by a proconsul in 257, as a result of which Cyprian was sent into exile ; then the official report of the arrest and a second examination in 258 ; finally the account of the martyrdom. In the authentic Acts the martyr does not pose ; one hears only the words of the judge and the martyr, and one is present at the carrying out of the sentence ; it is an official record ; the editor introduces nothing of his own into the words he puts into the mouths of the judge and the accused. Few such records exist ; the Passion of the Scillitan martyrs is one of the best of them.

II. The second category of authentic Acts comprises *unofficial* accounts of eye-witnesses. They may be (1) Documents in which the accused alone speaks in his own name ; (2) those in which a contemporary chronicles the evidence ; (3) those in which he in addition adds testimony of his own, as in several chapters of Eusebius' *Martyrs of Palestine*, and in the life of Cyprian by Deacon Pontius. With these we may compare the narratives of Bede concerning such of the missioners of his time as were personally known to him, and the chroniclers of the martyrdom of Edmund, king of the East Angles, and Edward, the young king of Wessex.

III. The third category is composed of Acts of which the principal source is a written document or documents belonging to the first or second category. This document may be abridged, amplified, interpolated, or recast to any extent, small or great. The difficulty is to pick out the original document. Thus the life of the Empress Helena is based on genuine historical documents ; but as we have seen, these were later on amplified, recast, and falsified to a large extent. To this category a great mass of biography is to be referred. It cannot be questioned for one moment that there is adequate evidence in documents of early date that S. Martin, S. Leger, S. Remigius, S. German, S. Boniface, not only are real historical personages, but did actually do missionary work at the times and in the districts and very much in the fashion that they are reported to have done ; the same is true of S. David in Wales ; SS. Patrick, Columba, Brandon, in Ireland ; SS. Aidan, Cuthbert, Ninian, Hilda, Wilfrid, in Northumbria ; and of SS. Birinus and Chad

24

in the South of England and the Midlands. Strip off the later embellishments, and a solid substratum of historic fact remains. The proportion of fact to embellishment varies immensely, from say 90 per cent. to nearly *nil.* From the large proportion of fact in the biography of a saint of late date, such as S. Francis, we pass, as time recedes backward, to an ever-decreasing amount of fact, and an ever-increasing amount of myth : the earlier the date at which the saint lived and worked, the more difficult it is to obtain anything beyond a bare modicum of satisfactory evidence. There can be little doubt that SS. Hubert, Leonard, Sebastian, Vincent, Lawrence, Botolph, Giles, Nicholas, were once living men, and did some such work as they are credited with ; but the longer ago it is since they lived, the greater is the accretion of additional and false elements with which their story has been encrusted. It is to be noted also that though the documentary evidence of a biography may be of quite late date, yet it may be based on ancient data known to the biographer, though not to ourselves, *e.g.*, the Lives of S. Bridget of Kildare were mostly written centuries after her death, but they are based on ancient material, for they contain numerous references to an ancient state of things in the numerous references to archaic tribe-law, wizards and wizardry, and the presence of the cow in the kitchen.

IV. The fourth category consists of Acts of which the kernel is not a document, but certain facts, which if few, are real ; *e.g.*, the name of the saint, the locality where he worked or perished, the existence of his shrine, the date of his feast. Round this the writer constructs what nowadays is termed a historical romance. And of course, then as now, the proportion of history and fiction may vary very considerably, as it does in *Esmond* as compared with *The Virginians,* or *Hypatia* compared with *Westward Ho,* or in Sir Walter Scott's novels. Among such historical romances we may place the legends of the mission work of the apostles Andrew, Matthew, Thomas, and James the Greater, and the legends of Edward the Confessor, the two Maries, Lazarus and Mary Magdalene, and many other undoubtedly real personages, among whom we should like to include S. George.

In this, as in the following categories, the legends contain a large amount of repetition. When imagination failed the writer, as not infrequently happened, he calmly transferred to his own hero or heroine the details that belonged to another : wholesale plagiarism is exceedingly common. The biography of S. Remachus is servilely imitated from that of S. Lambert ; and of the Lives of S. Hubert, S. Eustace, S. Meinulf, S. Arnold of Metz, and S. Lambert several portions are shared in common ;

the passion of S. Martina is literally the same as that of S. Tatiana; S. Castissima owns the same acts as S. Euphrosyne, and so with many others.

The passion of S. Vincent and S. Lawrence is borrowed from that of the martyrs of Phrygia, as told by Socrates and Sozomen. The miracles of the ship that comes to a halt and that of the oxen who refuse to go further are of common occurrence; they are told of the arrival of S. James the Greater in Spain, of S. Lubentius at Dietkirchen, of S. Maternus at Rodenkirchen, of S. Emmerammus at Ratisbon, of the girdle of the Blessed Virgin at Prato, of the Volto Santo at Lucca.[1]

V. To the next class belong those imaginative romances in which there is no kernel at all, not the least substratum of fact; in which we cannot accept that the saint even existed. Such imaginative romances were written, like modern novels, to edify, instruct, and please, and there is no more sinister motive at the back of the composition than in a modern novel, such as *Treasure Island* or *The Delectable Duchy*. To this class we may refer such legends as those of SS. Ursula, Catherine, Barbara, Margaret, Dorothy, and Roch. The probability is that these are no more real personages than the characters in a modern novel. In this class the personages, as well as the incidents, are invented, and the only question we are entitled to ask is whether they are *ben trovato*. Such stories were written with as innocent a motive as any modern work of fiction.

VI. A special subdivision may be devoted to those saints whose legend is suggested by the etymology of their names; *e.g.*, S. Agnes ("a lamb"), S. Hippolytus ("torn by horses"), S. Christopher ("Christ-bearer"), S. Petronilla ("Peter's little daughter"); to which we may perhaps add Havering ("Have a ring") in the story of the Confessor and the Evangelist.[2]

VII. Another subdivision includes explanations of pictorial representations. S. Denis, S. Osyth, and others suffered death by decapitation. This the pictorial artist depicts in a forcible way by showing them with their head in their hands. Then comes the legend-monger, and starts them walking, head in hands; *e.g.*, S. Denis to Montmartre.

VIII. The last category comprises those legends in which the direct aim is not the edification or amusement of the reader, but the selfish personal interest of the writer or of the society to which he belongs. These narratives may be catalogued simply

---

[1] Delehaye, *Ibid.*, 31, 102, 104.
[2] To these may be added SS. Sidwell and Cornelius. In Flemish glass S. Cornelius is shown with the papal triple tiara, but with a bishop's cross; in his right hand he holds a horn. As S. Corentin, he protects Breton cattle.

as Downright Deliberate Forgeries. At such work the early mediæval chroniclers were adepts. They were in constant practice. Living in religious houses, and being the only people who could read or write, or who could understand Latin or Norman-French, it was the easiest thing in the world to palm off forgeries on the laity. If there was a link loose in a monastery's title to property, it was the most natural thing in the world to supply it by inventing a charter from some bygone monarch, or a grant from some defunct landowner; thus the house was able to secure to itself with the greatest ease manors and tolls and fishing rights, and the like, to which it had little, if any, right at all. It was only natural then to transfer this system of swindling and forgery to the province of legendary history, with a view to aggrandising the house to which the writer belonged. Sometimes, however, two religious houses were at variance, and each side brandished forgeries in the other's face, as for instance, on the question whether the relics of S. Alban had been returned to S. Albans monastery or were still at Ely. Among forgeries perpetrated to increase the kudos of a monastery we may without doubt include those of the visit of Joseph of Arimathea to Glastonbury and that of S. Peter to consecrate the new abbey church at Westminster.

CHAPTER XIV

Compound Dedications—Change of Dedication—Lost Dedications—
Dedications to Unknown Saints—Dedications to Little Known Saints
—Doubtful Alternative Dedications—Spurious Dedications.

COMPOUND DEDICATIONS

IN a large number of churches the dedication is not to one saint,
but to two or more. Sometimes the dedication, *e.g.*, to SS. Peter
and Paul, SS. Philip and James, was from the first a compound
one. But more frequently a single has become a compound
dedication by process of accretion. Some of these compound
dedications arise naturally from family relationship. The relationship may be that of mother and child; thus the church of
Beaulieu, Hampshire, is dedicated to the Blessed Virgin and
Child. Or the child's name may precede the mother's; there
are 5 dedications to Christ and Blessed Mary the Virgin; and
3 to SS. Cyriacus and Julitta. Husband and wife are commemorated together, but not in an English church, in the dedication to SS. Julian and Basilissa. The dedication SS. Gervase
and Protasius is of twin brothers; so are the three dedications
to SS. Cosmas and Damian. On the other hand, there are no
compound dedications to the apostolic brothers, James and
John, or Andrew and Peter.

Some compound dedications are due to natural association;
e.g., 1 to All Saints and All Angels; 3 to S. Helen and the
Invention of the Cross. Others are simply due to the fact that
the saints in question were bracketed together in some one of
the calendars; *e.g.*, SS. Fabian and Sebastian, 20th January, 1
dedication; SS. Simon and Jude, 28th October, 3 dedications.
Of compound dedications, that of SS. Peter and Paul is far away
the most common; it occurs 286 times. The reason for this is
to be found not so much in the desire to bracket together the
Apostle of the Jews and the Apostle of the Gentiles, as in the
fact that both were believed to have been executed on the same
day, 29th June.

Or again, where the dedication was not really to a saint at
all, but to the man whose preaching had organised the first
Christian congregation or whose money had built the first church,

the name of an authentic saint was not infrequently added in
after days, *e.g.*, SS. Menaacus and Dunstan (3 dedications), the
Blessed Meran and Thomas-à-Becket, SS. Pandiana and John
the Baptist ; while S. Bees was re-dedicated to God, S. Mary of
York, and S. Bega.

The addition of the name of a Biblical to that of a non-
Biblical saint is very frequent, especially when the fame of the
latter had paled ; *e.g.*, S. Candida and Holy Cross. Waltham
abbey originally commemorated only the miraculous trans-
portation of a portion of the Holy Cross ; afterwards the name
of S. Lawrence was added. In similar fashion probably may
be explained dedications to SS. Andrew and Eustachius, Holy
Trinity and S. Osyth, SS. John and Alkmund, SS. Mawnanus
and Stephen, SS. Peter and Etheldreda, SS. Peter and Wilfrid.
Most of all was it desired to obtain in addition the intercession
of Our Lady, whose name therefore appears in a vast number
of compound dedications. In the case of several cathedrals
complexity was produced by the addition of the favourite dedication names of Henry VIII., viz., Holy Trinity, Christ, or the
Blessed Virgin. Winchester cathedral illustrates the process of
accretion. There is a vague tradition that it was originally
dedicated to S. Amphibalus, the priest who was sheltered by
S. Alban, conjointly with SS. Peter and Paul and S. Swithun.
At the Conquest the dedication was changed to " SS. Peter and
Paul and Swithun." Henry VIII. re-dedicated it to The Sacred
and Undivided Trinity. Now it is described in the Clergy List
as the church of the Holy Trinity, SS. Peter, Paul, and Swithun.

In other cases the compound form is simply due to the
consolidation of parishes. The process of consolidation has
been carried furthest in the City of London, producing such
cumbrous compounds as " SS. Anne and Agnes with S. John
Zachary," and most complex of all, " S. Nicholas Cole Abbey,
S. Nicholas Olave, S. Mary Somerset, S. Mary Mountshaw, with
S. Benet, Paul's Wharf, and S. Peter, Paul's Wharf " ; here six
parishes have been consolidated.

In such churches of monks or canons as were parochial,
there was a special reason why a double dedication might arise,
that while the whole church was dedicated to one particular
saint, the parochial nave or aisle might have a special dedication
of its own, *e.g.*, Bridlington priory church was dedicated to the
Blessed Virgin, but the parochial part of it to S. Thomas of
Canterbury. So also the priory of Nunburnholme, Yorkshire,
was dedicated to the Blessed Virgin, but the parish church to
All Hallows.[1]

---

[1] Raine in *Yorkshire Archæological Journal*, ii. 182.

CHANGE IN DEDICATION

Not infrequently an entirely new dedication has been sub-stituted. The occasion for it no doubt was frequently a re-consecration following a rebuilding of a church or important additions made to it. Sometimes the very existence of the dedication had passed out of memory. Sometimes the name had become unpopular because identified with superstition, the reason given by Henry VIII. for suppressing dedications to S. Thomas of Canterbury. Henry seems to have meant to abolish all dedications except his three favourites; for in 1536 he issued a proclamation that every saint's day should be abolished, and that in future every parish feast should be held on the first Sunday in October, a proclamation which fortunately was pretty generally disregarded. Again, 15th August is a feast day still observed in many villages; in all these there is a presumption that the original dedication was to the Assumption of the Virgin, and was afterwards changed as being without scriptural warrant. A very complex series of changes is seen in the great and beautiful church of Milton Abbas; it was dedicated to " SS. Mary, Michael, Samson, and Branwallader." Later this was reduced to " SS. Mary and Samson "; later still to " S. James the Great." This last change illustrates what had become increasingly common in the fourteenth and fifteenth centuries, and of course still more so after the Reformation, viz, the addition or the substitution of names of Biblical saints; and above all, of " All Saints " or " All Hallows," the dedications to whom reached the great number of 1,217. In some cases a wealthy and popular chantry overshadowed the church in which it was founded, its name ultimately taking the place of the original dedication. Thus the church at Cambridge, now called " Little S. Mary's " to distinguish it from the University church of " Great S. Mary's," was originally S. Peter's church, from which the adjacent college got its name of " Peterhouse." The parish church of Hitchin is now dedicated to S. Mary; but in 1475 a licence was issued by the Bishop of Lincoln to found a "gild of S. Mary in the church of S. Andrew, Hicchyn, co. Hertford." Here the original dedication to S. Andrew has been supplanted by the guild dedication.

LOST DEDICATIONS

Every ancient church once had its patron saint. Sometimes the church has disappeared, and the dedication with it. Nowadays, in many a parish, there are few villagers who can tell one to whom the church is dedicated; to them it is simply " the

church" or "the parish church" or "t'owd church." No wonder
that so many churches are anonymous ; there are said to be over
500 ancient churches and over 150 ancient chapelries without a
known dedication.   Many, however, have been recovered of late.
Burial in the parish church was formerly not forbidden ; and in
such case the legal title of the church will be mentioned in the
will of the deceased.   Sometimes the name of the patron saint
has been retained in the name of the village, while it has been
lost in the dedication of the church ; thus the name of Peakirk,
once written Pegkirk, is in itself quite sufficient to show that the
dedication of the little old church is to S. Pega, sister of S.
Guthlac of Crowland.   But this does not always follow.   From
the form of the name of a Kentish parish, Bethersden or
Betrysden (Beatrichesdenne), it has been argued, erroneously,
that the parish church was dedicated to S. Beatrice ; whereas the
village feast, which is nearly always on dedication day, is on
20th July, the festival of the famous S. Margaret of Antioch,
who is known by documentary evidence to be the patron saint.
The date of the parish feast is of great importance in settling
dedications, *e.g.*, the church of Wimborne is dedicated to S.
Augustine; the village feast is kept on the day of S. Augustine
of Canterbury ; therefore the dedication is not to S. Augustine
of Hippo.   It should be remembered, however, that the village
feast may be held according to the Old or the New Style, so that
it may be necessary to deduct from the date of the present feast
day from ten to thirteen days.   Sometimes the date of the
village feast is no guide at all ; for if dedication day fell at some
busy period of the year or in winter, it was not seldom changed
to one of the greater feast days or holidays.   Arranged in
order of demerit, the following English counties had most
dedications untraced in 1899 :—

Devon -	- 60	Somerset -	- 37
Dorset -	- 50	Sussex	- 37
Essex -	- 37	Yorkshire -	- 29

By researches among wills, Canon Raine added greatly to our
knowledge of Yorkshire dedications, and reduced the unknown
dedications of Nottinghamshire to 6.

DEDICATIONS TO UNKNOWN SAINTS

In the case of some saints, especially of those of Celtic blood,
all memorial of them has passed away except the dedication ;
e.g., SS. Alwys, Breward, Dilpe, Erney, Torney, Gomonda, Kuet,
Materiana, Merther, Metherian, Newlyn, Onslow, Stedian,

Tallan, whose churches are in Cornwall and Devon; and SS. Dinabo, Mapley, Weonard in Hereford and Monmouth.

DEDICATIONS TO LITTLE KNOWN SAINTS

In this class Celtic proprietary dedications naturally bulk large. Some of the least known saints are SS. Merryn or Meran, Cleer, Grada, Creed, Sanscreed, Day or Dye, Eval or Uvell or Noell, Just, Winnow, Pinnock, Twinnock, all in Cornwall; and elsewhere SS. Briavel, Elphin or Elgin, Eadnor, and Ruthin.

DOUBTFUL ALTERNATIVE DEDICATIONS

Where a dedication is not given full-length, it is often impossible to know for certain to which of two saints it should be credited; e.g., it is very often difficult to decide between S. John the Apostle and S. John the Baptist, or S. Mary the Virgin and S. Mary Magdalene, or S. Thomas the Apostle and S. Thomas of Canterbury, or S. Margaret of Antioch and S. Margaret of Scotland, or S. Augustine of Hippo and S. Augustine of Canterbury. Bede says that S. Paulinus built a stone church at Lincoln; this church, or rather one of its successors, probably occupies the original site; but here, as at S. Paul's Cray, Paulinus' name has been shortened to " Paul," thus confusing him with the apostle. No doubt many a minor saint has been ousted by one with a bigger reputation, who happened to have a name identical or similar.

SPURIOUS DEDICATIONS

Lastly, there are dedications which are no dedications. These are particularly common in the City of London, where S. John Zachary has nothing to do with Zacharias. It is a church of S. John Baptist which had been conveyed by the Dean and Chapter of S. Paul's to one Zachary, and to which people added Zachary's name to distinguish it from S. John Baptist on Walbrook. So it is with S. Andrew Hubbard, S. Lawrence Pountney, S. Catherine Coleman, S. Margaret Moses (= Moyses), S. Benet Finck (or Finch), and S. Benet Sherehog; there was living in the City in 1122 a certain " Wilhelmus Serehog," and later, an " Alwinus Serehog." [1]

[1] For Compound, Changed, Lost, Alternative, and Spurious Dedications, see Arnold-Foster, *Ibid.*, chaps. 50 and 51.

25

CHAPTER XV

Uncanonised Saints— King Henry the Sixth—Sir John Schorn.

UNCANONISED SAINTS

IN early days there was no formality whatever about canonisation. The conditions of sanctity were of a most uncertain character. No formal process, certainly no reference to Rome, was required to put a departed worthy on the roll of the saints. Piety and blamelessness of life were *desiderata* ; but the proofs of holiness in the technical sense were miracles, and these proofs were estimated simply by the *vox populi*. A good man died ; signs were believed to be wrought at his tomb or by his intercession; the multitude flocked to the place, and his claim to sanctity was carried by acclamation. Eadmer records a conversation between Anselm and Lanfranc, in which the former supports the canonisation of Archbishop Alphege on substantial reasons alone. The first step taken to regularise canonisation was to require for it *episcopal* sanction.[1] The next step was to refer all proposals for canonisation to Rome, where counsel for prosecution and defence were formally appointed, and the departed worthy was sat upon with all the formalities of a court of law ; it is not long since this process was gone through to secure the canonisation of Joan of Arc. In the later Middle Ages the power of canonisation was one of the most valuable perquisites of the pope ; enormous sums being levied by the Papal Court on the friends of the candidate, so much so that not infrequently, as in the case of Bishop William De Marchia of Wells, the process had to be abandoned, though heavy expenditure had already been incurred. The present system or process of canonisation dates back to Benedict XIV., who was pope from 1740 to 1758.

Among English saints who obtained informal canonisation only, probably the one most venerated was King Henry VI. In a letter dated 1504, Pope Julius II. acknowledges to have heard that "some miracles, *ut pie creditur*, have been wrought by the intercession of King Henry VI. and crowds of people have begun to flock to his tomb." His sufferings and the rumours

---

[1] Forbes' *Kalendar of Scottish Saints*, xlix.

of a violent death had deeply impressed all England, and he was
venerated in every county, especially in the North.   His statue
on the rood-screen in York minster was an object of devotion,
and a Yorkist archbishop in 1479 had to forbid that it should

C. F. N.

Henry the Sixth.

Rood-screen, Barton Turf.

be venerated ; it was removed in the sixteenth century.   At
Alford, Lincolnshire, there was a bequest to " King Henry's
Light and S. Anthony's Light."   In Ripon minster, offerings
were made to King Henry VI. in 1502 and 1525.   At Windsor,

where was his tomb, as in the case of formally canonised saints, little signs or tokens[1] were manufactured, to be carried home by pilgrims. A list of miracles wrought by the saintly king is printed by Hearne as an addition to Otterburn's *Chronicle* ; and in the year 1500 his life had attained to the dignity of a legend, which was put forth by a monk at Windsor, prefaced by the following hymn :—

> Salve ! miles preciose
> Rex Henrice generose
>   Palmes vitis celice ;
> In radice caritatis
> Vernans flore sanctitatis
>   Viteque angelice.
>
> Salve ! forma pietatis,
> Exemplar humilitatis,
>   Decus innocentiæ !
> Vi oppressis vel turbatis,
> Moestis atque desolatis
>   Scola paciencie.

Cetera desint.

Henry VII. made formal demand for the canonisation of Henry VI., but declined to pay the extortionate sums demanded by the Papal Court. He had intended to remove the Windsor tomb to the easternmost recess of his new chapel at Westminster, which was made ready for it. Here is a Sarum prayer :—

" Præsta, quæsumus, omnipotens et misericors Deus, ut qui devotissimi Regis Henrici merita miraculis fulgentia pie mentis affectu recolimus in terris, ejus et omnium sanctorum tuorum intercessionibus ab omni peste, febre, morbo ac improvisa morte ceterisque eruamur malis, et gaudia superna adipisci mereamur. Per dominum nostrum Jesum Christum filium tuum."[2]

On the rood-screen at Gateley, Norfolk, the saintly king is depicted with Sir John Schorn.[3] The latter was never canonised, and came too late (he died in 1308) to get commemoration in dedications. He was a gentleman by birth, Rector of North Marston, Bucks., and Doctor of Divinity ; his greatest feat

[1] One of these is illustrated in the *British Archæological Journal* for 1845, p. 205.

[2] On the veneration of King Henry VI. see Edward Peacock in *Proceedings of the Society of Antiquaries*, 1891, p. 227 ; and Stanley's *Memorials of Westminster Abbey*, 3rd ed., pp. 162 and 616.

[3] The prefix " Sir " means " parish priest," not " knight " or " baronet."

N. R.

Sir John Schorn.

Rood-screens at Gateley and Cawston.

was that he once conjured the devil into a boot.[1] It was also
said of him that by reason of frequent prayer his knees had

---

[1] See drawing from the screen of Alphington, Devon, in Bond and Camm's
Rood Screens and Rood Lofts, ii. 238.

become horny ; also that during a drought, at the request of his distressed parish he struck the ground with his staff and a spring (now a well) broke forth. This spring was chalybeate, and among other purposes was good against gout, which may have been the devil in the boot. On the rood-screen at Cawston he is depicted with the cap, cloak, and hood of a Doctor of Divinity ; on the Gateley screen his name is annexed—

MAGISTER JOHANNES SCHORN

He was depicted in the east window of his own church, and had an image at Canterbury ; at first his shrine was in his church of North Marston, but when the living came into the possession of the college in 1481, it was removed at great cost to S. George's, Windsor. The Fabric Rolls for the 19th and 20th year of Edward IV. show heavy expenditure, which includes among other things "lintels for the enterclose of the chapel of Master John Schorne." This was placed in the east corner of the south aisle. Later on it was returned to Long Marston, and such was the resort of pilgrims during the century it remained there that at the Suppression the offerings were estimated to amount to not less than £500, say £6,000 in our money, each year. Erasmus says that there were nearly as many pilgrims to Long Marston as to Walsingham. In 1538 Dr Loudon writes that at Long Marston "Mr Johan Schorn standeth blessing a boot, whereunto they do say he conveyed the devil. He is much sought for the ague." On the 17th of September he writes that he is about to send up Mr Johan Schorn to London.[1]

Quite a long list might be drawn up of persons who obtained popular, but not formal canonisation.[2] Among them are Simon de Montfort; John of Bridlington; Bishop Dalderby of Lincoln ; Thomas, Duke of Lancaster, who was beheaded at Pontefract in 1322, and whose burial-place in the Cluniac priory there became a place of pilgrimage ; and Richard Scrope, Archbishop of York, beheaded by order of Henry IV. in 1398. Scrope's tomb was resorted to by thousands as that of a saint ; offerings were made at it, and miracles were said to have occurred before it.

[1] See *Norfolk and Norwich Archæological Society*, ii. 283, and the *Reliquary and Illustrated Archæologist*, vii. 37.

[2] In the illustration on p. 199 S. John of Bridlington is shown with S. William of York. The former was prior of the Augustinian priory of Bridlington, Yorkshire. He died in 1379 ; and at a later day his relics were removed to a shrine behind the high altar : moreover, a feast day was assigned to him in the calendar. An attempt to canonise him, however, was unsuccessful.

G. H. W.

SS. William of York and John of Bridlington.

From stained glass at Morley, Derbyshire.

Henry IV. forbade the offerings ; and the officials of the cathedral were ordered to pull down the wooden screenwork by which the tomb was enclosed, and to pile wood and stone over it so as to prevent access of the people. Offerings, however, were still made, and at the Reformation the treasures deposited in the adjoining chapel were among the richest in the cathedral.[1] At Wells too, the vaulting of the retrochoir was so planned as to enclose a saint's chapel for Bishop William de Marchia, whose canonisation the chapter desired to obtain, but were obliged to desist owing to the excessive demands of the Papal Court. Here is a Latin effusion of a pious versifier, indignant that the stories of his favourite saint are received with incredulity, though great works are still wrought at his tomb through his intercession :—

> " Tumba tamen protestatur
> Ubi vir hic veneratur ;
> Hæc non falsa, ut affatur,
> Preciosa pagina."
> " Licet non canonicatur,
> Adhuc autem operatur
> Per hunc Pater, cum precatur,
> Plura beneficia."

[1] For an inventory of these see *Monasticon Anglicanum*, viii. 1206, and Canon Raine's *Fabric Rolls of York Minster*, 225.

CHAPTER XVI

METHODS APPLICABLE TO THE STUDY OF DEDICATIONS

Dedications of Churches in selected counties—Northumberland, Durham, Yorkshire, Lincolnshire, Nottinghamshire, Kent, Wiltshire, Somerset, Devonshire, Shropshire, Pembrokeshire—Comparison of Saints commemorated in Dedications and on Bells.

So far we have spoken in the main of the dedications of English churches generally. It is of considerable interest to examine how far the general conclusions that have been obtained hold true of restricted districts. So far, however, in few English counties have the dedications been made the subject of serious study. It is a task peculiarly incumbent on the provincial archæological societies, and should be taken in hand at once. In most of the counties there are now complete and accurate accounts of the Church Plate and others of the Church Bells ; similarly investigations should be carried out into the dedications and patron saints of the churches of the county. A few suggestions may be offered as to the way to go to work. The first thing is to get a complete list of all the dedications, and where possible, of their dates. For this list resource may be had to the Diocesan Calendar, the Clergy List, the Postal Directory, and the like. Then the dedications must be tested, one by one. If they are only known by hearsay, say so. But they may be corroborated by mediæval wills or other documents. The date of the village feast or fair,[1] which was usually held on the

---

[1] In most of the towns and parishes of England (except where the privilege of new fairs had been obtained in ancient times), the old fairs, whether fixed by custom or by charter, depend upon the patron saint of the church. Thus the primitive fair of Oxford was on S. Frideswide's Day, October 19th, because that was Dedication day at the priory church. At Canterbury, S. Thomas was murdered on September 29th, and his body was translated on July 7th ; this occasioned two fairs annually in that city. On July 7th there is a fair at Bromhill, near Brandon Ferry, and another at Westacre, near Swaffham, both in Norfolk ; in both places are old ruinous chapels, which were dedicated to S. Thomas of Canterbury. The charters for fairs granted by kings of England were often a confirmation rather than

anniversary of the dedication of the church, may be evidence·
But it must be remembered (1) that the saints' days in the
calendar were sometimes moved to another date (as may be
seen below by comparing the calendars of Bede and Sarum);
(2) that the village feast day was sometimes altered, *e.g.*, by
enactment of Henry VIII., or to take it out of harvest time, or
to bring it to a time of year when good weather might be expected ;[1] (3) and that the date of the fair may be New Style or
Old Style, and the latter may vary as much as three days.

Then when the individual dedications have been as far as
possible verified, they should be grouped under the names of the
respective saints commemorated. The next thing is to arrange
the names of the patron saints in order of popularity. Then
comes the interesting attempt to explain the abnormal popularity
of some, and the abnormal unpopularity of others. Finally, the
order of popularity in the individual county should be compared
with that of the neighbouring counties, and with that of all
England, taking into account also diocesan boundaries and
changes in them.

It will probably be found desirable to divide the subject into
two parts : dedications before and dedications after the end of
the sixteenth century.

For the whole subject of dedications Miss Arnold-Forster's
book is the standard work.

If the district is Celtic, or if Celtic dedications are numerous,
then the dedications must be approached by a totally distinct
line of research, for which some knowledge of Welsh, and at any
rate a pretty thorough acquaintance with the literature which
has grown up on the subject of Celtic dedications and Celtic
saints, are desirable. A list of books dealing with this special
subject will be found in the bibliography prefixed to this volume.

The counties which have been selected for a cursory
examination in this volume are Northumberland, Durham,
Yorkshire, Lincolnshire, Nottingham, Kent, Wiltshire, Somerset,

a new grant ; thus King Richard gave a charter for a fair to be held
eight days in Peterborough, beginning on the feast of S. Peter ; but a fair
had been held on that day, June 29th, from time immemorial, because the
church was dedicated to S. Peter.

[1] Lawton mentions that at Bishop Wilton, Yorkshire, the parish feast, up
to the middle of the fifteenth century, was held on September 15th, the vigil
of S. Edith of Wilton, who therefore, and not S. Edith of Polesworth, is the
patron saint of the church : but since the said day fell at a time when Yorkshire people were busy with their harvest, John, Archbishop of York, translated the said feast until the Sunday the next ensuing, every year solemnly
to be celebrated.

Devonshire, Shropshire, Pembrokeshire. It is not attempted to forestall detailed and thoroughgoing research, but merely to present a few obvious surface conclusions.

YORKSHIRE DEDICATIONS

The following table has been compiled by the writer from the list of ancient dedications in Yorkshire, as set forth by Mr Lawton in his *Collectio rerum ecclesiasticarum de diocesi Eboracensi*, as verified and corrected by Canon Raine, from wills prior to 1560 preserved in York and those formerly kept at Richmond, Yorkshire, but now in London. It must be borne in mind that in this and all the county lists doubt often exists as to the real ascription of dedications to S. John, S. James, S. Peter, S. Paul, S. Thomas, S. Augustine, S. Edward, and others; that a good many dedications have not been determined with certainty, and several are still unknown. The order given below, however, is probably approximately correct, though not the exact figures. For Yorkshire the order of dedications is as follows:—[1]

1. All Saints or				22. S. Margaret -	7	11
All Hallows	144	2		23. S. Catherine -	6	26
2. Blessed Virgin				23. S. Edmund -	6	27
Mary	-	129	1	23. S. John Evan-		
3. S. Peter	-	50	3	gelist	6	14
4. S. Michael	-	41	4	26. S. Stephen	5	30
5. S. Andrew	-	38	5	27. S. Augustine -	4	40
6. S. Helena	-	34	19	27. S. George	4	20
7. S. John Baptist	33	6		27. S. Thomas of		
8. S. Nicholas -	29	7		Canterbury	4	22
9. S. Oswald	-	22	24	30. S. Anne	3	32
10. Holy Trinity	22	10		30. S. Clement -	3	32
11. S. James	-	21	8	30. S. German	3	50
12. S. Leonard	-	18	15	30. S. Gregory -	3	38
13. S. Cuthbert	-	16	23	30. S. John of		
14. S. Lawrence -	14	12		Beverley -	3	73
14. S. Martin	-	14	16	35. S. Agatha	2	100
14. S. Paul -	-	14	9	35. S. Alban	2	58
17. S. Wilfrid	-	13	29	35. S. Botolph -	2	25
18. S. Hilda	-	11	50	35. S. Christopher	2	60
19. S. Giles	-	10	18	35. S. Edward -	2	48
20. S. Mary Mag-				35. Holy Cross or		
dalene	-	10	13	Holy Rood	2	21
21. S. Bartholomew	8	17		35. S. Patrick -	2	68

[1] In all these tables the first column of figures gives the local order, the second the number of dedications, the third the general order as shown in Chapter III.

To the following only a single church is dedicated :—

42. S. Akelda
43. S. Alkeld (?)
44. All Souls
45. S. Benedict
46. S. Bridget
47. S. Columb
48. S. Cyprian
49. S. David
50. S. Denis
51. S. Edith
52. S. Everilda
53. S. Faith
54. S. Felix
55. S. Jude
56. S. Lambert
57. S. Matthew
58. S. Maurice

59. S. Olave
60. S. Osyth or Sithe
61. S. Quintin
62. S. Radegund
63. S. Richarius
64. S. Robert of Knares-
       borough
65. S. Ronald
66. S. Sampson
67. S. Saviour
68. S. Sepulchre
69. S. Simon
70. S. Swithun
71. S. Ursula
72. S. Werburga
73. S. William of York
74. S. Winifred

The first surprise is that the Blessed Virgin is ousted from her precedence in favour of All Saints. Secondly, there is a grateful remembrance, pleasant to notice, of Yorkshire saints. S. Cuthbert belongs rather to Lindisfarne and Northumberland, and the chief relics of him were in Durham cathedral and Bamburgh, but his fame had crossed the Tees, and his position rises from 23rd to 13th. S. Wilfrid, by his connection with Hexham, was Northumbrian, but as Archbishop of York and founder of Ripon minster, he was a Yorkshireman ; moreover, he had done in his day more than anyone else to secure that Christianity in England should be of the Roman, not of the Celtic type: his position rises from 29th to 17th. S. Hilda, the learned abbess of Whitby, rises from 50th to 18th : a cluster of little churches is dedicated to her in the Whitby district. Good John of Beverley was not forgotten in his own country ; he rises from 73rd to 30th. S. Oswald, the Christian king of Northumberland, gave his life fighting with the heathen, praying with his last breath for his soldiers : " Lord have mercy on their souls," said Oswald as he passed. He rises from the 24th to the 9th place. S. Robert, the Hermit of Knaresborough, has a single dedication. S. William of York came too late to have more than one church dedicated to him, and this has been demolished. Chiefest among local saints may be placed S. Helena, for it was known that her son spent considerable time in York, and it was believed that he was born there. Of Celtic saints few are commemorated. Of the Irish saints, S. Patrick has two dedications, one of them the magnificent church of Patrington ; S. Columb, S. Bridget, and S. Sampson have one each ; of the Welsh saints, S. David and S. Winifred also one each.

DEDICATIONS OF NORTHUMBERLAND AND DURHAM

In the following lists the churches of Northumberland and Durham respectively are arranged according to the number of dedications up to 1800 :[1] omitting dedications which occur but once :—

NORTHUMBERLAND				DURHAM			
1.	Blessed Virgin			1.	Blessed Virgin		
	Mary -	21	1		Mary -	23	1
2.	S. Michael -	13	4	2.	S. Andrew -	7	5
3.	S. Cuthbert -	10	23	3.	S. Michael -	6	4
4.	S. Bartholo-			3.	S. Cuthbert -	6	23
	mew - -	8	17	3.	All Saints -	6	2
5.	S. Andrew -	7	5	6.	John Baptist -	5	6
6.	Holy Trinity	6	10	6.	S. James -	5	8
7.	John Baptist -	5	6	8.	S. Peter -	4	3
7.	S. Peter -	5	3	8.	S. Mary Mag-		
9.	S. Nicholas -	4	7		dalene -	4	13
9.	All Saints -	4	2	10.	King Edmund	3	27
11.	S. Helen -	3	19	11.	Holy Trinity	2	10
11.	S. Giles -	3	18	11.	S. Nicholas -	2	7
13.	Holy Cross -	2	21	11.	S. Helen -	2	19
13.	S. Anne -	2	32	11.	S. Hilda -	2	50
13.	S. Maurice -	2	68	11.	S. Margaret -	2	11
13.	S. Paul - -	2	9	11.	S. Thomas of		
13.	S. Wilfrid -	2	29		Canterbury	2	22
13.	S. Oswald -	2	24				
13.	S. Mary Mag-						
	dalene -	2	13				
13.	S. Thomas of						
	Canterbury	2	22				

In both counties a very high position is held by S. Michael. It is possible that this dedication is a survival of Celtic Christianity. In Wales the dedications to S. Michael are outnumbered by those to the Blessed Virgin ; but the latter are mostly found in the English and Flemish districts, and in

[1] The statistics are those of Mr John V. Gregory in *Archæological Journal*, xlii. 381.

churches of modern foundation—the former in Celtic districts and churches of ancient foundation. In Cornwall the Blessed Virgin has 9 dedications, S. Michael 5. It is remarkable that S. Peter has sunk in Northumberland and Durham to the 7th and 8th position respectively, in spite of early and important dedications at Monkwearmouth, Jarrow, Lindisfarne, Bamburgh, and Brinkburn. S. Andrew may owe his high

St CATHERINE.
OF SIENA.
(TORBRYAN)

St VICTOR.
(TORBRYAN)

B. AND C.

position partly to the fact that he is the patron saint of Scotland, of which Northumberland for some time formed a part, and to the influence of the important churches of Newcastle, Hexham priory, and Auckland ; round Hexham is a cluster of dedications to S. Andrew. To S. Bartholomew there were 8 dedications in Northumberland, but only one in Durham ; some of the Northumberland dedications probably belong to the Bartholomew who was a hermit in the Farne Isles. S. Margaret has two churches in Durham; the christian name of Margaret is still very common in the district, perhaps not altogether without reference to S. Margaret of Scotland. Considering the excessive popularity in Yorkshire of the dedication to All Saints, it is a little surprising to find that in the two northern counties it occupies an exceptionally low position.

DEDICATIONS OF LINCOLNSHIRE

Of the Lincolnshire churches Precentor Venables gives the following list.[1] (Churches with but a single dedication are omitted.)

1.	All Saints	-	97	2	19. S. Leonard -	6	15
2.	S. Peter	-	89	3	19. Holy Cross -	6	21
3.	S. Andrew	-	68	5	19. S. Mary Mag-		
3.	Blessed Virgin		68	1	dalene -	6	13
5.	S. Nicholas	-	31	7	25. S. Benedict -	5	45
5.	S. Margaret	-	31	11	25. S. Guthlac -	5	60
7.	S. Helen	-	28	19	25. S. Stephen -	5	30
7.	S. Michael	-	28	4	25. S. Swithin -	5	28
9.	S. John Baptist		25	6	29. S. Edmund -	4	27
10.	S. James	-	19	8	29. S. Edward -	4	(?)48
11.	S. Martin	-	16	16	29. S. George -	4	20
12.	S. Lawrence -		15	12	29. S. Giles -	4	18
12.	Holy Trinity		15	10	29. S. Hybald -	4	100
14.	S. Clement -		10	32	29. S. Thomas		
15.	S. Bartholo-				Apostle -	4	30
	mew -	-	8	17	29. S. Vincent -	4	75
16.	S. Edith	-	7	(?)50	36. S. Chad -	3	36
16.	S. Oswald	-	7	24	36. S. Faith -	3	43
16.	S. Thomas of				36. S. German -	3	50
	Canterbury		7	22	39. S. Cuthbert -	2	23
19.	S. Botolph	-	6	25	39. S. Paul -	2	29
19.	S. Denis	-	6	32	39. S. Wilfrid -	2	29
19.	S. John Evan-						
	gelist	-	6	14			

Lincolnshire in early days was either treeless, untilled chalk wold or interminable swamp. The natives were said by unfriendly neighbours to be web-footed. Anyway, though they built many churches, they produced but few saints. Of these three appear in the dedications: S. Guthlac, who rises from 60th to 25th; S. Botolph, from 25th to 19th; and S. Hybald or Hygbald (4 dedications), whom Bede mentions,

[1] *Archæological Journal*, xxxviii. 390.

and who seems to have been a good pious man, and probably abbot of Bardney, in the seventh century. His mission centre was probably the village of Hibaldstow, and his dedications are in the village of Hibaldstow and its two neighbours at Manton and Scawby; a fourth dedication is at Ashby-de-la-Launde, in South Lincolnshire; there are no other dedications to him in England. A certain amount of northern influence is apparent: as in Yorkshire, All Saints takes the premier place in the dedications, ousting the Blessed Virgin, who stands exceptionally low; S. Helena advances from the 19th to the 7th position; and S. Oswald from the 24th to the 16th. On the other hand, S. Cuthbert and S. Wilfrid lose ground. Others who improve their position are S. Clement, S. Benedict, S. Vincent, S. Denis, and S. Edith: the latter two, and also S. Helen, because of groups of "cluster-dedications."

DEDICATIONS IN NOTTINGHAMSHIRE

The chief dedications of Nottinghamshire churches, as shown by Canon Raine, are as follows:—

1. S. Mary the Virgin	34	1	16. S. Andrew	-	5	5
2. All Hallows -	33	2	17. S. Edmund	-	4	27
3. S. Peter -	16	3	17. S. Leonard	-	4	15
4. S. Helen -	15	19	19. Holy Rood	-	3	21
5. Holy Trinity-	14	10	19. S. John of Beverley	-	3	73
6. S. Wilfrid -	12	29				
6. S. Peter and S. Paul -	12	29	19. S. John Evangelist-	-	3	14
8. S. John Baptist	11	6	19. S. Mary Magdalene	-	3	13
8. S. Michael -	11	4	19. S. Swithin	-	3	28
10. S. Giles- -	10	18	24. S. Catherine -		2	26
11. S. Nicholas -	7	7	24. S. Cuthbert -		2	23
12. S. James -	6	8	24. S. David	-	2	43
12. S. Lawrence -	6	12	24. S. George	-	2	20
12. S. Martin -	6	16	24. S. Margaret -		2	11
12. S. Oswald -	6	24				

This county is next door to Lincolnshire, but was in the diocese of York, having for its cathedral Southwell minster, adjoining which the Archbishop of York had a palace. It was natural, therefore, that the Yorkshire saints should be commemorated in Nottingham in numerous dedications; among them S. Helena stands fourth on the list with 15 dedications; S. Wilfrid has risen from 29th to 6th; S. Oswald from 24th to 12th; S. John of Beverley has 3 and S. Cuthbert has 2 dedications. S. Giles, S. Edmund, and S. Swithin have all improved their position; while S. Michael, S. Andrew, and S. Margaret have greatly receded.

KENTISH DEDICATIONS

The following list of dedications of Kent churches has been compiled from the lists of Mr Leland L. Duncan and Mr Arthur Hussey. Dedications which occur once only are omitted.

1.	Our Lady	-	116	1	15. Holy Cross -	5	21
2.	S. Peter	-	82	3	15. S. Andrew -	5	5
3.	All Saints	-	38	2	15. S. Augustine		
4.	S. Nicholas	-	30	7	of Canterbury	5	40
5.	S. John Baptist		21	6	15. S. Bartholo-		
5.	S. Margaret	-	21	11	mew - -	5	17
7.	S. Martin	-	18	16	19. S. Leonard -	4	15
8.	S. Michael	-	17	4	19. S. Clement -	4	32
9.	S. Lawrence	-	14	12	19. S. Dunstan -	4	45
10.	S. James	-	11,8&43		19. S. Mildred -	4	60
11.	S. Mary Mag-				23. S. Catherine -	3	26
	dalene	-	10	13	24. S. Alphege -	2	87
12.	S. George	-	7	21	24. S. Stephen -	2	30
13.	S. Botolph	-	6	25	24. Holy Trinity	2	10
13.	S. Giles	-	6	18			

The table shows a considerable rise in popularity of five saints. Four of these rise because they are local saints: Alphege and Dunstan were both Archbishops of Canterbury; so also was Augustine; it is possible, however, that some of his dedications belong to the theologian, Augustine of Hippo. Mildred is almost the typical saint of Kent.[1] But why should Botolph have six churches dedicated to him so far from the fenland? S. Nicholas rises from 7th to 4th; S. Margaret from 11th to 6th; S. Martin from 16th to 7th; S. George from 21st to 12th; Holy Cross from 21st to 15th; S. Clement from 32nd to 19th; S. Stephen from 30th to 24th. There is a drop in the position of dedications to the Holy Trinity from the 10th to the 24th place; of S. Michael from 4th to 8th; and of those to S. Andrew from the 5th to the 15th place; the latter is the more remarkable as S. Andrew is the patron saint of Rochester cathedral.

[1] For her pretty story see Bishop Stubbs in *Dictionary of Christian Biography*.

27

No Celtic saints appear above: and S. Botolph is the only non-Kentish local saint. Few counties offer so many departures from the normal; the Kentish men and the men of Kent had evidently strong opinions of their own on hagiography.

A comparison of dedications of Kentish churches with a list of the images known from wills to have existed in parish churches, naturally shows marked divergences, the dedication having usually been given centuries before images referred to in late wills were set up. In West Kent, Mr Leland L. Duncan found that after those of Our Lady, the most common images were those of—

IMAGES

2. S. Catherine	- -	48 (nearly half the number of churches)
3. S. Christopher	- -	43
4. S. Nicholas -	- -	41
5. Holy Trinity	- -	40
6. S. James	- -	34
7. S. John Baptist	- -	32

DEDICATIONS OF WILTSHIRE

The following tables show the dedications most in favour in Wiltshire: it includes several doubtful examples.[1]

1. Blessed Virgin Mary	73	1
2. All Saints	45	2
3. S. Peter	34	3
4. S. Michael	23	4
5. S. Andrew	22	5
5. S. John Baptist	22	6
7. S. Nicholas -	18	7
7. S. James	18	8
9. Holy Trinity	10	10
10. Christ Church	9	38
10. Holy Cross or Rood	9	21
12. S. Leonard	8	15
13. S. George	7	20
13. S. Paul	7	9
15. S. Giles	6	18
15. S. Margaret -	6	11

17. S. Catherine -	5	26
17. S. John Evangelist	5	14
17. S. Lawrence -	5	12
17. S. Martin	5	16
21. S. Swithun	3	28
21. S. Thomas of Canterbury	3	22
23. S. Aldhelm -	2	100
23. S. Anne	2	32
23. S. Bartholomew -	2	17
23. S. Edith of Wilton	2	114
23. S. Mary Magdalene	2	13
23. S. Stephen -	2	30

[1] The dedications are given on the authority of Mr J. E. Jackson.

This is an exceptionally normal county, the order of the first eight dedications being the same for Wiltshire as for all England. There were few local saints to break into the order, the only ones of importance being S. Aldhelm and S. Edith, each with only 2 dedications. The northern saints, S. Helen, S. Cuthbert, S. Wilfrid, S. Oswald, do not appear on the above list; nor the fenland saints, S. Guthlac and S. Botolph; nor the East Anglian saint, King Edmund; nor the Midland saint, S. Chad; nor does it contain any Celtic saint.

DEDICATIONS OF SOMERSET

Mr Bates has printed in vol. li. of the *Proceedings of the Somerset Archæological and Natural History Society* all the church dedications known in that county. Omitting dedications which occur once only, the following is the result :—

1.	Blessed Virgin	104	1	16.	S. Giles -	8	18
2.	All Saints -	43	2	17.	S. Bartholomew	6	17
3.	S. Peter -	41	3	17.	Holy Cross -	6	21
4.	S. Michael -	40	4	19.	S. Catherine -	5	26
5.	S. Andrew -	36	5	19.	S. John Apostle	5	14
6.	S. John Baptist	27	6	19.	S. Margaret	5	11
7.	S. Paul - -	19	9	19.	S. Thomas of		
8.	S. Nicholas -	17	7		Canterbury	5	22
8.	S. James -	17	8	23.	S. Augustine	3	30
10.	Holy Trinity	14	10	23.	S. Gregory -	3	38
10.	S. Mary Mag-			25.	S. Bridget -	2	47
	dalene -	14	13	25.	S. Edward -	2	(?)48
12.	S. George -	11	20	25.	S. Stephen -	2	30
12.	S. Leonard -	11	15	25.	S. Thomas		
14.	S. Lawrence -	10	12		Apostle -	2	30
15.	S. Martin -	9	16				

As in Wiltshire, the results are of quite normal character, the order of the first ten dedications of Somerset being almost identical with those of all England : this is largely due to the absence of local saints in this county. The special saints of other localities, S. Helena, S. Oswald, S. Wilfrid, S. Hilda, S. Aldhelm, S. Edith, S. Chad, S. Edmund, S. Botolph, S. Guthlac, S. Swithun, all fail to obtain a place in the above list. S. Bridget is the only Celtic saint. S. George, S. Catherine and S. Margaret all rise in popularity.

Devon Dedications

The following list has been drawn up from a paper by Mr B. Rowe :—

1.	Blessed Virgin	113	1	19.	S. John Apostle	8	14
2.	S. Peter -	50	3	19.	S. Lawrence -	8	12
3.	S. Michael -	37	4	22.	S. Gregory -	7	32
4.	S. Andrew -	34	5	23.	S. Nectan -	5	114
5.	All Saints or			23.	S. Pancras -	5 (?)	59
	All Hallows	29	2	23.	S. Stephen -	5	30
6.	S. John Baptist	28	6	23.	S. Thomas		
7.	Holy Trinity	22	10		Apostle -	5	30
8.	S. James -	20	8	27.	S. Bartholo-		
9.	S. George -	13	20		mew - -	4	17
10.	S. Martin -	12	16	27.	S. Edmund -	4	27
10.	S. Mary Mag-			27.	Holy Cross -	4	21
	dalene -	12	13	27.	S. Swithun -	4	28
10.	S. Paul - -	12	9	31.	S. Anne -	3	32
10.	S. Petrock -	12	53	31.	S. Bridget -	3	47
14.	S. Catherine -	11	26	31.	S. David -	3	43
15.	S. Leonard -	10	15	34.	S. Brendonus	2	180
15.	S. Nicholas -	10	7	34.	S. Clement -	2	32
17.	S. Margaret -	9	11	34.	S. Edward -	2	(?)
17.	S. Thomas of			34.	S. Helena -	2	19
	Canterbury	9	22	34.	S. Luke -	2	41
19.	S. Giles -	8	18	34.	S. Winifred -	2	75

No account is taken here of numerous cases in which a dedication appears in one church only. There are several churches of which the dedication is unknown.

Perhaps one of the most striking features of the list is the comparative paucity of Celtic dedications, which is the more remarkable as they swarm in the neighbouring county, Cornwall. This seems to point to the fact that the Tamar was an "oceanus dissociabilis" to the two counties, and that at the chief church-building periods the state of feeling between Devonian and Cornishman was such that the former had very little use for any saints of the latter. S. Michael, however, is to be regarded as largely a saint, if only by adoption, of the Celtic Church : and he occupies the third position in the list of Devon dedications.[1] S. Petrock, or Petrox, with 12 dedications, stands high on the list. He was of Cornish royal stock, and lived in the sixth century.

[1] On the screen at Ashton, Devon, S. Sitha bears a book in her right hand, and a bunch of keys in her left (213). At Mells, Somerset, she carries three loaves and a bunch of keys (217).

He studied in Ireland, and visited Rome. On his return he landed at Padstow, and then probably visited the parishes where

E. W. A.

S. Sitha.   S Michael.

Rood-screen at Ashton, Devon.

his dedications are now found. His relics were long kept in the famous ivory casket still to be seen at Bodmin ; in 1177 they were stolen and were carried off to an abbey in Brittany, and were only restored through the personal intervention of King Henry II. S. Nectan (5 dedications)was one of the many children of the Welsh saint, Brynach. It was at Hartland that Githa, mother of King Harold, founded a college in honour of S. Nectan, by intercession to whom her husband, Earl Godwin, had been saved from shipwreck; the relics of the saint were long preserved in Hartland church, which is dedicated to him, and his statue is still to be seen on the east side of the church tower. There are 3 dedications to S. Bridget of Ireland, 2 to S. Brendan, another Irish saint, and 3 to S. David of Wales. With the dedications of Devon we may compare those of Shropshire, which, though embedded in a Celtic district, has hardly one authenticated Celtic dedication, except perhaps that of S. Sampson and S. Owen's well at Wenlock.

In an interesting and valuable paper on *Celt and Teuton in Exeter*,[1] Mr Kerslake has shown that the interpretation put by Palgrave and Kemble on the statement of William of Malmesbury, that "King Athelstan found the Cornish Britons and the English settlers at Exeter living side by side under equal law," was erroneous. It was believed by these two historians that up to that time the river Exe divided the two nations. But the church dedications show that the dividing line was the Roman Fossway, to the north of which the Britons had been driven by the invaders coming from the estuary to the south. North of the Fossway are churches dedicated to S. Petrock, S. Kerian, S. Pancras, S. Paul (Pol de Leon), all distinctively Celtic dedications. At Kilkenny also there may be seen two nationalities, sharply divided, in what are called "Irishtown" and "Englishtown"; so also at Galway and elsewhere.

DEDICATIONS OF SHROPSHIRE

Mr Cranage, in the last volume of his *Churches of Shropshire*, arranges the known dedications as follows:—

1. Blessed Virgin	42	1		10. S. Margaret -	6	11
2. S. Michael -	28	4		10. S. Giles- -	6	18
3. S. Peter -	26	3		12. S. George -	5	20
4. S. John Baptist	20	6		12. S. Bartholomew	5	17
5. All Saints -	14	2		12. S. Lawrence -	5	12
5. Holy Trinity-	14	10		12. S. Mary Mag-		
7. S. Andrew -	11	5		dalene -	5	13
8. S. Chad -	7	36		12. S. James -	5	8
8. S. Paul - -	7	9		12. S. Leonard -	5	15

[1] *Archæological Journal*, xxx. 211.

18. S. John Evan-gelist -	-	3	14	29. S. Agatha	-	I	100
18. S. Nicholas	-	3	7	29. S. Calixtus	-	I	180
20. S. Alkmund	-	2	100	29. S. Eata	-	I	180
20. S. Catherine	-	2	26	29. S. Gregory	-	I	38
20. S. Cuthbert	-	2	23	29. S. Juliana	-	I	180
20. S. Edith	-	2	50	29. S. Lucy	-	I	137
20. S. Martin	-	2	16	29. S. Mark	-	I	75
20. S. Milburge	-	2	87	29. S. Ruthin	-	I	180
20. S. Oswald	-	2	24	29. S. Thomas Apostle	-	I	30
20. S. Swithun	-	2	28	29. S. Ethelbert	-	I	49
20. S. Thomas of Canterbury		2	22	29. S. Helen	-	I	19
29. Holy Cross	-	I	21	29. S. Sampson	-	I	75

In the Salop dedications some local saints naturally take a prominent place. S. Chad of Lichfield has no less than 7 dedications. S. Alkmund was a young king of Northumbria, who was murdered A.D. 800 ; somehow or other he was buried at Lilleshall in Shropshire, but his body was afterwards removed to S. Alkmund's, Derby, which subsequently became a famous place of pilgrimage.[1] Other of his churches are Whitchurch and Shrewsbury, Salop, Duffield (re-dedicated to "All Saints"), Blyborough, Lincolnshire, and Aymestry, Hereford. S. Edith has 2 dedications ; in the various English churches with this dedication it is not always possible to separate those of S. Edith of Polesworth from those of S. Edith of Wilton and those of S. Edith, the wife of Edward the Confessor and sister of King Harold, to whom the Herefordshire village, which still goes by the name of Stoke Edith, was granted. S. Milburga (2 dedications) was a granddaughter of the old heathen Penda, king of Mercia, who slew King Oswald. She seems to have spent most of her life at Wenlock, where she was abbess. When she was pestered by a wealthy suitor, the stream between rose high and effectually cut off his importunities. She died about 722.[2]

It is interesting to note that Shropshire gave a welcome to saints of other localities—S. Cuthbert, S. Oswald, S. Eata, all of Northumbria ; S. Ethelbert of Hereford ; S. Swithun of Winchester ; S. Thomas of Canterbury ; as well as three Celtic saints—SS. Juliana, Ruthin, and Sampson. S. Nicholas falls from the 7th to the 18th place, probably because Shropshire

[1] Arnold-Forster, *Ibid.*, ii. 324.
[2] Arnold-Forster, *Ibid.*, ii. 379.

is an inland county.   S. Giles, S. George, and S. Bartholomew
all rise in popularity.

Dedications of Pembrokeshire

With these English counties it may be interesting to
compare the Welsh county of Pembroke. Of its churches 24
dedications are unknown. Of the rest the dedications are
as follows :—

1.	Blessed Virgin	22	18.	S. Florence	1
2.	S. David	13	18.	S. Giles	1
3.	S. Teilo	8	18.	S. Gwyndaf	1
3.	S. Michael	8	18.	S. Gwynnog	1
5.	S. James	5	18.	S. Gwythwr	1
5.	S. Brynach	5	18.	S. Howel	1
7.	S. Dogfael	4	18.	S. Illtyd	1
7.	S. John Baptist	4	18.	S. Issels	1
7.	S. Ismael	4	18.	S. Justinian	1
7.	S. Nicholas	4	18.	S. Keyne	1
7.	S. Peter	4	18.	S. Leonard	1
12.	S. Andrew	3	18.	S. Llawddog	1
13.	S. Colman	2	18.	Holy Martyrs	1
13.	S. Cristiolus	2	18.	S. Mallteg	1
13.	S. Lawrence	2	18.	S. Meilyr	1
13.	S. Madoc	2	18.	S. Mynno	1
13.	S. Martin	2	18.	S. Oswald	1
18.	S. Aidan	1	18.	S. Petrox	1
18.	S. Ailbhe	1	18.	S. Rheithan	1
18.	S. Bridget	1	18.	S. Rhian	1
18.	S. Caradoc	1	18.	S. Teloi	1
18.	S. Catherine	1	18.	S. Thomas	1
18.	S. Cewyll	1	18.	S. Tudwal	1
18.	S. Clydei	1	18.	S. Tycefyn	1
18.	S. Decumanus	1	18.	S. Tysilio	1
18.	S. Edren	1	18.	S. Usyllt	1

In examining the Pembrokeshire list one is struck at once
with the vast preponderance of Celtic saints, the greater part of
unknown provenance. Among the best known of them S. David,
of S. David's cathedral, stands 2nd ; S. Teilo, of Llandaff
cathedral, is 3rd ; S. Brynach is bracketed 5th ; S. Dogfael and
S. Ismael are bracketed 7th ; S. Colman, S. Cristiolus, and
S. Madoc are bracketed 13th ; then come nearly thirty to whom
but a single church is dedicated. The chief position is held as
usual by the Blessed Virgin, with 22 dedications ; then come

successively S. Michael, S. James, S. John Baptist, S. Nicholas, S. Peter, S. Andrew, S. Lawrence, S. Martin, S. Aidan, S. Catherine, S. Giles, S. Leonard, Holy Martyrs, S. Oswald, S. Thomas the Apostle. These dedications, including those to the Blessed Virgin, are no doubt due to the immigration of Anglo-Normans and Flemings into the county (*c.* 1100). To this day Pembrokeshire is a double county: the northern half is Celtic, the southern half English ; the north folk are small men speaking Welsh, the latter are big men speaking English. The two districts were each protected of old by its own line of castles; and to this day when English and Welsh meet at market day, there is apt to be a free fight. Both in Pembrokeshire and in Glamorgan, which latter county was divided up among Norman adventurers (*c.* 1090), the number of dedications to the Blessed Virgin is far above the average of the Welsh counties generally ; and many of the parishes where her dedications occur have not even Welsh names. Indeed, a dedication to S. Mary the Virgin may be regarded *prima facie* as of late date. Welsh dedications to S. Michael are proportionally thrice as numerous as in England; and as they occur quite as much in purely Celtic as in semi-foreign districts, they are probably anterior to any foreign occupation. But, undoubtedly, the oldest dedications in Wales are those of native missioners.[1]

J. H. P.

S. Sitha or Zita.

From painted glass of the fifteenth century in Mells Church, Somersetshire.

DEDICATIONS OF BELLS

A comparison of dedications of mediæval churches and chapels with those of mediæval bells leads to some curious results. From the time of Charlemagne it was common to baptize bells and to give them Christian names, like human beings. This is definitely stated on some bells, *e.g.* :—

[1] Rev. J. T. Evans, *Church Plate of Pembrokeshire.*

28

SUM ROSA PULSATA MUNDI KATERINA VOCATA
" I that am struck am called Katherine, rose of the world."

VIRGINIS EGREGIE VOCOR CAMPANA MARIE
" I am called the bell of Mary the excellent virgin."

NOMEN PETRI FERO QUI CLAVIGER EXTAT IN EVO
" I bear the name of Peter who carries the keys for all time."

DICOR EGO THOMAS LAUS EST XRI SONUS O MAS
" I am called Thomas; my sound, O man, is the praise of Christ."

In some cases the tenor or other of the bells bears the name of the saint to whom the church is dedicated; but far more often this is not so. To some extent the order of popularity of the saints is similar in the dedications of churches and bells.

DEDICATION.	MEDIÆVAL CHURCHES AND CHAPELS.	DEDICATION.	MEDIÆVAL CHURCHES AND CHAPELS.
Virgin Mary -	2,335 (1)	S. Paul - -	326 (9)
All Saints and All Hallows -	1,255 (2)	Holy Trinity -	297 (10)
		S. Margaret -	261 (11)
S. Peter and S. Peter *ad vincula*	1,140 (3)	S. Mary Magdalene - -	187 (13)
S. Michael or S. Michael and All Angels - -	687 (4)	Our Lord - -	150 (19)
		S. Thomas of Canterbury -	80 (22)
S. Andrew -	637 (5)	S. Catherine -	62 (26)
S. John Baptist [1]	495 (6)	S. Anne - -	41 (27)
S. Nicholas -	437 (7)	S. Augustine -	30 (28)
S. James the Elder	414 (8)	S. Gabriel - -	6 (29)

DEDICATION.	MEDIÆVAL BELLS.	DEDICATION.	MEDIÆVAL BELLS.
Virgin Mary (1) -	900	S. Thomas of Canterbury (11)	Most of 80
S. John Baptist (2) - -	Most of 260	S. Andrew (12) - -	66
S. Catherine (3) -	170	S. Mary Magdalene (13) - -	52
Our Lord (4) - -	160	S. Nicholas (14)- -	48
S. Gabriel (5) - -	158	S. Augustine (15) -	43
S. Peter (6) - -	154	S. Paul (16) - -	41
S. Michael (7)- -	110	All Saints (17) - -	40
S. Margaret (8) -	106	S. James the Elder (18) - -	26
S. Anne (9) - -	90		
Holy Trinity (10) -	80		

[1] Frequently the Baptist and the Evangelist cannot be distinguished on bells.

Any very close coincidence, however, between the dedications of churches and church bells is hardly to be expected: the churches for the most part received their dedications hundreds of years before bells were placed in them. On the other hand, the minor altars are as a rule much later than the original foundation of the church, and in some districts, *e.g.*, in Norfolk, a large number of coincidences have been observed between the dedications of minor altars and those of the bells. As regards dedications of the bells, there were special reasons why particular saints were in favour. No less than 2,335 churches and chapels were dedicated to the Blessed Virgin. In all these and in every church one of the commonest representations was that of the Annunciation, in which the personages were the Blessed Virgin and S. Gabriel. Now every Christian person was wont at least once a day to repeat the words of S. Gabriel: "**Ave Maria, gratia plena, benedicta tu in mulieribus et benedictus fructus ventris tui**"; and a special bell was often set apart to be rung at those hours on which good Christians were expected to say their **Ave Maria**. S. Catherine, in church dedications, stands 26th; in bell dedications she is 3rd. For this there are two reasons. One is that the bells were rung by rope and wheel, and the wheel is the emblem of S. Catherine; the other is that she was apparently the patron saint of the London bell-founders, a large number of whose bells survive in Essex, Kent, and Sussex. A bell at Theddlethorpe, Lincolnshire, has the inscription—

CATERINA PIA PROTEGAS NOS A NECE DURA

and one at Shapwick, Dorset—

I KATERY(N)E GODDES DERLYNGE
TO THE(E) MARI SHAL I SYNG

The proportion of bell dedications depends very largely on the predilections of the founders. As the London founders favour S. Catherine, so the Bristol founders favour S. Anne and S. George; the Bury founders the Virgin Mary; the Nottingham founders the Holy Trinity and Our Lord; and so with the rest.[1] The most popular inscription to Our Lord at all periods, especially in the Midlands, is—

IHS NAZARENUS REX JUDEORUM

sometimes with the addition—

FILI DEI MISERERE MEI.

[1] On Bell Dedications see Walters' *Church Bells of England*, pp. 256-80.

CHAPTER XVII

CALENDARS

Saints Commemorated in Calendars

THE ecclesiastical calendar is but a Christianised version of the *Fasti* of Pagan Rome, feasts of the saints taking the place of

those of Pagan deities, and the Sunday Letter that of the *Litteræ Nundinales*. For a considerable time, no doubt, the two calendars existed side by side; the secular calendar or *Fasti*, and the ecclesiastical in which were noted the obits of bishops and the birthdays of martyrs. A small calendar, the earliest on record, records the death and burial of some of the popes down to Julius I. (337-352) and of some of the martyrs, chiefly Roman. Eusebius wrote the first important martyrology, *De Martyribus* (*c.* 372); it was scarce even in the sixth century, and seems no longer to exist. It is probable that this treatise of Eusebius was translated wholly or in part by S. Jerome (*c.* 400).[1] From this time onward a stream of calendars and martyrologies appeared in the Western Church.[2]

It may be of interest to see what opinion as to claims to saintship was held by those who compiled the Prayer Book of the Church of England.

B. AND C.

S. Genevieve.
Kenn rood-screen, Devon.

[1] See preface to Bishop Forbes' *Kalendars of the Scottish Church.*
[2] On p. 220 an angel is shown relighting S. Genevieve's taper, which had been blown out by a devil.

I. It includes all the apostles and evangelists.

II. It includes a large number of saints to whom English churches were dedicated before the end of the seventeenth century, as follows :—

S. Lucian
S. Hilary
S. Fabian
S. Agnes
S. Vincent
S. Blaise
S. Agatha
S. David
S. Chad
S. Gregory
S. Benedict of Cassino
S. Richard de Wych
S. Alphege
S. George
S. Dunstan
S. Augustine of Canterbury
S. Boniface
S. Alban
S. John Baptist's nativity
S. John Baptist's decollation
S. Martin's translation
S. Swithun
S. Margaret
S. Mary Magdalene
S. Anne
S. Lawrence

S. Augustine of Hippo
S. Giles
Holy Cross
S. Lambert
S. Cyprian
S. Michael
S. Jerome
S. Remi
S. Faith
S. Denis
S. Etheldreda
All Saints
S. Leonard
S. Martin
S. Britius
S. Hugh
Edmund, K.M.
S. Cecilia
S. Clement
S. Catherine
S. Nicholas
S. Lucy
S. Stephen
Holy Innocents
S. Silvester

So far there is a considerable amount of agreement between the calendar and the dedications.

III. On the other hand, a vast number of saints to whom ancient churches are dedicated find no place in the Prayer Book calendar. Even if we do not take into account those to whom few churches are dedicated, the omissions are still most serious. In most cases this is not due to the compilers ; they were not trying to draw up a brand-new list of saints, but to bring out an amended version of the English calendars already in use, especially that of the Sarum breviary. Whether it was their fault or that of their predecessors, or of both, a list was produced of very defective character. Crowds of Celtic saints are commemorated in English dedications, but not in the Prayer Book.

That was to be expected ; the history of the Celtic Churches was
a *terra incognita* till some half a century ago, and is still familiar
to but few. There are indeed hundreds of worthies of Wales
and Cornwall, Ireland and Brittany, whose absence we can well
put up with; but we strongly object to lose S. Patrick,
S. Columba, S. Bridget, S. Brandon, S. Teilo, S. Ninian,
S. Constantine. Equally sad was the fate of the history of
the Anglo-Saxon Church—there was little knowledge of it
and little interest in it till modern days; and so there are
omitted dozens of the good people who had introduced, or
worked for, or given their lives for Anglo-Saxon Christianity.
Among them are S. Cuthbert, S. Oswald, S. Botolph, S. Wilfrid,
Edward the Confessor, S. Ethelbert, S. Edith of Polesworth and
S. Edith of Wilton, S. Hilda, S. Werburga, S. Eadburga,
S. Milburga, S. Osyth, S. Mildred, S. Guthlac, S. Kenelm,
S. John of Beverley, S. Felix, S. Paulinus. Equal ignorance of
and indifference to Continental Church history led to the
omission of S. German of Auxerre, S. Rémi, S. Radegund,
S. Leger, and S. Theobald. Then having shown their contempt
for the Celtic Church, the Anglo-Saxon Church, and the Gallican
Church, the calendars omit also a bevy of saints connected with
the earliest struggles of the infant Christian Church ; so we lose
the Empress Helena, S. Pancras of Rome and S. Pancras of
Taormina, S. Eustace and S. Maurice, S. Julian the Hospitaller,
S. Julitta, SS. Cosmas and Damian, S. Cyril, S. Christopher,
Anthony the Great, and, finally, the archangel Gabriel. On the
other hand, the sixteenth-century calendar kindly supplies us from
the York and other calendars with new saints to whom no
churches are dedicated; these are S. Perpetua of Carthage ;
S. Bede ; S. Crispin of Agincourt ; S. Prisca, a virgin martyr
of the third century ; S. Valentine, a Roman priest of most
uncertain history, but with pleasant modern associations ; S.
Nicomede, a Roman priest and martyr ; S. Enurchus, a printer's
error for Evortius, Bishop of Orleans in the fourth century ;
and S. Machutus, Bishop of S. Malo in the seventh century,
the only Celtic saint, except S. David, honoured with a place
in the Prayer Book calendar — altogether a most oddly
assorted company. We must not forget to add the name
of King Charles, Martyr, who was included in all calendars
up to 1859, when the special form of prayer for January 30
was given up.

The Prayer Book calendar, as we have it now, owes its
form to two sets of revisers. Those of 1561 comprised Parker,
Archbishop of Canterbury ; Grindal, Bishop of London ; Dr
William Bill, and Mr Walter Haddon; it was practically a

revised version of the Sarum calendar. A second revision, in 1661, added the names of S. Alban, S. Bede, and S. Enurchus.

It should be added that for a long time the Prayer Book version had a rival in such calendars of the Church of England as were not bound up with the Prayer Book. These were published by the Stationers' Company under the authority of the Archbishop of Canterbury ; this authority was not given up till 1832. The Stationers included in their calendars All Souls, S. Patrick, and S. Thomas of Canterbury.

As an example of the utter carelessness which characterises the revisions of our calendars we may cite the words of *O Sapientia* on 16th December. Many people stoutly believe that this is a dedication, and is equivalent to that of the great church *Santa Sophia* at Constantinople. The phrase is simply the first two words of the first of seven anthems, which were to be sung before the Magnificat at Vespers, from the 16th of December to Christmas Eve. The whole antiphon is :—

" *O Sapientia quæ ex ore altissimi prodisti, attingens a fine usque ad finem, fortiter suaviterque disponens omnia ; veni ad docendum nos viam prudentis.*"

Putting the results together, the calendars of Sarum, York, and Hereford, and those of the Reformed Church, can but be regarded as a record of ignorance of, or indifference to, Church history, discreditable alike to the mediæval churchman who drew them up, to the churchmen of the sixteenth and seventeenth centuries who revised them, and to the churchmen of the following centuries who have retained them unamended.[1]

But though English churchmen have still to put up with this wretched production, attempts to revise it have been made here and there. The most drastic is that of the Irish Church, which has solved the difficulty of selection by expunging all names of saints except those who have " red-letter days," and for whom a special collect, epistle, and gospel are provided.

The Episcopalian Church of Scotland, on the other hand, has enriched its calendar by the addition of Celtic saints, S. Columba, S. Cuthbert, S. Mungo, S. Patrick, King David, Queen Margaret, and others, and one outsider, Bishop Cyril.

An attempt has also been made to supply the English Church with a full-blown calendar. This is printed in the first appendix to the sixth volume of *Lives of the English Saints*, entitled a " Provisional Catalogue of English Saints," and was compiled in 1843 by J. H. Newman, afterwards Cardinal, and

[1] An excellent account of the Prayer Book calendar by F. E. Warren will be found in the third volume of *Hierurgia Anglicana*, pp. 245-59.

includes a few "eminent or holy persons, who, though not in the Sacred Catalogue, are recommended to our religious memory by their fame, learning, or the benefits they have conferred on posterity."

Two draft calendars in MS. by Archbishop Cranmer, which were never issued, are printed by Messrs Gasquet and Bishop in *Edward VI. and the Book of Common Prayer*, pp. 32-34, 388-394. In the first of these there are 58 holy days, in the second 162. In a book of Latin prayers of the time of Elizabeth (1560) the number rises to 303 ; this calendar is practically identical with that of the Latin Prayer Book of 1560.

An interesting calendar of the eighth century is attributed to Bede ; it is entitled *Calendarium Floriacense*, and is printed by Martene ; and probably dates from the last year of Bede's life, A.D. 735 : it is reprinted below.

Between the calendar of Eastern and Western Christendom there is the striking difference that the former introduces saints freely from the Old Testament. The list includes the whole of the prophets, Moses, Joshua, David, Elijah, Job, and very many others. A Byzantine calendar is printed in Neale's *Introduction to the History of the Holy Eastern Church*, ii. 768.

But to the student of English dedications the calendars of primary importance are those of Sarum, York, and Hereford ; the first of these is printed below : any additions made to it in the Uses of York (1526) and Hereford (1502) are noted (but not the omissions that occur in these calendars). Many variations occur in the different versions of the Sarum calendar, as may be seen by comparing the Sarum calendars printed in Maskell's *Monumenta Ritualia Ecclesiæ Anglicanæ* with that printed by Dr Blunt from a Missal of 1514 in the library of Bishop Cosin of Durham. Editions of the calendars for the York and Hereford Uses were printed by the Surtees Society : they are given *in extenso* in Blunt's *Annotated Prayer Book*, pp. 130-76. In an appendix to Husenbeth's *Emblems of the Saints* eight calendars are printed in parallel columns, viz., the Roman, Sarum, Scottish, Old English,[1] French, Spanish, German, Greek. Mr Maskell, in *Monumenta Ritualia Ecclesiæ Anglicanæ*, pp. 186-225, prints two Sarum calendars ; the first, in English, may be of the end of the fourteenth century. He also prints two months of an English rhymed calendar.

---

[1] This calendar occurs in the *Catholic Almanack* for 1687, and in old *Manuals* of 1706 and 1728 ; also in the *Paradise of the Soul* in 1720. It is much fuller than that of Sarum, every day of the year being filled up. It is reprinted in Geldart's *Manual of Church Decoration and Symbolism*.

In the sixteenth volume of the second edition of Baring-Gould's *Lives of the Saints* is printed a "Celtic and English Kalendar of Saints proper to the Welsh, Cornish, Scottish, Irish, Breton, and English People," accompanied by notes.

Canon Christopher Wordsworth has printed in *Archæologia*, vol. li., two calendars, apparently transcripts of mediæval documents. One is the kalendar of Lincoln, and was probably drawn up late in the fifteenth century; the other is that of Peterborough, and probably belongs to the last half of the fourteenth century.

Other examples of calendars will be found in various editions of the Post-Reformation *Services* and *Primers* published by the Parker Society. R. T. Hampson's *Medii Aevi Kalendarium* includes calendars dating from the tenth to the fifteenth century. In the fifth appendix to Stanton's *Menology of England and Wales* is a list of 108 calendars.

CHAPTER XVIII

THE CONSECRATION AND DEDICATION OF CHURCHES

THE object of consecration of churches, says Hooker,[1] is twofold; first of all it makes them public, *i.e.*, no longer private property, but the property of God; and secondly, it signifies the use to which the property is to be put—it is to be a divine use. So also Bingham (viii. 9), that by the consecration of a church is meant the devoting or setting it apart peculiarly for divine service. Perhaps the earliest definite reference to a consecration service is in the rebuke addressed by the Emperor Constantine to Athanasius in 335, because "he had celebrated the holy mysteries in a church before it was consecrated"; for this he humbly apologised to the emperor. There is a sermon extant of S. Ambrose (A.D. 380) entitled *De Dedicatione Basilicæ*, and in a letter to his sister he speaks of having dedicated a church. The great church at Tyre was demolished in the Diocletian persecution, and many others shared its fate. But after the Peace of the Church they were rebuilt, and Eusebius speaks of the solemnisation of "festivals of dedication of churches" in every city. Eusebius also describes in detail the dedication services of Constantine's great church of the Holy Sepulchre at Jerusalem, in which the historian himself took part. Pope Hyginus is reported as saying in 138, "Omnes basilicæ cum Missa debent consecrari." In 324 Pope Sylvester decrees in a general synod, "Nullus presbyter Missas celebrare præsumat, nisi in sacratis ab episcopo locis." In the seventh century Theodore, Archbishop of Canterbury, gives directions as to the consecration of a church, and in 816 the Council of Chalcuith passed a canon *De modo consecrandi ecclesias*: and in 1076 it was ordered at a Council in Winchester "that mass should not be celebrated in churches unless they had been consecrated by bishops."

For all these Christian consecrations there were of course Old Testament precedents in the dedications of Solomon's

[1] Hooker, Book V., chap. xii.

temple (1 Kings, chap. viii.), the dedication of the second temple (Ezra vi. 16), the solemnities and feasts of dedication in the time of Judas Maccabeus, and the dedication of the temple built by Herod, of which Josephus gives an account (Book XV., chap. xiv.).

The religious part of the ceremony was performed by clergy of episcopal rank. There were indeed occasional instances of consecration in emergency by priests, but these were always censured and condemned. It was also laid down that a church should be consecrated by the bishop of the diocese in which it was situated, and not by the bishop of another diocese.

Special services were prepared and were used—(1) When the corner stone or foundation stone of the church was laid. (2) At the dedication. (3) At each anniversary of the dedication. At the dedication the following hymn was sung :—

1.

Urbs Jerusalem beata
Dicta pacis visio,
Quæ construitur in cœlis
Vivis ex lapidibus,
Ut angelis coronata,
Ut sponsata comite.

2.

Nova veniens e cœlo,
Nuptiali Thalamo
Præparata, et sponsata
Copuletur Domino ;
Plateæ et muri ejus
Ex auro purissimo, etc.

In Cornwall procedure of dedication was quite different from that of mediæval days, at any rate, so long as the usages of the ancient British Church prevailed. " It was customary when any holy man, were he bishop or priest, wished to found a church or a monastery, that he should come himself to the spot on which the future edifice was to be raised, and here continue forty days in the exercise of prayer and fasting. This done, the ceremony was completed, and all that was required by way of consecration was effected." [1]

Very similar was the process of consecration of Anglo-Saxon churches in the seventh century. About the year 678, Bishop Cedd consecrated the monastery and church of Lastingham,

[1] Borlase's *Age of the Saints*, 44.

purposely placed in a remote hollow of the wild Cleveland moors of the North Riding. Bede tells us[1] that he resolved to follow the ancient ritual of fasting and prayer before consecration in order to purge the site from taint of sin ; and fasted for forty days, Sundays excepted, till eventide, when his meal was a crust of bread, an egg, and a little milk mixed with water.

Becon (1512-67), in his *Reliques of Rome*, gives an account[2]

A. W. S.

Consecration Cross.

Ottery S. Mary.

of the ceremonies of consecrating a church, which, from its date, is worth transcribing :—

"When any church is to be hallowed, this order must be observed. First all the people must depart out of the church, and the deacon must remain there only, having all the doors shut fast unto him. The bishop with the clergy shall stand without before the church door and make holy water mingled with salt. In the mean season, within the church there must be set up twelve candles burning before twelve (consecration)

---

[1] Plummer's *Bede*, i. 175.

[2] Quoted in Maskell's *Monumenta Ritualia Ecclesiæ Anglicanæ*, vol. i.

crosses[1] that are appointed upon the church walls. Afterward the bishop, accompanied by the clergy and people, shall go thrice about the church without ; and the bishop, having in his hand a staff with a bunch of hyssop on the end, shall with the same cast holy water on the church walls. And the bishop shall come unto the church door, and strike the threshold with his crozier staff, and shall say, *Tollite portas* (Psalm xxiv. 7). Then shall the deacon that is within say *Quis est iste Rex gloriæ?* To whom the bishop shall answer, *Dominus fortis, dominus fortis in prælio.* At the third time the deacon shall open the church door, and the bishop shall enter into the church accompanied with a few ministers, the clergy and the people abiding still without. Entering into the church, the bishop shall say, *Pax huic domui.* And afterwards the bishop, with them that are in the church, shall say the Litany. These things done, there must be made in the pavement of the church a cross of ashes and sand, whereon the whole alphabet or Christ's cross shall be written in Greek and Latin letters.[2]

"After these things the bishop must hallow another water with salt and ashes and wine, and consecrate the altar. Afterwards the twelve crosses that are painted upon the church walls, the bishop must anoint them with chrism, commonly called cream. These things once done, the clergy and the people may freely come into the church, ring the bells for joy, etc."

Since the Reformation there has been no prescribed form of dedication of churches ; but early and important precedents are to be found in the consecration by Bishop Andrewes in 1620 of a church near Southampton ; that of Fulmer church, Buckinghamshire,[3] by Dr Barlow, Bishop of Lincoln, in 1610 ;

[1] "On Consecration Crosses" see Rev. E. S. Dewick in *Archæological Journal*, lxv. 1-34.

[2] Alphabets were sometimes inscribed also on bells and fonts. See the writer's *Fonts and Font Covers*, 117, and Walters' *Church Bells of England*, 329. There may be a reference to Our Lord's stooping and writing on the ground (John viii. 6). In the Sarum ritual the cross seems to be the cross saltire, or S. Andrew's cross ; each alphabet begins at the top : on the left begins the Greek, on the right the Latin alphabet. There was thought to be in the alphabet a mystical reference to the beginnings or elements of Christian doctrine : "Lac vobis potum dedi, non escam," said S. Paul. A very similar ritual is mentioned by S. Gregory in the sixth century. See Maskell's *Monumenta Ritualia*, i. 208, who gives the Sarum ritual in full in i. 196. Durandus on *Symbolism* (edit. Neale), p. 237, gives the form of dedication used by S. Dunstan. Martene gives ten forms.

[3] For the Fulmer dedication, see Stow's *Chronicle*, pp. 997-99, where there is a full and very interesting account. The text of Bishop Andrewes' form of consecration is printed as an appendix to Harington, *On the Consecration of Churches*, p. 145. The consecration of S. Katherine Creed is described in Rushworth's *Historical Collections*, ii. 77 ; the so-called

and S. Katharine Creed, London, and Stanmore, Middlesex, by Bishop Laud in 1630 and 1634.

A form of consecrating churches, chapels, and churchyards was passed by the Lower House of Convocation in 1712, "with a design to have it established among the offices of the Liturgy"; it was compiled chiefly for the consecration of the (50) new churches; it was never, however, legalised. It is printed in Harington, *Ibid.*, 179.

The Irish forms of the Consecration and of the Restaurations of churches, dated 1666, are printed in the third volume of *Hierurgia Anglicana*, pp. 188-220 (London, 1904).

"Popish ceremonies" employed thereat were urged against Laud at his trial : one of them was that "as soon as the Bishop came within the church door, he fell down upon his knees." "True," said Laud : "it was no more than my duty, being a House of Prayer." For the form of consecration used at Stanmore Magna, see Oughton's *Ordo Judiciorum*, ii. 249, and Harington, *Ibid.*, 195.

PART II

CHAPTER XIX

ECCLESIASTICAL SYMBOLISM

Symbolism of the Plan and Fabric of Churches—Orientation of Churches—
Deviation of the Axis of the Chancel—Emblems of the Trinity—The
First Person of the Godhead—The Second Person of the Godhead—
The Agnus Dei—Vesica Piscis—The Pelican in Piety—Monograms of
Christ—The Fish—The Third Person of the Godhead—The Blessed
Virgin—The Apostles—The Evangelists—The Doctors of the Church—
The Magi—The Sibyls—The Church—The Gallant Ship of Christendom
—The Devil—Heaven—Hell Mouth—The Soul—The Cross—The
Crucifix—The Crown of Thorns—Instruments of the Passion—The
Nimbus—The Aureole—Prayer—Symbolism of Numbers—Symbolism
of Colours—Geometrical Figures—Pentalpha—Fylfot—Months and
Seasons—Zodiac—Sagittarius—Emblems of Mortality.

"ALL things," says Durandus, "as many as pertain to matters
ecclesiastical, be full of divine significations and mysteries and
overflow with a celestial sweetness, if it be that a man be diligent
in his study of them, and know how to draw 'honey from the
rock and oil from the hardest stone.'[1] Wherefore I, William,
by the alone tender mercy of God, Bishop of the holy church
which is in Mende, will knock diligently at the door, if so be
that the key of David[2] will open unto me, that the King may
bring me in and show me the heavenly pattern which was shown
to Moses in the mount." With which pious prœmium Durandus
set forth to expound in his *Rationale* the inward and spiritual
purport of the church and every part of the church, and of each
and all of its rites and ceremonies and observances. With like
solemnity, six centuries later, Mr Walcott rebukes those who
should venture to question the symbolic origin of the planning
of the Christian church. "It would be difficult," he says,[3] "to
assign any other reason than symbolical consideration as that
which influenced our forefathers in laying out the ground-plan
of their churches; and he is not to be envied who should

---

[1] Deuteronomy xxxii. 13.   [2] Apocalypse iii. 7.
[3] Walcott's *Church and Conventual Arrangement*, 61.

attempt to impugn their attempt to embody holy doctrines in external objects and to make the material fabric suggestive of Christian verities." Mr Poole[1] goes further still : while by the translators of Durandus we are told that not only the plan of a church but every detail has symbolic import :—

"The whole fabric of a church, its general plan, and its many details, are capable of expressing religious truth in a symbolical language of its own. The earthly building is but the symbol of the spiritual church, the Heavenly Jerusalem. A Christian church always embodied mysteries of the Christian religion ; always shadowed forth ecclesiastical polity ; always conveyed instruction in religion and morals. A Gothic church, in its perfection, is an exposition of the distinctive doctrines of Christianity, clothed upon with a material form ; in Coleridge's words it is a 'petrifaction of our religion.' Very beautiful is the vision of the mediæval church of England to the eye of faith. Far away, long before we catch our first glimpse of the city, the three spires of the cathedral, rising high above the smoke and stir, preach to us of the most Holy and Undivided Trinity. As we approach, the transepts, striking out crosswise, tell of the Atonement ; the Communion of Saints is set forth by the chapels clustering round choir and nave ; the weathercock bids us watch and pray ; the hideous forms that seem hurrying from the eaves speak the misery of those who are cast out from the Church ; spire, pinnacle, and finial, the upward curl of the sculptured foliage, the upward spring of the flying buttress, the sharp rise of the window-arch, the high-thrown pitch of the roof, all these, overpowering the horizontal tendency of string-course and parapet, teach us that, vanquishing earthly desires, we also should ascend in heart and mind. Deep down, profound, unseen, the Church is seated upon the Rock ; its foundations are the apostles and prophets, Jesus Christ being the chief corner-stone. We enter. The triple breadth of nave and aisles, the triple height of pier-arch, triforium, and clerestory, the triple length of choir, transepts, and nave, again set forth the Holy Trinity. And what besides is there that does not tell of our Blessed Saviour : Him First, in two-fold nature, in the double western door ; Him Last, in the distant altar ; Him Midst, in the great Rood ? Close by us is the font, for by Regeneration we enter the Church ; it is deep and capacious, for we are buried with Christ in Baptism ; it is of stone, for He is the Rock ; its spiry cover teaches us, if indeed we be risen with Him from its waters, to seek those things which are above. Before us in long-drawn vista are massy piers, which are the Bishops and Doctors of the Church ; each is of many members, for many are the graces in each saint ; round the head of all is delicate foliage, for all were plentiful in good words. Beneath our feet are the badges of worldly pomp and glory, the charges of prelates and nobles and knights, in the presence of God as worthless dross. Overhead rises indistinct in the gloom the high-pitched roof ; angels on the hammerbeams, angels on the collars, angels on the

---

[1] Poole's *Appropriate Character of Church Architecture*, pp. 18, 19, 40.

cornice ; a great host of faithful witnesses, arrested as it were midway in heavenward flight, spirits of those who, generation after generation, have gathered within the sacred walls, cherubim and seraphim, thrones and principalities and powers, quick and dead, church militant and church triumphant, gathered together in common prayer and worship, with psaltery and lute and harp singing the praises of Him who is worthy to receive blessing and glory and wisdom and thanksgiving and power and might.[1] Down below, in the rich deep glass of the windows, is yet another multitude of saintly forms, each in fair niche enshrined. Here is the glorious company of the Apostles ; the goodly fellowship of the Prophets ; the noble army of Martyrs ; the jubilant chorus of the Virgins ; Kings who have exchanged an earthly for a heavenly crown ; Doctors of the Church who have taught the faith ; Bishops who have given in a glad account to the Shepherd and Bishop of Souls. Passing up the nave, through serried ranks of the Church Militant, we reach the Rood Screen, the barrier between it and the Church Triumphant, thereby typifying Death, the portal of Life Eternal. High above it hangs on His triumphal cross the image of Him who by His death has overcome death ; on it are portrayed Saints and Martyrs, His warriors, who fighting under their Lord have won their rest, and have entered into immortality. The screen itself glows with gold and crimson ; with gold, for they have on their heads golden crowns ; with crimson, for they passed through the Red Sea of Martyrdom. Through the delicate traceries of the screen we catch faint glimpses of the Sanctuary beyond. There are massy stalls, for in Heaven is eternal rest : there are the sedilia, emblems of the seats of the Elders round the Throne ; there is the piscina, for they have washed their robes and made them white ; there, heart and soul and life of all, is the altar with the ever-burning lights and golden carvings and precious jewels ; even Christ Himself, by whose only merits we have admission to the inheritance of Heaven."

Such is an English church as seen by the eyes of a pious churchman.[2]

Much of its mysticism and of its beauty dissolves in analysis. Transept and aisled nave, pier-arcade and clerestory originally were not designed to express the dogma of the Trinity ; aisles and clerestories were employed in basilicas in pre-Christian times ; the triforium arose from the necessity of roofing a vaulted

---

[1] More than a hundred carved figures ornament the cornice of the roof of Carlisle choir, and many texts in black letter may still be read. " Lift up your hands in the sanctuary and bless the Lord." " Praise ye the name of the Lord." " Praise God in His sanctuary." " Exalt ye the Lord our God, and worship at His footstool." " O magnify the Lord with me, and let us exalt His name together."

[2] Introduction to Neale and Webb's translation of the first book of Durandus' *Rationale*.

aisle ; the arch was pointed to make that vaulting easier ; the pinnacle is there to load the buttress ; the flying buttress to transmit the thrusts of a cross-ribbed vault ; the roof is high-pitched to throw off the rain and snow of a northern clime ; sedilia, piscina, altar, chapels all find their origin in the needs of ritual, not in symbolism ; and so with the rest.   Though, however, it is possible greatly to exaggerate the mystical significance of the planning of the mediæval church, yet it would be a mistake to imagine that all symbolism is *ex post facto*.   Of all emblems that of the Cross is of pre-eminent sanctity to the Christian. There can be no doubt that many great churches were built cruciform that their very plan should make the ground bear everlasting witness to the manner of the death of Christ.   Again and again we see the express instruction given that such and such church shall be built " *in modum crucis.*"   Such an ever-present remembrance of the Crucifixion could not but find favour with the mediæval ecclesiologist.   Yet, strange to say, this lively and abiding symbolism of the cross-plan is the exception, not the rule.   Even in early Christian days the great majority of the basilicas, whether in Rome or Ravenna, show no signs of the cruciform plan.   In mediæval days, indeed, almost all the greater churches were cruciform in plan.   With the parish churches it was not so.   In the twelfth century, indeed, and here and there sporadically in the following centuries in England and in Normandy, small cruciform churches occur.   But far more common from the first was the non-transeptal plan ; and as in later days the parish churches grew in size and importance, the tendency was more and more to increase their area by the addition, not of transepts, but of aisles.   Boston church, not S. Mary Redcliffe, Bristol, was the normal type of the English parish church in the later Gothic.   Even in the greater churches respect for the cruciform plan seldom hindered the builders from obliterating it to the eye by a conglomeration of later chapels. In many a parish church also, originally cruciform, *e.g.*, S. Martin's, Leicester, in later days the aisles were rebuilt as broad as the transept was deep, and the transept was thrown into the broadened aisle, thus obliterating the cruciform plan.   Uni-versality then is lacking in the symbolism of the cruciform plan, where above all it might be expected to be present.

Next to the symbolism of the cross, perhaps nothing presents itself of more mystic import than the orientation of the plan, with altar to the east.   Yet, strange to say, the orientation of the church was precisely the reverse in many early Christian basilicas ; in the great majority of these it was the main entrance, not the altar, which was at the east.   At Rome the churches of

S. Peter, S. Paul *extra muros*,[1] and S. Lorenzo as they were originally built, as well as over forty others, including the patriarchal basilicas of S. John Lateran, "*omnium urbis et orbis ecclesiarum mater et caput*," and S. Maria Maggiore, had the altar to the west; only about half a dozen of the Roman basilicas had an eastern apse. In fact the first churches followed the orientation of the Roman temples, in which Vitruvius recommended that the entrance should be to the east. It was not till the eighth century that the eastern replaced the western apse generally. At all times the Italians attached little importance to orientation. At Caen also, while the Abbaye-aux-hommes, S. Nicolas and S. Jean, all point to the east, the Abbaye-aux-dames, S. Gilles, S. Pierre, and Notre Dame all point to the south.

But whether a church is orientated west or east, the orientation is often inaccurate. Thus at Rome, out of forty-one basilicas which point to the west, only twenty-one point due west. Similarly, of mediæval churches which are set eastward, a considerable number are some points north or south of east. It has been suggested that in these latter the chancel is orientated to the point where the sun rises on the festival of the saint to which the church is dedicated. This may be true in some cases, but the number of contrary instances is too large to warrant so wide-sweeping a generalisation.

Another curiosity of planning is the not infrequent occurrence of a deviation of the axis of the eastern limb of the church to north or south. This is thought to be symbolical of the fact that Our Lord, dying on the cross, "bowed His head and gave up the ghost." And as the tradition is that His head sank on His right shoulder, the axis of the chancel was deflected *in memoriam* to the north. This hypothesis has received much support; *e.g.*, recently from M. Victor Mortet, M. Brutails, M. Mâle, M. Anthyme S. Paul, and to some extent from De Caumont, Viollet-le-Duc, and M. Camille Enlart. It is rejected by M. Choisy[2] and by Comte Robert de Lasteyrie.[3] An almost

---

[1] The first church of S. Paul, that of the Emperor Constantine, had its doorway to the east in the Via Ostiensis. Its foundations have been found; it was a small church. But in 386 it was rebuilt on a much larger scale, and the altar was set eastward. The Bollandists have a legend that Dunstan, Archbishop of Canterbury, seeing a church that had been built on another axis, swung it round to the east by a push from his shoulder, thus placing it in its right position.

[2] *Histoire d'Architecture*, ii. 473.

[3] For an exhaustive account of the facts and theories see Comte de Lasteyrie's "*La deviation de l'axe des églises, est-elle symbolique?*" in the *Mémoires de l'académie des inscriptions et belles-lettres*, vol. xxxvii., 2nd Part; Paris, 1905 (305).

fatal objection is that not one of the liturgists of the Middle Ages mentions the deviation of the axis.   Now it is a first principle of ecclesiastical symbolism not to suppose symbolical intent or to accept an explanation founded on such supposition if it be not proved to be contained in the writings of the Fathers or of the ancient liturgists.   So far from this, Durandus, one of the most eminent of the latter, says that the chancel ought to look *straight* to the east, "*recte inspiciat versus orientem, videlicet versus ortum solis equinoctialem.*"   Nevertheless, if the deviations were always to the north, the hypothesis would be admissible ; one could only conclude, not that it was not there, but that it had in some unaccountable way escaped notice by the ancient liturgists.   In most cases where it occurs the deviation is to the north.   It is curious that out of twenty Roman basilicas which do not point true west, only two lie to the south of west ; all the rest tend more or less to the north-west.   M. Brutails[1] asserts that almost invariably the deviation is to the north in the mediæval churches. De Caumont[2] observed a deflection to the north in more than a hundred churches of the twelfth and thirteenth century.   In England also a marked deviation to the north is common ; *e.g.*, in the cathedrals of Lichfield, Bristol, and Old S. Paul's, and the abbey churches of Whitby, Bridlington, and S. Mary's, York. On the other hand, in several important English churches, *e.g.*, the cathedrals of Canterbury and York and the abbey churches of Tynemouth and Selby, there is an equally marked deflection to the *south*.   So also in France, Comte de Lasteyrie gives a long list of churches with a southern deviation of axis, including Domfront, La Trinité at Angers, Le Dorat, S. Gilles, S. Germer, the Kreisker, Vézelay, S. Germain-des-Prés, Nîmes cathedral, and S. Hilaire de Poitiers, S. Nicholas-du-Port near Nancy, Preuilly, and S. Savin.   If, then, deviation of axis be significant of the inclination of the head of Our Lord, we can only say that the tradition is by no means uniform.   Moreover, representations of the agony of Our Lord on the cross were exceedingly rare till the twelfth century or later ; in that century Our Lord was still usually represented on the cross with body straight and head high, not leaning on the right shoulder.   Now of the churches mentioned above, some were set out in the eleventh century.   Is it likely that their planning had reference to a scene which it still pained good Christians to represent ?

What, then, is the rationale of a phenomenon of so frequent occurrence ?   In some few cases, doubtless, especially in town churches, the deviation of the axis of the chancel was due, like numerous other irregularities of plan of common occurrence,

---

[1] *L'archéologie du moyen age*, 9.   [3] *Abécédaire*, 299.

simply to the cramped nature of the site. Such an explanation, however, would hardly hold of a monastic church, built in the open country on an unencumbered site. In such a case as this some other explanation must be looked for. Now in mediæval building bad work was done as well as good, just as at present; some churches were built with rock-like foundations, like Amiens; others, like the nave, choir and transept of Peterborough in the twelfth century, the west front in the thirteenth, the eastern chapels in the fifteenth, with hardly an apology for a foundation. So it was also with the planning. Of two twelfth-century churches, Dorchester priory and Romsey abbey, the former is set out with perfect accuracy, while the latter is casual in the extreme, varying almost from bay to bay. Some of this was due simply to carelessness, though some allowance must be made for lack of instruments of precision. With the aid of these it is now possible for two gangs of miners starting many miles apart to bore through the Alps, and make their tunnels meet within a few inches. Without such aid the old men found it difficult to keep a long church straight. In some English churches more than 500 feet separates east and west. A slight initial error in the setting out would assume formidable dimensions. There was besides a special difficulty nearly always present when a new choir was built; this was the survival of the old choir. Nowadays we pull down before we build up. But in the Middle Ages it was the rule to retain the old building for worship while the new one was being built. If the plans of Canterbury be examined, it will be found that the original choir, that of Lanfranc, was of the same breadth as the nave. But the next choir built, that of Conrad, is broader than the nave. This was to allow its being built on either side of and around Lanfranc's narrow and low choir. The same is the case at Selby, Lincoln, York minster, Tideswell church, and frequently elsewhere. In such a case it was impossible to see whether the axis of the new choir was being set out precisely in the line of that of the old nave. With modern instruments there would be little difficulty. But the old men had not modern instruments. In most cases, not in all, they did their best. Certainly the better of the builders had no wish to build a crooked church. Indeed it is recorded that the architect of a church at Metz, built between 1371 and 1409, in which there is a pronounced deviation of axis, "*ashamed of having made his work so crooked, died of grief and distress.*" Mr Choisy [1] reminds us that at S. Peter's, Rome, the builders had a narrow escape of getting the nave out of line with the choir. Nor is such a contingency

[1] *Histoire d'Architecture*, ii. 437.

impossible even now, in spite of our modern appliances. At Aberystwyth, there has been built recently *by degrees* a rather long, cruciform church. When the temporary east wall was taken down, it was found that the new choir had a most perceptible list to the south. If that can happen nowadays, we need not be surprised that many a mediæval church is crooked. When the present choir of York minster was set out late in the fourteenth century, measurements to the west were stopped by the still existing twelfth-century choir. In this last-mentioned choir again, it had been equally difficult to obtain correct alignment ; for when it was begun, there was standing an eleventh-century choir. Before that there had been one, if not more, Anglo-Saxon choirs. Every one of these choirs tended to produce errors of alignment in its successor, and these errors are summed up in the crookedness of the present choir. With such a history as this behind it, is it surprising that there is in York choir the insignificant deviation to the south of two feet four inches? Selby abbey choir, in the same way, is the successor of the Norman choir and that probably of one or more Pre-Conquest choirs ; here there is a deviation of five feet to the south. So with many others.

There is, however, a class of churches to which these considerations apply with less force, viz., homogeneous structures, built "*d'un seul jet.*" Some few of our smaller churches fall into this category, but very few indeed of the great cathedral, monastic, or collegiate churches ; of the latter Salisbury cathedral is the chief example. In the Ile de France Gothic, on the other hand, this class is comparatively large ; it includes great cathedrals, such as Notre Dame, Paris. But even these churches are hardly ever, if ever, homogeneous throughout. Closer inspection reveals, *e.g.*, in Notre Dame, that the church was really built in sections. Now when a section was built, *e.g.*, the choir, or the choir, transepts, and eastern bays of the nave, then, in order to enable the section completed to be used for worship, it would be enclosed to the west by temporary walling, and the presence of this screen of masonry would make accuracy of alignment difficult. On the whole, we conclude that it is quite unnecessary to invoke symbolism as an explanation of the deviation of the axis of the eastern limb of a church.

While, however, symbolism cannot be proved to have had any considerable influence in determining the plan of the mediæval churches, it was undoubtedly employed to a very great extent elsewhere ; and a very great amount of mediæval art is quite unintelligible without some acquaintance with the symbolic import of the representations. To some of the more important of these we now turn.

THE TRINITY

The Trinity is hardly ever represented in Norman sculpture. In Gothic days the Trinity is a group in which the First Person in human form holds in front of him the crucified Son, and a dove issues from his mouth, or from the mouths both of Father and Son. This is very common in the later stained glass, and on fonts and bosses (3).

A favourite geometrical emblem is that shown below; which reads—"The Father is not the Son, the Son is not the Holy Ghost; the Holy Ghost is not the Father; the Father is God, the Son is God, and the Holy Ghost is God." Another device consists of three circular rings interlaced, and inscribed *Trinitas Unitas. Cf.* 288, 276.

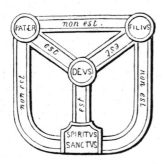 

THE FIRST PERSON OF THE TRINITY

God the Father is not represented by a full-grown figure before the thirteenth century; in the sixteenth century He often wears pontifical robes and a tiara. The First Person occurs more often in Old Testament than in New Testament scenes; of the latter the chief are the Baptism, the Transfiguration, the Agony in the Garden, and the Transfiguration. The earliest representation is that of the Divine Hand issuing from a cloud: this occurs in a tomb in the Catacombs, dated A.D. 359, in which Moses is shown receiving from God the tables of the Law. The reference may be to such texts as " His right hand and His holy arm hath gotten Him the victory "; " Thy hands have made and fashioned me "; " Thou openest Thy hand, they are filled with good "; " The works of His hands are verity and judgment." The Divine hand appears in the Bayeux tapestry over the church of S. Peter; in the Romsey crucifix; on the Norman font in Lenton church, Notts.[1]

The Second Person of the Trinity

The Second Person of the Trinity is represented symbolically in early Christian art as Orpheus and as the Good Shepherd; also as the Lamb of God; by the Cross, by the Alpha and Omega, by the fish, rarely by the lion, and by various monograms. In Anglo-Norman sculpture three representations alone occur: the Lamb, the Cross, and I.H.C. In the early days of Christianity Christ is always represented as a youth, a beardless youth, an Orpheus, or a Good Shepherd; in mediæval art He is no longer a youth: He is the Man of Sorrows. One marvels at the change. Unspeakable were the horrors of the mediæval life; but were they worse than life in the Catacombs, with daily prospect of torture and martyrdom? Nor is it easy to comprehend why Orpheus was such a favourite of symbols of Christ in the Catacombs. It is true that his return from the shades with his lost Eurydice was taken in later days to typify Christ's sojourn in Hades as amplified in the Gospel of Nicodemus; but in the Catacombs this scene never occurs. It is always the same, Orpheus with his lyre among the listening beasts. After the third century Orpheus disappears from Christian art. Perhaps the reason was that this representation had great vogue under the last Antonines, especially Alexander Severus, and was depicted with such frequency in Pagan mosaics and pavements all over the empire that it did not present to censorious eyes any Christian significance. Even in remote Britain, Roman pavements had the conventional representation of Orpheus; *e.g.*, at Barton, Wilts., Horkstow and Winterton, Lincolnshire. The most ancient symbol of Christ is the Good Shepherd bearing on His shoulder the sheep that was lost; in the end this entirely supplanted that of Orpheus. This symbol also was without import to a Pagan, and might escape the outrage which would have followed any attempt to portray Our Lord in person. The symbol of the Good Shepherd died out before the eleventh century, and does not reappear till the sixteenth century; even then it is rare. But in the Catholic Liturgy the imagery of the Good Shepherd has never disappeared, for the "Ordo Commen-

---

[1] In modern Jerusalem may be seen rudely painted (or colour-washed) over the main doorway of many houses a large representation of a hand. It is called the "hand of power," the idea being that it is the Hand of God stretched forth in blessing.—G. C. N.

dationis Animæ" runs—"*Constituat te Christus Filius Dei vivi intra paradisi sui amœna virentia et inter oves suas verus ille Pastor agnoscāt.*"

Another very ancient symbol is that of the Vine—a symbol which had been employed greatly in the Old as well as in the

Agnus Dei.

South Brent, Devon.

New Testament. It was very common in the decorations of the Roman houses, and could therefore be employed with a Christian import without danger. The vine is exceedingly common in the early Christian art of the West; it is yet more common in Byzantine art; so much so that when one sees the vine in western Romanesque there is almost a *prima facie* reason to believe that it is of Byzantine origin. So sacred was the vine to the early Christians that its presence alone was sufficient to symbolise the Christian faith ; *e.g.*, on the tomb of Constantia at Rome.

Naturally Christ appears very frequently as the Lamb of God, "Agnus Dei." In the Apocalypse this symbol occurs no less than twenty-nine times. It is to be noted, however, that in early Christian art the Lamb was not a symbol of Christ, but of the soul of the Christian here on earth, or brought back to the fold by the Shepherd, or listening to the instruction of the Church at the feet of his gentle Master ; more rarely it represents the soul in Heaven. It is not till much later that the Lamb became the symbol not of the Christian, but of Christ. In the twelfth century the Lamb occurs with cross and nimbus. In the twelfth and thirteenth centuries the Lamb occurs with cross, nimbus, and chalice, *e.g.*, Kirkburn font, Yorkshire ; or with cross, nimbus, and banner of victory, *e.g.*, Helpringham font. In the thirteenth century occurs the Lamb of the Apocalypse with seven horns and seven eyes opening the book with the seven seals ; also, rarely a Lamb with horns. In the fifteenth century a Lamb with nimbus occurs, resting on a closed book. It was common to regard the sacrifice of Isaac as typifying that of Christ. This was rendered more plausible by a little "accommo- dation " of the two scenes. On the one hand Isaac may be seen bound on a *cross*, with a ram whose horns are caught in the thicket ; on the other the " Agnus Dei " may be a *horned* lamb or even a goat.

CHRIST IN GLORY

In the Romanesque of the Continent lintelled doorways are far more common than in England. Where such exist, the tympanum above the lintel and below the relieving arch affords an excellent field for sculpture. From the thirteenth century our doorways were less and less frequently constructed with lintel and tympanum, and consequently sculptured ornament above doorways ceases. Where the tympanum has figure sculpture, the favourite representation is the glorified Christ, seated on a throne, and holding a book in His left hand, while His right hand is raised in the act of benediction ; *e.g.*, Adel, Yorkshire ; Prestbury, Cheshire ; Essendine, Rutland—all of the twelfth century. " I am the door," said Our Lord ; it was natural, therefore, that the usual sculpture above the doorway should be that of Our Lord. Above the porch the Crucifixion is not

Chartres Cathedral : central western doorway.

infrequent; but over doorways it is nearly always the Glorified not the Crucified Saviour that is depicted.

VESICA PISCIS

As has been said, Our Lord in Glory is represented as seated on a throne. Now the prophet Ezekiel (i. 26) writes— "And above the firmament there was the appearance of a throne; and upon the likeness of the throne there was the likeness as the appearance of a man above upon it. . . . And I saw as it were the appearance of fire, and it had brightness round about. As the appearance of the bow that is in the cloud in the day of rain, so was the appearance of the brightness round about. This was the appearance of the likeness of the Glory of the Lord." In the Apocalypse (iv. 2) the Great White Throne is again described—"And behold, a throne was set in heaven, and One sat on the throne. . . . And there was a rainbow round about the throne, in sight like unto an emerald." Now in Norman and Gothic sculpture the figure of Our Lord is very frequently enclosed in a border of pointed oval shape. It may well be that this *oval* or *mystic almond*, as it is also called, may be intended to symbolise the Glory of God. In later Gothic art, instead of a geometrical border, it often becomes a glowing, nebulous splendour, such as can well be represented in stained glass. Another name for it is *vesica piscis*, given to it because of its supposititious resemblance to the bladder of a fish—the fish being one of the emblems of Christ. The *Vesica Piscis* is used both of the three Persons of the Godhead and of the souls of the blessed [1] (255).

THE PELICAN IN PIETY

The symbol of the PELICAN is exceedingly common in mediæval art. It had been noticed that at the top of its long bill the bird has a crimson spot. This was enough for the mediæval naturalist, ὁ Φυσιολόγος. The pelican, he says, feeds its young with blood from its own breast. And when mediæval naturalist and mediæval theologian join hands, we get this edifying comment from S. Augustine and others on Psalm cii. 6: "*I am like a pelican in the wilderness.*" "The pelican," we are told, "fervently loveth her young birds. Yet when they be

---

[1] It may be noted here that it was usual to represent God the Father, Our Lord, and the apostles with *bare feet*, but not the Blessed Virgin or the saints.

haughty and begin to wax hot, they smite her in the face and
wound her, and she smiteth them and slayeth them. And
after three days she mourneth for them; and then striking
herself in the side till the blood runs out, she sprinkleth it upon
their bodies, and by virtue thereof they quicken again. In like
manner Christ was beaten and buffeted by the children of men,
and yet shed His blood to give them eternal life." So, in

W. M.

Pelican in Piety.

Aldington, Kent.

memory of the love and sacrifice of Christ, He is called by
Dante *nostro pelicano*. Shakespeare, in *Hamlet*, re-echoes the
ancient fable :—

> "*To his good friends thus wide I'll ope my arms,*
> *And like the kind, life-giving pelican,*
> *Refresh them with my blood.*"

The *Rites of Durham* describes "*a goodly fine lectern of
brass, with a great pelican richly gilt, billing her blood out of her
breast to feed her young ones.*"

33

SACRED MONOGRAMS

Various monograms arose from the selection of different

J. J. C.
Labarum of Constantine.

letters of the name of Jesus Christ, whether written IHCOUS XPICTOS, or Ἰησοῦς Χριστὸς. Of these the most famous is that which appeared to the Emperor Constantine, outshining the sun in splendour, while a voice was heard, "*In hoc signo vinces.*" This the emperor placed on the standard or *labarum* of the Roman legions in place of the ancient eagle. It remained in use under all the Byzantine emperors. It consists simply of the first two letters of the word XPICTOS; X = *ch*, and P = *r*. Instead of this, from the beginning of the twelfth century a monogram taken from the first three letters of IHCOUS, or Ἰησους, becomes common ; *i.e.*, I.H.C. or I.H.S. When the latter of the two became common in the Western Church, it was taken to mean also "Iesus Hominum Salvator," "Jesus the Saviour of Mankind," and became in consequence yet more popular. Another monogram, found in the Catacombs, is formed by combining the initial letters of Ἰησοῦς Χριστὸς. Numerous other combinations occur.

W. M.

East Harling, Suffolk : Rood-screen.

THE FISH

The fish is employed as a symbol of Our Lord with great frequency in Early Christian and Early Romanesque art. There is nothing Biblical about its origin ; and it is as far removed as

J. H. P.

Monograms of the Sacred Name.

1, 2. From mediæval embroidery.   3. From painted glass, Thaxted Church, Essex.   4, 5. The mystical fish, from the Catacombs at Rome.

possible from the poetical imagery of the Lamb, the Vine, the Lion. It is of purely literary origin. It was found that the letters of the Greek word for "fish," IXΘΥΣ, could be amplified into Ιησοῦς Χριστὸς Θεοῦ Υἱὸς Σωτήρ ; *i.e.*, "Jesus Christ, Son of

God, Saviour." Augustine, Tertullian, Clement of Alexandria, all accept this interpretation, and speak of the fish as a symbol of Our Lord. The Greek Church never adopted it.

THE THIRD PERSON OF THE TRINITY

The Holy Ghost appears chiefly in representations of the Creation, moving on the face of the waters, and at the Annunciation and the Baptism. The Holy Spirit is usually represented by a dove ;[1] *e.g.*, on the Norman font at Kirkburn, Yorkshire. An instance occurs as early as A.D. 359. From the tenth century the Holy Spirit sometimes appears in human form, with a roll or book held in the hand. A dove of carved wood was often placed on the summit of a font cover. But since it was written, "*Be ye harmless as doves*," the dove is also one of the symbols of the Christian believer. It was also an emblem of peace and rest ; for it is written, " *O that I had wings like a dove ; for then would I flee away and be at rest.*"

M. L.

Coronation of the Blessed Virgin.
Boss in York Minster.

[1] Matthew iii. 16 ; Luke iii. 22.

THE BLESSED VIRGIN

The emblem of the Blessed Virgin, especially in the scene of

S. Peter.   S. Andrew.   S. James ye more.   S. Johan.   S. Thomas.   S. James ye less.

J. H. P.

S. Phylypoe.   S. Barthylmew.   S. Mathewe.   S. Jude.   S. Symon.   S. Mathyas.

the Annunciation, is the lily, which signifies spotless purity. But in the Song of Songs the mouth of the Beloved is compared to a lily, the reference being plainly to red lips. The flower referred to is probably neither the *Lilium candidum* nor the Lily of the Valley, but the scarlet anemone, which grows plentifully round Jerusalem and in Galilee. Often she is crowned. The Coronation of the Virgin is very frequently represented, *e.g.*, on bosses in York minster (260), Worcester cloister, and Gloucester nave.[1]

THE APOSTLES

In Early Christian art the apostles appear as sheep, six on either side of the Good Shepherd or of the Lamb of God. But in mediæval art they are human figures distinguished by their emblems, of which the following are the most common :—

In the illustration, taken from an ancient print (261), the apostles are depicted as follows:—*S. Peter* holds keys; *S. Andrew*, the cross saltire on which he was crucified ; *S. James the Greater*, a pilgrim's staff, wallet, and scallop shell ; *S. John*, the poisoned chalice ; *S. Thomas*, the spear by which he was slain ; *S. James the Less*, a fuller's club, the instrument of his martyrdom ; *S. Philip*, the cross on which he was crucified (sometimes he has a basket of loaves, as on p. 61) ; *S. Bartholomew*, the large knife with which he was flayed ; *S. Matthew*, an axe, instrument of his martyrdom ; *S. Jude*, a tall cross-staff (often he holds a boat, as on p. 82) ; *S. Simon*, the saw with which he was reputed to have been sawn asunder longitudinally ; *S. Matthias*, the battle-axe by which he suffered death.

THE EVANGELISTS

Of the various representations of the four evangelists, by far the most common in mediæval sculpture is that of the four beasts of the Apocalypse, which may be memorised as ALOE : A being the angel or man, S. Matthew ; L the lion, S. Mark ; O the ox or calf, S. Luke ; E the eagle, S. John. They are exceedingly common in East Anglian fonts of the fifteenth century, *e.g.*, at Saxmundham, Suffolk. At first they were not applied with exact uniformity, S. Matthew or S. Mark each being represented at times as man or lion. This symbolism is drawn from Revelation iv. 6 : "*And in the midst of the throne and round about the throne were four beasts. . . . And the first beast was like a lion, and the second beast like a calf, and the third*

---

[1] In the York vault angelic hands are placing the crown on the head of Our Lady, while another hand swings a censer behind Our Lord, who holds the orb of sovereignty in His left hand.

beast had a face as a man, and the fourth beast was like a flying eagle." The Apocalyptic imagery is plainly drawn from the first chapter of the prophet Ezekiel, who, being among the captives by the banks of a tributary of the Euphrates, saw visions of God ; when out of a whirlwind and a fiery cloud there came "*the likeness of four living creatures. . . . And every one had*

J. H. P.

Ancient Altar Cloth.

Steeple Aston, Oxon.

four faces and every one had four wings. . . . As for the likeness of their faces, they four had the face of a man and the face of a lion on the right side; and they four had the face of an ox on the left side; they four also had the face of an eagle." Ezekiel's imagery again is drawn from the winged bulls and the other strange composite creatures which he saw around him, and which we may still see in the Assyrian rooms at the British Museum.

The evangelistic symbols are set forth in an ancient hymn :—

"Circa thronum Majestatis
Cum Spiritibus Beatis
Quattuor diversitatis
Astant animalia.

"Formam primam Aquilinam,
Et secundam Leoninam,
Sed Humanam et Bovinam
Duo gerunt alia.

"Hi sunt Marcus et Matthæus
Lucas, et quem Zebedæus
Pater tibi misit Deus,
Dum laxaret retia."

In the concluding verse the meaning of the symbols is declared as follows :—

"Natus Homo declaratur,
Vitula sacrificatur,
Leo mortem depredatur,
Sed ascendit Aquila."

THE DOCTORS OF THE CHURCH

In the Eastern Church these are SS. Athanasius, Basil, Gregory Nazianzen, and Chrysostom ; in the Western, S Augustine, who is usually represented holding a heart ; S. Ambrose, with a scourge or a beehive ; S. Gregory, with a cross and dove ; S. Jerome, with a lion and inkhorn. The Doctors of the Church are often provided with distinctive dress ; S. Gregory with that of a Pope, S. Jerome with that of a Cardinal, S. Ambrose with that of a Bishop, while S. Augustine has Doctor's robes. In a window at All Souls, Oxford, S. Gregory has the ox of S. Luke, S. Jerome the lion of S. Mark, S. Ambrose the angel of S. Matthew, S. Augustine the eagle of S. John. Statues of the Doctors occur or used to occur as pinnacles on the towers of several East Anglian churches ; on the tower of Wiggenhall S. Peter, Norfolk, the evangelistic symbols formed the pinnacles. In the Eastern Church the term saint is applied to holy men of the Old Testament also ; and we hear of S. Abel, S. Noah, S. Moses, S. Samuel, and many others.

W. P. W.

SS. Ambrose, Jerome, Augustine.

Pulpit at Trull, Somerset.

34

W. S. W.

S. Jerome.

Westminster.

E. K. P.

S. Ambrose.   S. Augustine.

Ashton Rood-screen, Devon.

THE MAGI

Of the three Wise Men, Gaspar is usually aged, and has a long grey beard ; Melchior is in the prime of life, and has a short beard ; Balthazar is young and beardless ; sometimes he is a negro, with thick lips and curly hair (95). In the scene of the Adoration they are generally crowned kings ; for it is written : *" The kings of Tarshish and of the isles shall bring presents ; the Kings of Sheba and Saba shall offer gifts ; yea, all kings shall fall down before Him."* In similar fashion, to show the fulfilment of ancient prophecy, an ox and an ass appear in the scene of the Nativity.[1] They are not mentioned in the New Testament

---

[1] The illustration is from the thirteenth-century wall arcading in Worcester cathedral : the figures comprise the Blessed Virgin, S. Joseph, and the Child, an ox and an ass (268).

G. G B.

The Nativity.

Worcester Cathedral.

account; but Isaiah had written—"*The ox knoweth his owner and the ass his master's crib.*" And so, in the words of an old carol—

> "*Ox and ass before Him bow,*
> *And He is in the manger now;*
> *Christ is born to-day.*"

THE SIBYLS

The Sibyls are frequently represented in mediæval art, especially in company with the Prophets. They are ten, or more often twelve, in number, and were supposed to have prophesied the coming of Christ. A detailed account of them, with illustrations, is given in the first appendix to Husenbeth's *Emblems* The Sibyls form part of the famous pavement of the cathedral of Siena, where they are incased in white marble. Complete sets of twelve remain on the painted rood-screens of Bradninch and Ugborough, and nine on that of Heavitree, Devon.

The Church

A ship riding safely amidst the storms of life was a favourite early symbol of the Church ; sometimes S. Peter is at the helm, so that the reference may be to Our Lord walking on the sea. Sometimes instead of a ship a floating chest, or *arca*, appears, in which kneels a saint, the prototype being the ark of Noah.[1]

Norman examples of the ark building and the ark afloat occur on the west front of Lincoln minster. Also in Salisbury chapter house, Noah is seen in the ark.[2] Sometimes the Church

J. H. P.

The Christian Church. The Synagogue.

From painted glass in Bourges Cathedral.

[1] "With its ship-like character," said Durtal, "Chartres strikes me as amazingly like a motionless vessel with spires for masts and the clouds for sails, spread or furled by the wind as the weather changes. It remains the eternal symbol of Peter's boat which Jesus guided through the storm."

"And likewise of Noah's ark—the ark outside which there is no safety," added the Abbé.—J. K. Huysmans, *La Cathédrale*.

For a more sober account of the symbolism of Chartres cathedral, see paper by Mr G. H. Birch on "Christian Iconography" in *S. Paul's Ecclesiological Society*, i. 9.

[2] It may be mentioned here that Jews were generally represented with the conical caps they were compelled to wear in the Ghetto.

A. G.

Synagogue.

Rochester : doorway of Chapter House.

appears as a crowned female figure, holding a cross in one hand and in the other a chalice or church. Opposite may be another female figure, symbolising the Synagogue, sometimes blindfolded; with broken spear or banner, a crown falling from her head, and the broken tables of the Law from her hands; *e.g.*, in the doorway of Rochester chapter house, where the figure at a recent restoration was supplied with a moustache.

This is how Mr W. J. Blew sings of "The Gallant Ship of Christendom" :—[1]

"Up to the wind, nor wild nor free
　She steers; her course right on is set;
Though crags lie low upon her lee,
　The headland shall be weathered yet."

"To windward all; look up and hail
　The blowing of that goodly breeze;
Fresh life it gives to hearts that fail,
　And strength unto the feeble knees."

"So—steady so—like winged sea-fowl
　She breasts the wind; on each broad sail,
Through stay and shroud, the white squalls howl,
　And rattles the sharp spray like hail."

"Yet stands she, as on Lebanon
　The trees that be her fellows stand—
Time-worn and stained as years roll on,
　Yet staunch as from the builder's hand."

"Though weed and wave have dimmed the gold
　Of Judah's lion on her prow,
Sound is the treasure in her hold,
　Her sheathing shines like gold below."

"The Red Cross from her topmast flies,
　And white as snow her silver field;
Her Ancient—blue as summer skies—
　Bears the Lamb crowned and pennonceled;
While charged with richest blazonries
　Hangs aft S. Michael's dragon-shield."

---

[1] In appendix to his translation of *Medea* (Rivington, 1887). The verses quoted are but a small part of a noble poem, which should be known to all churchmen.

" Bear on, brave bark, with forward shoot
    Cleave the curled wave, the billowy swell ;
The high mast trembles to her root,
    She feels it ! that her keel can tell,
As it lifts to the leap of her merry forefoot
    At the cry of the watch, ' All's well.' "

" Her taut spars like a Cretan bow
    Arch with the wind ; taut stands each stay ;
He slumbers not nor sleeps who now
    Holds the brave galley on her way."

THE DEVIL

is only represented in the Catacombs as the Serpent tempting Eve ; but from the tenth century appears as the conventional hideous monster, or as a dragon in the scene from the Apocalypse, in which he is described as " *that great dragon*," and is overcome by S. Michael. On the west front of Lincoln minster and elsewhere he may be seen on his back with fetters round his arms and legs, while Christ tramples on him, and holds him down by thrusting into his mouth the butt end of the Cross. This scene is from the apocryphal Gospel of Nicodemus, and was termed the Harrowing, *i.e.*, the Harrying or Spoiling of Hell.

T. N. B.

Hell Mouth.

Horning Church, Norfolk.

H. C. B.

Hell Mouth.

Bench end, Barming, Kent.

HEAVEN AND HELL

The Early Christian Church delighted in depicting Paradise ; the Mediæval Church in graphic realisation of the torments of Hell.

In the Catacombs Hell is not represented ; but they are full of the joys of Paradise, green pastures by still waters, where the birds flutter in the branches of olive and palm and rose, or peck at the grape or fig, or drink from limpid fountains, and the saints are gathered together at the table of their Lord, waited on by Irene and Agape, " Peace " and " Love." In mediæval art Hell appears as a seething caldron or as the open mouth of a monster from which issue flames.[1]

[1] The scene on the bench end at Barming, Kent, is the normal one of the Spoiling of Hell, as given in the Gospel of Nicodemus. Our Lord in cruciferous nimbus and holding a staff tipped with a cross (not seen in the photograph) is taking Adam by the right hand, Eve being behind. The treatment of the subject at Barming is determined by the peculiar shape of the base and the curve behind, the figure of Eve being magnified to fill up the space behind Our Lord. She is not mentioned in the narrative in the Gospel of Nicodemus, which runs as follows : xvii. 13, " Then the King of Glory trampling upon death . . . and took an earthly father, Adam, to his glory." xix. 1, " Then Jesus stretched forth His right hand and said,

H. C. B.

Hell Mouth.

North Cray, Kent.

'Come to me, all ye my saints.'"   3, " Then presently all the saints were joined together under the hand of the most high God ; and the Lord Jesus laid hold on Adam's hand and said to him " . . . 12, "And taking hold

It is to be noted that the representation of Hell Mouth as the jaws of a monster is foreign to Byzantine art; in Western art the earliest examples appear to occur in English MSS. of the tenth and eleventh centuries.

THE SOUL

In the Catacombs the soul is represented as an *Orante*, a slender girl, tall and dignified, and heavily draped, with hands uplifted to heaven. A medal in the Vatican, depicting the martyrdom of S. Lawrence on the gridiron, shows an Orante by his side rising to heaven. In mediæval art the soul is generally depicted as a tiny babe, usually naked, issuing from the mouth

F. H. C.

Boss in the Vault. S. Mary's, Beverley.

of a dying person, or standing in the lap of Our Lord, as in Lady Percy's tomb in Beverley minster. If there are several babes, the bodies may be omitted. In an interesting example illustrated in Mrs Barber's *Drawings of Ancient Embroidery*, the souls are in the lap of *Abraham*, commemorating the fact that Lazarus was taken up into Abraham's bosom.

of Adam by his right hand, He ascended from Hell, and all the saints of God followed Him." c. xx., "Then the Lord, holding Adam by the hand, delivered him to Michael the archangel." The following plates in vol. lxvi. of the *Archæological Journal* should be consulted, vii. 321; viii. 323; ix. 325; x. 327; xiii. 333 (G. C. D.). The same scene is represented in stone in a window at Dorchester, Oxon., illustrated in the writer's *Introduction to English Church Architecture*, vol. i., p. 261.

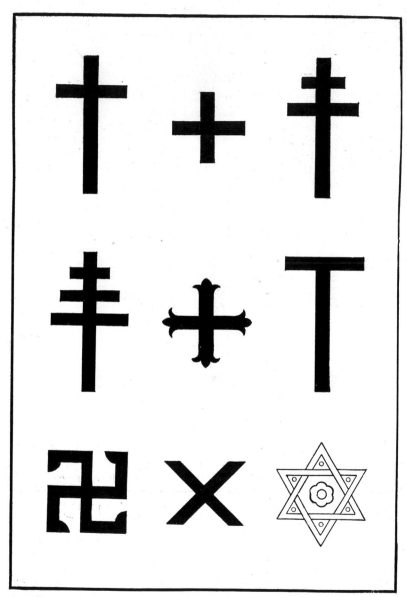

W. E.

The Cross

Though the cross was held in the greatest reverence by the Early Christians, the symbol of the cross is hardly ever found in the Catacombs before 312 A.D., perhaps because it was dangerous to exhibit a symbol known to be associated with a proscribed religion. It appears in a mosaic at Ravenna about 440, and is thenceforth common. The Tau cross was the symbol of eternity with the Egyptians, and was borne by Thoth. It may have been introduced as a Christian symbol by the Coptic Christians. The Tau cross is an emblem of S. Anthony of Egypt, and is worn by the Order of the Knights of S. Anthony, instituted in 1352.

In Norman sculpture the Maltese cross is usually employed ; it has arms of equal length which expand at the end ; as a rule it is enclosed in a circle, *e.g.*, Wold Newton, Yorkshire. Other types of cross are figured on p. 276.[1]

The Crucifix

The crucifix does not occur till the fifth century ; and till the eleventh century the body of the Crucified is always shown clothed, sometimes in the robes of the High Priest. The object of the early representations was rather to depict the triumph of the Son of God over death than the sufferings of the Son of Man.

The Crown of Thorns

is associated not only with Our Lord, but with S. Francis of Assisi, S. Catherine of Siena, and others.

Instruments of the Passion

These may include the ladder, the thirty pieces of silver, the dice-board and the dice, the seamless robe, the cock, the spear,

---

[1] It is a common error to suppose the cross of an archbishop to be the equivalent of the crook or crosier of a bishop, and to have been carried by him. As a matter of fact he carried a crosier like other bishops. The cross he did not carry ; it was borne before him in processions. But in brasses and memorials an archbishop is sometimes represented as holding in his hand his cross as an emblem. In the upper line of p. 276 are shown a Latin cross, a Maltese cross, and the cross of an archbishop ; in the second line a papal cross, a cross fleuri, and a Tau cross ; in the third line a fylfot, a cross saltire, and a pentalpha or pentangle.

the sword, the pillar and scourges, the hammer and nails, the crown of thorns, the cross, the goblet of vinegar, the fist that buffeted Him, the ewer used by Pilate, the cup of wine and

From Poppies in the Chancel of Cumnor Church, Berks.

Crown of Thorns and Nails,   S. Peter's Sword,
in stained glass.   from a MS. in the Bodleian Library.

J. H. P.

Scourges, from Abbot Ramrigg's Chantry, S. Albans Abbey.

myrrh, the lantern, the lance, the pincers, a rope or chain for the deposition of the body, winding sheet and spices in a vase. A very elaborate set is painted on the wooden vault of Winchester choir ; they are common on East Anglian fonts ; fine examples occur at the back of a bench at Fressingfield, Suffolk (283) ;

E. K. P.

Passion Emblems.

Bench end at Sutcombe, N. Devon.

others at Swaffham, Norfolk, Horsham, Sussex, Mildenhall, Suffolk, Llanrwst, Wales (280), and elsewhere.[1]

[1] At Fressingfield, Suffolk, is the best carving on bench ends in England. On the back bench, locally known as the " Passion bench," the subjects are as follows : (1) Cock crowing ; (2) the buffet and jug of vinegar ; (3) I. H. C. ; (4) whipping pillar, cords and scourges ; (5) the cross, crown of thorns, and nails ; (6) the spear and sponge ; (7) hammer, pincers, and ladder ; (8) seamless coat and dice-board (284). On the screen at Llanrwst the subjects are : (1) The cross and crown of thorns ; (2) Agnus Dei ; (3) hammer, pincers, nails, lantern, ladder, cock, pillar and cords, spear ; (4) I. H. C. (280). At Sutcombe, Devon, the five wounds are shown (279) ; also the hand of Judas grasping a purse (290). *Cf.* p. 102.

Rood-screen, Llanrwst, N. Wales.

F. H. C.

The Nimbus

In the religious art both of Buddhism and of Greece a golden halo round the heads of gods and saints is quite familiar. At first it was an emblem of power rather than of sanctity; for among those who possess it are the emperors Trajan, Justinian and Charlemagne, King Herod and Satan himself. It may also occur on allegorical personages such as Charity and Poverty. The nimbus does not occur on Christian monuments till the sixth century. All early nimbi were circular; the triangular form is not found before the eleventh century, and the square nimbus, as characteristic of a living person, is not employed before the eleventh century. The nimbus in the form of an

J. H. P.

The Assumption of the Virgin.

From sculpture in Sandford Church, Oxfordshire.

36

equilateral triangle does not occur before the fifteenth century, and is usually reserved for the First Person of the Trinity, or for the dove symbolising the Holy Spirit. The cruciferous nimbus, a cross inscribed in a circle, is almost invariably restricted to Our Lord [1] (255).

THE AUREOLE

This is not so common as the nimbus ; it came into existence later, and disappeared earlier. The nimbus surrounds the head, the aureole the whole person. The aureole is emblematic of the encircling radiancy of the Divine Glory, and is based on the account of the Transfiguration and various other passages.[2]

The aureole is especially devoted to the Deity, though it is associated with the Blessed Virgin. It is possible that the *vesica piscis* (p. 256) is a variant of the aureole. The aureole is seen in a representation of the Assumption of the Virgin at Sandford, Oxon. (281), and at Tideswell (3).

PRAYER

In Pagan and in Early Christian art, the attitude of prayer was with uplifted hands. In mediæval art also this may occur ; and is perhaps the explanation of the strange figure on a capital of the doorway of S. Woolos, Newport, Wales.[3]

Even in late days the primitive attitude of prayer survived ; for Ælfric, writing at the end of the tenth century, says of King Oswald, M., that

> "Wherever he was, he worshipped God
> With the palms of his hands uplifted heavenward."

NUMBERS

In Christian symbolism by far the most significant number is seven. It is written of Job, "*In seven troubles there shall no evil touch thee*" ; and in Proverbs, "*Wisdom hath hewn out her seven pillars.*"

---

[1] On the Nimbus, see Geldart's *Manual of Church Decoration and Symbolism* and *British Archæological Association*, x. 332.

[2] "The sight of the glory of the Lord was like devouring fire" on Mount Sinai (Exodus xxiv. 17). So also at the dedication of Solomon's temple, "the glory of the Lord had filled the house of the Lord" (1 Kings viii. 11). And in the Apocalypse John saw one "like unto the Son of Man ; and His countenance was as the sun shineth in his strength" (Revelations i. 16).

[3] Illustrated in *Gothic Architecture in England*, 421.1.

C. F. N.

Passion Bench, Fressingfield.

There were seven days of creation. On the seventh day of the seventh month a holy observance was ordained to the children of Israel, who fasted seven days and lived seven days in tents. The seventh day was to be observed as a Sabbath, and at the end of seven times seven years came the great year of Jubilee. Pharaoh in his dream saw seven oxen and seven ears of corn. The Israelites compassed the walls of Jericho seven times. Samson was bound with seven bands. Naaman was told to bathe seven times in the Jordan. Jacob bowed himself seven times before his brother. Balaam built seven altars and prepared for sacrifice seven oxen and seven rams. In the Apostolic Church seven men were appointed deacons. The week has seven days, and the seventh day is the Sabbath. The Catholic Church has seven sacraments: Baptism, Confirmation, Penance, Eucharist, Orders, Matrimony, Extreme Unction; these are represented on many fonts. The seven-branched candlestick of the Jewish temple may still be seen at Rome on the Arch of Titus. In a Christian church a seven-branched candlestick or a group of seven lamps is illustrative of the passage, "*There were seven lamps of fire burning before the throne, which are the seven spirits of God*" (Revelations iv. 5).

The prophet Isaiah (xi. 2) enumerates the gifts of the Spirit as *"the spirit of wisdom and understanding, the spirit of counsel and might, the spirit of knowledge and of the fear of the Lord."* To these the Vulgate adds a seventh, Piety. Psalms vi., xxxii., xxxviii., li., cii., cxxx., cxliii. are penitential psalms, seven in number. There are seven deadly sins: Avarice, Pride, Quarrel-someness, Envy, Drunkenness, Luxury, Anger, Lust. There are seven cardinal virtues: Generosity, Humility, Piety, Pity, Modesty, Temperance, Patience, Chastity. The seven joys of

C. O. R.

Fressingfield.

the Blessed Virgin were the Annunciation, the Visitation, the Nativity, the Adoration of the Magi, the Presentation in the Temple, the finding of Christ among the doctors in the Temple, the Assumption. The seven dolours are the Prophecy of Simeon, the Flight into Egypt, losing Christ in the Temple, the Betrayal of Christ, the Crucifixion, the Deposition from the Cross, and the Ascension. At the consecration of a Catholic church the altar is sprinkled seven times in remembrance of the seven outpourings of the precious blood of Christ; the first whereof was at circumcision; the second in prayer in the garden; the third at the scourging; the fourth from the crown of thorns;

the fifth from the pierced hands ; the sixth when His feet were nailed to the cross ; the seventh when His side was pierced with the spear.   Moreover, there are seven champions of Christendom: S. George of England, S. Andrew of Scotland, S. David of Wales, S. Patrick of Ireland, S. Denis of France, S. James of Spain, S. Anthony of Italy.   No wonder that in the eyes of the

C. O. R.

Fressingfield, Suffolk.

mediæval churchman a special sanctity attached to the number seven.   But not to the Christian only was seven the mystic number of perfection.   There were seven wise men in Greece. Shakespeare distinguishes seven ages of man.   At Mecca the pious Moslem passes round the sacred stone seven times.   Jacob served an apprenticeship seven years for the love of Rachel ; and gave the precedent for the seven years of apprenticeship to a trade which till recently were customary.   The lease of a house is wont to be for seven, fourteen, or twenty-one years ; seven years of penal servitude used to be a customary sentence for crime.   We come of age when our years are three times seven ; when our years are three score and ten it is time to go.

On the other hand the number nine, in spite of its marvellous mathematical properties, was of little account to the Christian. Outside Christianity we hear of the nine tailors, the nine lives of a cat, the nine points of the law, the-cat-o'-nine-tails, and the cheer of three times three.

C. O. R.

Fressingfield.

With the number forty there were many associations.   The Deluge lasted forty days, and Noah was shut up forty days in the ark.   The Israelites wandered forty years in the wilderness, and forty years were they in bondage to the Philistines.   Moses was forty days on the Mount.   Elijah lay in concealment forty days.   Jonah preached "yet forty days, and Nineveh shall be overthrown."   Our Lord fasted forty days in the wilderness. Forty days of rain are due after a wet S. Swithin's.   Sanctuary privilege was good for forty days, and quarantine used to last the same period.

Fressingfield.

Fressingfield.

Colours

The symbolism of colours is far too intricate to be worked out here. An extraordinarily minute and fanciful account of the symbolism of colours, jewels, and odours, and indeed of ecclesiastical symbolism in general, especially as found in the cathedral of Chartres, will be found in *La Cathédrale*, by J. K. Huysmans, translated by Clara Bell (Kegan Paul, 1898).

C. O. R.

Fressingfield.

Geometrical Figures

Two may be of mystic import. Naturally the *Equilateral Triangle* is sacred, as expressive of the doctrine of the Trinity. The *Pentalpha* or *Fuga Dæmonum* had a great repute among exorcists ; it is not uncommon as a centre-piece in window tracery. It is formed by connecting two equilateral triangles ; which being done, the figure is found to contain the letter A repeated five times. It occurs on a slab at S. Laurens, Jersey, and the tomb of Cœur de Lion at Fontrevault (276).

THE FYLFOT OR SWASTIKA

This mysterious emblem has a literature of its own; it is fully discussed in vol. xlviii. of the *Archæologia*. It occurs in the mediæval churches and the Catacombs; it was found also at Troy by Dr Schliemann, and is common in Indian and Chinese art (276).

C. O. R.

Fressingfield.

THE MONTHS AND SEASONS

These are favourite subjects, especially on Norman doorways, tiles, misericords, and stained glass. The Four Seasons occur on a Norman font at Thorpe Salvin, Yorkshire. Perhaps the most complete set of the months is that on the fourteenth-century capitals in the choir of Carlisle cathedral. Many examples, in fine preservation, may be seen on the west front of Amiens and on the great west doorway of S. Mark's, Venice.

THE ZODIAC

The signs of the Zodiac are particularly common over Norman doorways, *e.g.*, Barfreston, near Dover. They are well

seen on a Norman lead font at Brookland, Kent.[1] The sign of the Zodiac, Sagittarius, is often represented by a Centaur shooting with a bow and arrow; very frequently in company with Leo or other animals, *e.g.*, West Rounton font and capitals at Adel, Iffley, and Lullington, Somerset. The Months and the Zodiac have been treated exhaustively by Rev. S. Pegge in *Archæologia*, x. 177 ; Mr James Fowler, *ibid.*, xliv. 137 ; and Mr R. Brown, *ibid.*, xlvii. 337. See also *Arch. Cantiana*, iv. 89, and *Journal of British Archæological Institute*, vi. 159.

EMBLEMS OF MORTALITY

It was not till the later days of Gothic art that repulsive representations of Time and Death, skeletons and skulls,

E. K. P.

The hand holding the bag of silver.
Bench end at Sutcombe, Devon.

[1] Illustrated in *Arch. Cantiana*, iv. 87.

came into vogue. In the Greek Church Time had been represented as a beardless youth; and in the Campo Santo of Pisa
Death is a stately angel. On the Elizabethan and Jacobean
monuments the emblems of mortality are exceedingly common.
In Broxbourne church, Hertfordshire, on a monument of 1609,
Sir Henry Cock, his two wives, his daughters, and four grand-
daughters, all hold skulls in their hands. To the Puritan, a little
later, death was a yet more repulsive idea. With the Renaissance came in also Pagan symbols : the broken column, and the
cinerary urn in which there were no ashes.

W. D.

Poppy Head.
Barningham Parva, Norfolk.

PART III

CHAPTER XX

EMBLEMS OF THE SAINTS

Early Christian Emblems—Eucharistic Vestments—Processional Vestments—Generic Emblems—Specific Emblems.

IN this chapter a list is given of the chief emblems of the mediæval saints. The emblems of the Early Christian saints are omitted, simply because they were for the most part unknown to mediæval people. Vast numbers are still to be seen in the Roman Catacombs, and they have been described and illustrated with scrupulous care.[1] But in the Middle Ages the Roman Catacombs, with a few insignificant exceptions, were unknown, till on May 31st, 1578, workmen engaged in excavation fell through the roof of one of the underground chambers, and attention was called to the existence of these long-forgotten *incunabula* of the Christian Church. From that time much study was devoted to their contents, which, mainly through the work of Marchi and the brothers De Rossi, are now familiar. But since the abandonment of the Catacombs commenced as early as the invasion of the Goths in A.D. 537, and since the rediscovery of them did not take place till A.D. 1578, the mediæval symboliser had and could have no direct knowledge of their contents. In this chapter, therefore, little reference is made to Symbolism in Early Christian Art ; it forms a subject in itself.

The emblems of the saints may be divided into two classes, the Generic and the Specific. The former are emblems of a class ; the latter of an individual martyr or of individual martyrs. Thus usually a crown or a palm merely means that the saint who has them was a martyr. But a basket of apples is a specific emblem of S. Dorothy, and a scythe of SS. Sidwell and Walstan. In many cases the emblem is sometimes used generically, and sometimes specifically. The latter is the case when a crown is worn by persons who are of royal blood ; *e.g.*, Edward the Confessor, S. Etheldreda of Ely, S. Catherine of Alexandria, not because they have won the crown of martyrdom.

---

[1] See Northcote and Brownlow's *Roma Sotteranea* and the bibliography affixed to the article on "Catacombs" in Smith and Cheetham's *Dictionary of Christian Antiquities.*

It is not to be supposed that the saints were invariably depicted with their emblems. Sometimes the emblem would be unknown to the artist; especially would this be the case where such inconspicuous saints as Januarius, Prosdecimus, Gildard, and Desiderius are represented, as in the north aisle windows of Wiggenhall S. Mary Magdalen, Norfolk; or where, as in this church, there was attached a label or scroll to the representation of each saint; *e.g.*, in these windows SS. Aldhelm, Sixtus, Sampson, German, Cuthbert, Botolph, Januarius, Giles, Swithun, and others all wear mitres and the eucharistic vestments of bishop or abbot, and hold a crosier in one or both hands, or a crosier and a book, or the left hand holds a crosier and the right is raised as in the act of benediction. Evidently these are conventional representations intended merely to signify that the saint was an abbot or bishop, and not specific emblems. Moreover the emblems vary: *e.g.*, S. Matthew.

As the eucharistic vestments are so commonly represented, especially in stained glass, in which as a rule they are shown with great care and accuracy, it may be worth while to give a short description of them. Then, as now, Catholic priests were buried in their eucharistic vestments, well-worn vestments being reserved for that purpose. Naturally, therefore, most brasses of priests show them thus habited. As a large proportion of them are brasses of parish priests, they are usually of moderate size. The Mass vestments are put on in the following order, a short prayer being said while each vestment is being put on: 1, the Amice; 2, the Alb; 3, the Girdle; 4, the Stole; 5, the Maniple; 6, the Chasuble.

1. THE AMICE.—The amice was always of linen, and was a mediæval invention. Originally it must have been a hood; for still the priest first places it upon his *head*, with the prayer, "Impone, Domine, capiti meo *galeam* salutis (the 'helmet of salvation') ad expugnandum diabolicos incursus"; moreover, in effigies at Towyn and Beverley minster the amice is drawn over the head as a hood. In shape it was rectangular, about 36 inches by 25 inches, and was fastened by strings encircling the body. On the upper edge of it was sewn a strip of embroidery called an *apparel*, which, when the vesting was complete, formed a stiff standing collar. A glimpse is sometimes obtained of the linen portion of the amice in front of the neck between the two ends of the apparel. See SS. Martin (69), Dunstan (68), Lambert (125).

2. THE ALB.—In Pagan Rome under the early empire a common form of tunic was the flowing robe with sleeves called the dalmatica. In time this went out of fashion among laymen, but was retained in the Church by the conservatism of the ecclesiastics. Sylvester, Bishop of Rome, 253-257, ordained "ut diaconi dalmatica uterentur in ecclesia." A loose flowing robe, however, must have been very inconvenient during baptism by immersion, and by the ninth century it is found in illuminations as a tight-fitting robe convenient for baptismal and other offices as well. The material was usually but not always linen, nor was the colour invariably white. Sometimes the alb was plain, but

usually there were sewn or otherwise fastened to it rectangular strips of embroidery or *apparels*, *e.g.*, S. Dunstan (68). In brasses apparels are shown between the feet and upon the wrists. In the early albs the apparel invariably encircles the whole wrist; later it shrinks to a small square patch sewn on the part of the sleeve which is toward the back of the hand. It should be noted that the term "apparel" is applied only to a strip of embroidery on the alb or amice; when used elsewhere it is called an *orphrey*.

3. THE GIRDLE.—As the alb was always of great length, it was necessary to pull up the lower part of it through the girdle and let it hang over above it. The girdle is therefore not visible; but its presence implied by the disposition of the alb and stole when the latter can be seen, as in a brass at Upwell, Norfolk.

4. THE STOLE.—The stole is a descendant of the *Orarium*, which seems to have been a narrow strip of cloth, originally, perhaps, in the early empire merely a napkin used to wipe the face, "ora," but granted to the Roman people by the Emperor Aurelian as a favour or badge of distinction. In the seventh century this is found in the form of the present stole worn by deacons, priests, and bishops alike, and worn precisely in the same fashion as at present. The stole is a narrow strip of embroidery or orphrey work nine or ten feet long, and two or three inches wide. In the thirteenth and fourteenth centuries it is widened out at each end; afterwards it was uniform in width. By a priest the stole is crossed over the breast and secured in that position by the girdle of the alb. Deacons secured it over the left shoulder and under the right arm; thereby approximating the disposition of the stole to that of the ancient Roman orarium. Bishops generally do not cross the stole. Usually only the fringed ends appear, except where, as in brasses at Upwell, Norfolk, and Sudborough, Northants, the priest is not wearing the chasuble.[1]   See SS. Thomas (130), Dunstan (68).

5. THE MANIPLE.—The *maniple, fanon,* or *sudarium,* was also originally a napkin. Its use was enjoined on deacons as early as 253 to 257 by Sylvester, Bishop of Rome. Its object is plainly stated by S. Ivo of Chartres and Amalarius of Metz; it was to wipe off perspiration and moisture from the face and eyes. At first it was worn over the fingers of the left hand; later, probably because it was constantly liable to slip off, it was placed over the left wrist, and buttoned or sewn to the sleeve. In form it resembled the stole, but was only about three feet long. It was fringed and decorated with orphrey work. See S. Thomas (130).

6. THE CHASUBLE.—In Pagan Rome the outer dress of the Roman citizen was originally the toga; but for outdoor wear it was ultimately superseded by the penula, casula, and planeta. In the sixth century of our era the last was worn by nobles and senators. It was a sort of large poncho, passed over the head through a hole in the middle. As early as the time of Sylvester, the alb, orarium, and planeta were worn

---

[1] For Sudborough, see illustration in Haines' *Brasses*, lxv.; for Upwell, see illustration in Boutell's *Series of Monumental Brasses*.

by priests. Except when worn folded at certain seasons, its use was confined to the celebrant at Mass ; it is therefore the Eucharistic vestment *par excellence* ; in fact the word *vestimentum* applies strictly, not to a set of Mass vestments, but to the chasuble only. It was usually of the most costly materials and richly decorated. The earlier chasubles are circular in front, the later ones are usually, but by no means always, pointed. Mr Macalister estimates the cost, according to the present value of money, of a set of vestments purchased by Henry the Third as follows :—A cope, £361. 2s. 6d. ; tunic and dalmatic, £269. 2s. 6d. ; two chasubles, £265 ; an alb, £5. 7s. 6d. ; a mitre, £1,230. The inventories of Lincoln minster in 1536 enumerate 265 copes, 52 chasubles, 2 dalmatics, 94 tunicles, and 131 albs (68, 69).

EPISCOPAL VESTMENTS.—The above are vestments of a priest, worn at the most solemn moments of his life and at death. Those of a bishop are more elaborate still. On the principle that the clergy of the higher orders do not cease to belong to the various orders through which they have passed, they are entitled to wear the insignia of the lower orders to those of the higher. A bishop's vestments, when celebrating on greater and more solemn occasions, comprise (1) those of the priest, viz., the amice, alb, girdle, stole, maniple, chasuble ; (2) the dalmatic of the deacon ; (3) the tunicle of the sub-deacon ; (4) the episcopal insignia, viz., stockings, sandals, gloves, ring, mitre, pastoral staff or crosier. In addition to all these an archbishop adds, (1) the pall, (2) the cross staff, which, though shown sometimes in his hand, as a matter of fact was not carried by himself, but by his chaplain. The order in which the vesting took place was—1, amice ; 2, alb ; 3, girdle ; 4, stole ; 5, maniple ; 6, tunicle ; 7, dalmatic ; 8, chasuble ; 9, pall.

1. THE DALMATIC.—The dalmatic is the Roman *tunica dalmatica*, of which, as has been said, the alb is a tight-fitting variant. When worn by the bishop, it was shortened so as to allow the tunicle to be seen. For the dalmatic see S. Stephen (55).

2. THE TUNICLE.—This was another variant of the Roman *tunica dalmatica*. Both tunicle and dalmatic were richly embroidered and fringed. For the tunicle and dalmatic see S. Dunstan (68).

3. THE STOCKINGS.—These were originally appropriated to the pope. They were richly ornamented.

4. THE SANDALS.—The open sandal of the Roman citizen was retained by the monastic orders. On a brass at Kilkenny Bishop De Ledrede is represented (*c.* 1350), though in episcopal dress, with the Franciscan sandal. The tradition of the sandal survived in the open-work patterns in the upper portion of the shoe, through which the bare flesh appeared, or, in later days, the colour of the episcopal stocking. About the fourteenth century open-work shoes were abandoned in favour of a closed shoe of modern character.

5. THE GLOVES.—Originally, no doubt, their object was to keep the hands warm in a damp and unheated church ; later they came to be of white netted silk with a jewel or plate of gold on the back. They had

quite lost their utilitarian purpose *c.* 1130. See SS. Martin (69), William (138), Dunstan (68).

6. THE RING.—The episcopal ring proper was only one of a large number of rings which might be worn by a bishop, the others being probably purely ornamental and secular. It was worn on the third finger of the right hand, and *above* the second joint of that finger, not being passed, as rings are now, down to the knuckle. It was usually kept in place by a plain guard ring. It was always a circlet, with a precious stone, never engraved, which was usually a sapphire, but sometimes an emerald or ruby.

7. THE MITRE.—The mitre is not represented before the beginning of the eleventh century, when it is a simple cap, low and hemispherical, without a cleft, *e.g.*, S. William (138). Very soon, however, the cleft appears, producing the double-pointed mitre. Till the fourteenth century mitres were low. Afterwards, with the exception of those of the brasses of Bishops Pursglove and Bell, they become tall, and were richly ornamented with embroidery and jewels, *e.g.*, SS. Martin (69), Dunstan (68). Henry VIII. removed from Fountains abbey a silver gilt mitre set with pearls and stones which weighed seventy ounces.

8. THE PASTORAL STAFF.—The pastoral staff is also termed crosier, a word which has nothing to do with "cross." From the top of the staff was suspended the *infula*, which was not a survival of Constantine's banner, but was placed there to keep the moisture of the hand from tarnishing the plated staff. The crook is turned to the right or left at random; and is not significant, as is often stated, of external or domestic rule.

9. THE CROSS STAFF.—The pastoral staff is significant of the dignity of bishop or abbot, the cross staff of that of archbishop. On some foreign brasses an archbishop is represented carrying both in accordance with the principle stated above.

10. THE PALL.—The pall is of uncertain origin: it was already in use *c.* 820. In form it was a loop of white lambs' wool passing round the neck, with two tails, one in front and one behind. It was fastened to the chasuble by pins, *e.g.*, S. Dunstan (68), but sometimes a plummet of lead was attached to its extremities instead, to keep it in place. On it were always crosses, four to eight in number, originally worked in purple but now in black. It appears in the shape of a **Y** or **T**. An archbishop was expected to go to Rome on election to receive the pallium in person, and not to wear it outside his province; when he died, it was buried with him. The pallium is the only vestment which may not be lent by one cleric to another.

Memorials of mitred abbots show them as a rule in the episcopal vestments described, *e.g.*, the brass of Abbot Delamere at S. Albans.

Quite distinct from the Eucharistic were the PROCESSIONAL or CHOIR VESTMENTS. Above the underclothing was worn (1) the *Cassock*, which originally was lined with fur. Unlike modern cassocks, it was not worn with a sash, nor had it a row of buttons from neck to hem like "a boiler with a close row of rivets." (2) Above the cassock was worn the *Surplice*, which is practically an alb. Both the surplice and the alb were slipped over the head till enormous wigs came in fashion in the seventeenth and eighteenth centuries, when they were made open in front, and secured at the neck with a button. (3) Then came the *Almuce*, a fur-lined hood, which was worn turned back. (4) Then came the great *Cope*, or cloak, fastened in front of the breast by a big *morse* or brooch. See S. Martin (95).

GENERIC EMBLEMS

ARROW.—This usually means that the individual saint was shot with arrows, *e.g.*, SS. Sebastian, Edmund, Christina. But it is probable that the presence of an arrow, an axe, a halbert, a dagger, a club, a spear, a lance, a saw, etc., often means merely that the martyr was tortured before finally being put to death; *i.e.*, it is an emblem of torture in general.

ASPERGE.—Used for sprinkling holy water; and as a symbol of holiness of life.

BOOK.—This may mean specifically that the saint was an Evangelist or was a Doctor of the Church; or merely that he was learned, like S. Catherine, or a constant attendant at the services of the Church, like S. Sitha.

CHALICE.—This, with or without the Host and paten, may mean that the saint was a priest, the cup from 1215 being forbidden to the laity. But the chalice is a specific emblem in the case of SS. John Evangelist, Benedict, Richard of Chichester, and Barbara.

CHURCH.—A church may mean that the saint founded a church or a monastery; or may be merely a symbol of high rank in the Church.

CROSS.—A cross at the top of a long wand often signifies a missionary or preacher; *e.g.*, John Baptist and S. Alban (13).

CROWN OR SCEPTRE.—Royal rank on earth; or a saint in heaven.

DOVE.—The presence of the Holy Spirit, inspiring writers and preachers; or purity of heart; or a Christian.

FOUNTAIN SPRINGING UP.—This may mean nothing more than that good results followed the saint's preaching and example. But see S. Peter, p. 327.

HEAD CARRIED.—This may mean merely that the saint suffered death by decapitation, the usual form of capital punishment in the Roman Empire, *e.g.*, S. Denis.

LILY.—Symbol of the Blessed Virgin; also of virginity; also of a pure heart.

PALM.—The palm of victory of a martyr.

SCOURGE OR DISCIPLINE.—Self-mortification; *e.g.*, SS. Boniface and Guthlac. But specific in the case of S. Ambrose, p. 309.

SKULL.—Contemplation of mortality and preparation for death; *e.g.*, S. Jerome.

SWORD.—Death by decapitation.

Sometimes a symbol is merely a rebus ; *i.e.*, a play on the name of the saint—*e.g.*, SS. Cornelius, Agnes, Holofius, Sidwell, Hippolytus : the last name signifies " torn by horses."

SPECIFIC EMBLEMS OF INDIVIDUAL SAINTS

ALMS.—S. Elizabeth of Hungary.
ALTAR.—Prayer at or before, S. Clement and S. Canute, K.M. Murdered before, SS. Thomas of Canterbury and Winifred.
ANCHOR.—SS. Clement, Felix, Nicholas.
ANGEL.—S. Matthew, etc.
ANVIL —SS. Giles and Adrian ; his wife holding Adrian's hands on an anvil to be chopped off.
APPLES.—SS. Dorothy and Nicholas.
ARMS AND LEGS CUT OFF.—S. Adrian.
ARMOURED.—SS. George, Michael, Maurice, Pancras of Rome, Victor, Armil, Eustace.
ARROW.—SS. Sebastian, Edmund, Cosmas and Damian, Ursula, Giles, Christina.
ASPERGE.—SS. Benedict, Peter, Robert of Knaresborough, Martha, etc.
AXE.—Laid to the root of an oak, S. Boniface.
BAG OR BAG-PURSE.—SS. Matthew, Sitha ; Judas Iscariot.
BALL OF FIRE.—S. Benedict.
BALLS, Three or Six.—S. Nicholas.
BARN.—S. Bridget of Kildare.
BASKET.—SS. Philip, Dorothy, Sitha, Elizabeth of Hungary.
BATTLE-AXE.—SS. Olave, Alphege, Thomas of Canterbury.
BEARDED WOMAN.—SS. Wilgefortis, V.M., Barbara, Galla.
BED OF IRON OR BRASS.—S. Faith.
BEEHIVE.—SS. Ambrose, Bernard, John Chrysostom.
BEGGAR.—SS. Elizabeth of Hungary, Martin, Alexis, Giles, Medard.
BELL.—SS. Anthony, Benedict.
BELLOWS.—S. Genevieve.
BLIND RESTORED TO SIGHT.—SS. Magnus, Birinus, Vedast, Wulstan.
BIRDS.—SS. Macentius, Paul the Hermit, Remigius, Blaise, Erasmus.
BOAR, Wild.—SS. Anthony, Blaise.
BOAT.—SS. Jude, Mary Magdalene, Julian Hospitaller.
BOATHOOK.—S. Jude.
BODKIN OR BORER.—S. Leger, S. Simon of Trent.
BOTTLE AND SHEARS.—SS. Cosmas and Damian.
BOW.—S. Sebastian.
BOWELS.—SS. Erasmus, Vincent.
BOX, Money.—S. Matthew.
BOX OF OINTMENT.—SS. Mary Magdalene, Joseph of Arimathea, Cosmas and Damian.
BOYS IN TUB.—S. Nicholas.
BRANCH.—SS. Brandan, Bridget of Kildare, Kentigern.
BREAD.—See LOAF.

BREAST.—Serves as altar, S. Lucian.   Pierced or cut off, SS. Agatha, Sophia and her daughters.

BRIARS.—S. Benedict.

BROOM.—SS. Petronilla and Sitha.

BULL, Brazen.—SS. Eustace and Polycarp.

CALVES.—S. Walstan.

CANDLE.—SS. Genevieve, Beatrix, Blaise.

CANOE IN HAND.—S. Vincent.

CARDINAL.—SS. Jerome, Mark.

CARPENTER'S SQUARE.—SS. Thomas, Jude, Matthew.

CART DRAWN BY HORSE.—S. Bavo.

CASKET.—SS. Cosmas and Damian, Mary Magdalene.

CAULDRON.—SS. Lucy, Cecilia, Erasmus, Cyriacus, John Evangelist, Felicitas, Boniface, Cyprian.

CAVE.—SS. Benedict, Blaise, Leonard, Giles.

CHAIN.—SS. Leonard, Ninian, German, Ignatius, Radegund, Leonard, S. Peter *ad vincula*, S. Bridget of Sweden.

CHAFING DISH.—S. Agatha.

CHALICE.—SS. John Evangelist, Benedict, Barbara, Giles, Richard of Chichester, Thomas Aquinas, Bruno.

CHASUBLE.—Filled with stones, S. Alphege.   Red chasuble, S. Thomas of Canterbury.

CHEST.—Standing before open chest, S. Etheldreda.   Filled with gold, S. Rumold.

CHILDREN, Three.—S. Nicholas.

CHRISM.—S. Remigius.

CHURCH.— SS. Botolph, Helena, Osmund, Peter, Withburga, Martin, etc.

CLOAK.—Dividing, S. Martin.   Spread out before him, S. Alban.

CLUB, Fuller's.—SS. James the Less and Simon.

CLUB.—In his hand, SS. Jude, Boniface, and Fabian.   Set with spikes, SS. Nicomede and Vitalis.   Beaten with, SS. Lambert, Magnus, and Valentine.

COALS.—Hot coals in lap or hand or vestment, S. Brice.   Brought by acolyte in his surplice, S. Lambert.

COCK.—Crowing, S. Peter.

COFFIN.—In a boat, S. Ouen.

COLT.—Near, S. Medard.

COMBS.—Iron, S. Blaise.

COOK.—Wearing an apron, S. Evortius.

CORONATION.—Edward the Confessor.

CORPSE.—In a coffin before him, S. Silvester.

COW.—Wild, S. Perpetua.   Red, SS. Bridget and Morwenna.

COWS AND OXEN.—S. Cornelius.

CRIPPLE.—Clothed, S. Elizabeth of Hungary, S. Martin.

CROCODILE.—Under feet, S. Theodore.

CROW.—See RAVEN.

CROSS, Triple.—Any Pope.   Cross in the air, S. Ouen.

CROWN OF THORNS.—SS. Francis of Assisi, Catherine of Siena, William of Norwich, and King Louis.

CRUCIFIX.—SS. Bruno, Dunstan, Thomas Aquinas, Columba, Francis, etc.

CRUCIFIED HEAD DOWNWARD.—SS. Peter and Philip.

CRUETS, Two.—S. Vincent.

CUP.—Poisoned, with dragon or serpent issuing from it, SS. John Evangelist and Benedict. With dagger, King Edward, M. Covered cup, S. Mary Magdalene.

DAGGER.—SS. Olave, Canute, King Edward, M., Agnes. It is often the generic symbol of death by assassination.

DALMATIC.—SS. Gervase and Protasius, Vincent, Leonard.

DART.—SS. Lambert, Cosmas and Damian.

DEACON.—SS. Lawrence, Vincent, Quintin, Leonard.

DISH.—Silver dish broken and given to the poor, S. Oswald.

DISTAFF.—S. Genevieve, etc.

DOES.—S. Giles. Two does looking up to S. Withburga.

DOG.—With loaf in his mouth or licking the wounds of S. Roch.

DOVE.— SS. Bridget of Sweden, Catherine of Alexandria, Fabian, Lo, Remigius, Evortius, Hilary, Gregory, etc.

DRAGON.—SS. George, Michael, Margaret, Armil, Guthlac, Silvester, Martha, Julian, German, etc.

EAGLE.—SS. John Evangelist, Gregory, Medard, Augustine of Hippo.

EARS.—Three or five ears of corn, S. Walburge or S. Bridget of Kildare.

ESPOUSAL, to the Saviour.—S. Catherine, M., and S. Catherine of Siena.

EWER.—S. Vincent.

EYES.—Carrying, S. Lucy. Plucked out, S. Leger. Executioner's eyes fall out, S. Alban.

FALCON.—SS. Bavon, King Edward, M.

FAWN.—S. Blase.

FEATHER.—Instead of palm, S. Barbara.

FERRYMAN.— S. Julian Hospitaller.

FETTERS.—Holding, SS. Leonard, Quentin, Egwin. SS. Ninian (chain), German.

FIRE.—Before him, S. Patrick. Near him, S. Barnabas. Extinguished by prayer, S. Aidan. Passing through unhurt, S. Boniface. Above the head, SS. Lo, Martin, Bridget of Kildare. See FLAME.

FISH.—SS. Raphael Archangel, Andrew, Simon, Jude, Boniface, John of Bridlington, Eanswith, Egwin, Peter, Zeno.

FISHING ROD.—S. Zeno.

FLAMES. —Walking on, S. Anthony. Stabbed in flames, S. Polycarp. In his hand, S. Vincent. Near or over her, S. Bridget of Kildare. Flames and sword at her feet, S. Agnes. See FIRE.

FLOWERS.—SS. Dorothy, Cecilia and Zita.

FONT, near him.—SS. Patrick, Remigius, Silvester.

FOOTSTEPS, Imprinted on Stone.— S. Medard.

FORGING HORSE SHOES.—-S. Eligius or Eloy.

FOUNTAIN.—SS. Clement, Boniface, Julitta, Augustine of Canterbury, Ives, Riquier, Leonard, Humbert, Paul, etc.
FRANCISCAN HABIT.—SS. Anthony of Padua, Bonaventura, Francis.
FRUIT.—SS. Dorothy and Anne.
FURNACE, Thrown into.—S. Victor of Marseilles.
GEESE.—Three, S. Martin. Wild, S. Milburga. In wolf's mouth, S. Vedast.
GIANT.—S. Christopher.
GIRDLE.—SS. Thomas, Margaret, Thomas Aquinas.
GLOBE, at his feet.—SS. Bruno, Francis of Assisi, Ignatius.
GOAT, Devil in shape of.—S. Anthony.
GOOSE.—In wolf's mouth, S. Vedast. By side, S. Martin.
GOSPEL of St Matthew in hand.—S. Barnabas; of S. John, Edward the Confessor.
GRAIL, Holy.—Joseph of Arimathea.
GRAVE, Stepping into.—S. John Evangelist.
GRIDIRON.—SS. Lawrence, Vincent, Faith, Cyprian.
HAIR, Flowing.—SS. Mary Magdalene, Agnes.
HALBERT.—SS. Matthias, Matthew, Jude.
HAMMER.—SS. Adrian, Eloy, William of Norwich.
HANDS CHOPPED OFF.—S. Martha, etc.
HANDKERCHIEF.—S. Veronica.
HARP.—SS. Cecilia, Dunstan.
HATCHET.—SS. Matthias, Matthew.
HAWK.—S. Julian Hospitaller, S. Edward, K.M., etc.
HEAD.—Carried in hand or in platter, or on the ground, SS. John Baptist, Clair, Denis, Alban, Firmin, Winifred, Sidwell, Osyth, Decuman, etc.
HEAD of S. Oswald carried by S. Cuthbert.
HEART.—SS. Augustine of Hippo, Benedict, Clare, Francis, Quintin, Catherine of Siena.
HEART WITH I.H.S.—S. Ignatius.
HERMIT.—SS. Christopher, Jerome, etc.
HILL, Preaching on.—S. David.
HIND.—S. Giles, S. Withburga, etc.
HOLY WATER VESSEL AND ASPERGE.—S. Martha.
HOOK.—SS. Vincent, Agatha, Leger, Hippolytus.
HORN.—SS. Cornelius, Oswald, Hubert.
HORNS.—Moses.
HORSE LEG, shoeing of.—S. Eloy.
HORSES, torn by.—S. Hippolytus.
HORSE AND CART.—S. Bavo.
HUNTER.—SS. Eustace, German, Hubert.
IDOL, Broken or Falling.—SS. Philip, George, Wilfrid.
INFANT.—SS. Brice, Elizabeth.
INKHORN.—SS. Jerome, Matthew.
INSTRUMENTS OF THE PASSION.—SS. Bridget, Gregory, Bernard.
ISLAND OF SERPENTS.—S. Hilary.

JUG.—S. Vincent.

KEYS.—SS. Peter, Hubert, Sitha or Zita, Egwin, Petronilla, Hippolytus, Riquier, Genevieve, Blessed Virgin Mary, Dominic, Martha, James the Great, etc.

KNIFE.—SS. Bartholomew, Peter Martyr (in his head or shoulder).

LADDER.—SS. Olave, Perpetua, Leonard, Alexis.

LADLE.—SS. Martha.

LAMB.—SS. Agnes, Genevieve, John Baptist, Catherine.

LAMP.—SS. Lucy, Francis.

LANCE OR SPEAR.—SS. Hippolytus, Matthias, German, Oswin, Thomas, Lambert, Michael, Barbara, Philip.

LETTER BROUGHT BY DOVE.—S. Oswald.

LIGHT, Pillar of.—SS. Cuthbert, Bede.

LILY.—SS. Joseph, Gabriel, Kenelm, Sebastian, Clare, Dominic, Our Lady, Catherine of Siena.

LIMBS CUT OFF.—S. Adrian.

LION.—SS. Mark, Jerome, Adrian, Dorothy, Ignatius, Prisca.

LOAF OR LOAVES.—SS. Olave, Philip, Nicholas, Sitha or Zita, Cuthbert, Roch, Gertrude, Paul the Hermit.

LUTE.—S. Cecilia.

MALLETS.—S. Denis.

MANACLES.—S. Leonard.

MASS.—SS. Martin, Gregory.

MEDAL ROUND NECK.—S. Genevieve.

MEDALLION.—S. Jude.

MILK, Pan of.—S. Bridget of Kildare.   MILKING.—Ditto.

MILLSTONE.—SS. Vincent, Christina, Crispin and Crispinian, Victor of Marseilles, etc.

MONEY.—SS. Matthew, Philip, Martin.

MONEY BOX OR BAG, OR TABLE.—S. Matthew.

MONOGRAM, Sacred.—Ignatius.

MONSTRANCE.—S. Clare.

NAILS.—SS. Giles, Eloy, Quintin, King Louis, William of Norwich, etc.

NAPKIN.—SS. Stephen, Veronica.

NECK.—Pierced, S. Agnes.   Wounded behind, S. Cecilia.

OAK, Felling of.—S. Boniface.

OAR.—SS. Jude, Julian Hospitaller, Aubert.

OATS, Field of.—S. Radegund.

OIL.—SS. Walburge, Remigius, Vitus.

OINTMENT BOX.—SS. Mary Magdalene, Joseph of Arimathea, Cosmas and Damian, Joanna.

ORGAN.—S. Cecilia.

OTTERS.—S. Cuthbert.

OX.—SS. Luke, Cornelius, Silvester, Leonard, Medard, Julitta, Frideswide, Polycarp, Lucy.

PAINTING.—S. Luke.

PALM.—SS. John Evangelist, Catherine ; often a generic symbol of martyrdom.

PEACOCK'S FEATHER.—S. Barbara.
PHYSICIANS.—SS. Cosmas and Damian, Luke.
PICKAXE.—S. Leger.
PIG.—SS. Anthony, Blaise.
PILE OF WOOD.—SS. Polycarp, Agnes, Agatha.
PILGRIM.—SS. James the Greater, Roch, etc.
PINCERS.—SS. Apollonia, Dunstan, Agatha, Lucy.
PITCHER.—S. Bede.
PLAGUE-SPOT.—S. Roch.
PLOUGH.—SS. Richard, Kentigern.
POTSHERDS, Bed of.—S. Lucian.
PURSES.—SS. Nicholas, Edward the Confessor, etc.
PYRE.—See PILE.
RACK.—S. Vincent.
RAIN, Shower of.—S. Swithun.
RAVEN OR CROW.—SS. Benedict, Erasmus, Oswald, Vincent, Adrian,
    Paul the Hermit, etc.
RING.—SS. Edward, K.C., Barbara.
ROCK, Chained to.—SS. Martin, Gregory.
RODS.—SS. Benedict, Faith.
ROPE.—S. Beatrice, etc.
ROSARY.—SS. Sitha, Dominic, etc.
ROSES.—SS. Dorothy, Barbara, Elizabeth of Hungary, etc.
SALMON AND RING.—S. Kentigern.
SARUM MISSAL.—S. Osmund.
SAW.—SS. Simon, James the Less, etc.
SCALES.—S. Michael, etc.
SCALLOP SHELL ON HAT.—S. James the Greater, S. Roch.
SCEPTRE.—The kings Olave, Oswald, Edmund, Edward, C., Edward, M.,
    Louis ; Queen Margaret of Scotland and others.
SCOURGE.—SS. Ambrose, Boniface, Guthlac, Gervase and Protasius,
    Simon Stylites.
SCYTHE.—SS. Walstan and Sidwell.
SERPENT.—SS. John Evangelist, Benedict, Guthlac, Francis, Patrick,
    Hilary, Magnus, Christina, etc.
SEVEN SONS OR HEADS.—S. Felicitas.
SHACKLES.—S. Leonard.
SHEARS.—SS. Agatha, Cosmas and Damian.
SHEEP.—SS. Margaret, Genevieve, etc.
SHELL, Scallop.—S. James the Greater, S. Roch.
SHELLS, Lying on.—S. Felix.
SHIP.—SS. Jude, Ursula, etc.
SHOEMAKERS.—SS. Crispin and Crispinian, Theobald.
SHOEING A HORSE'S LEG.—S. Eloy.
SHRINES.—SS. John of Beverley, Omer, Louis, etc.
SICK PATIENT.—SS. Luke, Cosmas and Damian.
SIEVE.—SS. Benedict, Hippolytus.
SKIN FLAYED OFF.—SS. Bartholomew, Crispin and Crispinian, etc.

SKULL.—SS. Jerome, Mary Magdalene, Thomas of Canterbury.

SNAKES.—See SERPENTS.

SQUARE, Carpenter's.—SS. Matthew, Matthias, Thomas, Jude, Joseph.

STABBED on horseback in the back or shoulder with a dagger.—
S. Edward, K.M.

STAFF BUDDING.—SS. Joseph of Arimathea, Etheldreda, Ninian,
Christopher, Aldhelm.

STAG.—SS. Aidan, Julian Hospitaller, Kentigern.

STAG WITH CRUCIFIX.—SS. Eustace, Hubert.

STAR on, or over head, breast, or in hand.—SS. Dominic, Bruno,
Thomas Aquinas, Hugh of Grenoble, etc.

STIGMATA.—SS. Francis, Catherine of Siena.

STONE OR STONES.—Emblem of torture or martyrdom, SS. Pancras,
Matthew, Timothy, Stephen, Alphege, Barnabas, Bavon. Employed
in beating the breast in contrition, SS. Jerome, Barnabas. Loaves
turned into stones, S. Olaf.

SUNBEAM.—S. Bridget of Kildare and others.

SWAN.—SS. Hugh of Grenoble, Cuthbert, Leger.

SWORD THROUGH NECK OR THROAT.—SS. Agatha, Agnes, Lucy.

TAPER.—SS. Genevieve, Blaise, Bridget, Felix.

TAU CROSS.—SS. Anthony, Philip.

TEETH DRAWN.—S. Apollonia.

TEMPLE IN THE SEA.—S. Clement.

THORN.—Extracted by Joseph of Arimathea from lion's foot, SS. Mark,
Jerome. Lying on thorns, SS. Benedict, Jerome, Dominic.

TIARA.—Any Pope.

TONGS.—S. Dunstan, etc.

TONGUE CUT OFF.—S. Leger, etc.

TOOTH.—S. Apollonia.

TORCH.—SS. Blaise, Medard, Aidan, Barbara, Dorothy.

TOWER.—SS. Barbara, Ambrose, etc.

TRAMPLING.—SS. Catherine of Alexandria, Pancras of Rome, Barbara,
Theodore, Optatus, Cyprian.

VANE.—S. Leonard.

VASE.—SS. Mary Magdalene, Cosmas and Damian, etc.

VEIL.—SS. Veronica, Remigius, Agnes, etc.

VERNICLE.—S. Veronica.

VIAL.—SS. Walburge, Cosmas and Damian, etc.

VIATICUM.—S. Petronilla, etc.

VIOLIN.—S. Cecilia.

WALLET.—SS. James the Greater, Jerome, Roch.

WASHING FEET OF POOR OR LEPERS.—SS. Louis, Editha, Thomas of
Canterbury.

WELL.—SS. Sebastian, Sidwell, Sitha, Cyr, etc.

WHEEL.—SS. Catherine, Quintin, etc.

WILD BEASTS.—SS. Blaise, Magnus, German, Radegund, Columba.

WILD BOAR.—SS. Anthony, Cyr, Blaise.

WILD GEESE.—S. Milburga and S. Martin.

WINDLASS.—S. Erasmus.

WINDMILL.—SS. James the Less, Victor of Marseilles. Above S. Christopher in Ludlow stained glass.

WINE, Flagon of.—S. Elizabeth of Hungary.

WOLF.—SS. Vedast, Blaise, Columba, Edmund, Kentigern, Radegund, etc.

WOOL COMB.—S. Blaise.

WOUNDS IN THE NECK.—SS. Lucy, Cecilia.

WREATH IN HANDS OR ON HEAD.—S. Cecilia.

WRITING.—S. John Divine and other Evangelists.

F. B.

Deviation of Axis of Quimper Cathedral.

S. Ursula and her Companions.
Holy Trinity, Goodramgate, York.

M. L.

CHAPTER XXI

SAINTS AND THEIR EMBLEMS

THE following is a list of the chief saints to whom English churches are dedicated ; it also includes those who are retained in the Prayer Book Calendar, and a few of those who appear frequently in the paintings of rood-screens, wall paintings, and the like. On the other hand, it excludes numerous saints who are commemorated abroad, but very seldom, if ever, in England ; it also excludes nearly the whole of the great crowd of Celtic saints.

In the second column the following abbreviations are employed :—

A. = Abbot or Abbess.	E. = Evangelist.
Ap. = Apostle.	H. = Hermit.
Ar. = Archbishop.	M. = Martyr.
B. = Bishop.	P. = Pope.
C. = Confessor.	Q. = Queen.
D. = Doctor of the Church or Deacon.	V. = Virgin.

In the third column the feast days in many cases are not taken from the Prayer Book Calendar, but from the Calendars of Sarum, York, Hereford, and others.

The fourth column gives the date of the saint's death, in some cases only approximately ; the fifth column gives the number of English churches in whose dedication the saint is commemorated ; the sixth the page of the present volume in which the saint is referred to, and the page on which an illustration will be found.

	Title.	Day.	Date.	Ancient Dedications.	Text, Illustration.	
Acca -	B.	Aug. 6	740	1		Disciple of S. Wilfrid and his successor as Bishop of Hexham. With cope, mitre, and crosier, and right hand raised in benediction on Hexham screen.
Adeline	V.	Oct. 20	c.1125	1		Knight in armour, with hammer, anvil, and sword.
Adrian	M.	Dec. 2	290	0		A Sicilian maiden who suffered martyrdom because she rejected the proposals of the governor of the province, and refused to abjure her faith.
Agatha	V. M.	Feb. 5	253	4	20, 111	A sword is pointed at, or is passed through her breasts, or they are on a book or in a dish, or a nipple is held in pincers or shears. Or has a long veil.
Agnes	V. M.	Jan. 21	304	5	22, 180	An early legend relates that, when but thirteen, she refused to marry the son of a Roman prefect, and was tortured and stripped, but angels veiled her with her hair. Then she was thrown on a pile of burning faggots, but the fire went out. Then she was beheaded. She is represented with long hair; or angels cover her with their hair; or she kneels on a burning pyre; or holds a sword; or a sword is thrust through her neck. Near, or on a book, is a lamb, emblem of purity. Or a dove brings a ring to her as the bride of Christ.
Aidan	B.	Aug.	651	1		A stag crouches at his feet that fled to him for refuge

Title	Day	Date	Ancient Dedications	Text, Illustration	
Anthony -	A. H.	Jan. 17	251	4	13, 85, 141, 153	Tau staff with bell, or bell and book, or asperge, and wild boar, sometimes belled, at his feet or near. On a screen in Carlisle cathedral is painted— "Then liveth he in wilderness XX year or more Without any company but the wilde boar."
Apollonia -	V. M.	Feb. 9	249	0	123	Pincers and tooth, or with pincers holding a tooth.
Armil or Armagillus	C.	Aug. 16	551	0	93	A Breton saint, in armour under a chasuble, and leading a dragon.
Athanasius -	B. D.	May 2	372	0		Patriarch of Alexandria.
Aubert -	B. C.	Dec. 13	669	0		Baker's shovel. Ass with panniers of bread.
Aubyn -	B.	March 1	549	1		Monastic robes; shovel and book. Member of a noble English family settled in Brittany. Became Bishop of Angers.
Augustine of Canterbury	Ar.	May 26	604	? 30		Obtaining by prayer a fountain for baptizing (Cahier). In Ludlow glass vested as archbishop with double cross.
Augustine of Hippo	D.	Aug. 28	430	? 0	15, 265, 257	In doctor's robes. Holding a heart flaming or pierced with an arrow; or child before him with shell or spoon, or with pen and book.
Barbara -	V. M.	Dec. 4	c. 306	1	7, 22, 47, 144, 149	Holding a tower, sometimes with three windows, in one of which may be a chalice and Host. Holding a palm, a feather, or a sword. Has the crown of martyrdom. Trampling on her father or on a Saracen.
Barnabas -	Ap. M.	June 11	1st cent.	13		He holds the Gospel of S. Matthew, the evangelist's own copy, with which S. Barnabas healed the sick. Stones may be shown, as he was stoned to death at Salamis in Cyprus.

Title.	Day.	Date.	Ancient Dedications.	Text, Illustration.	
Botolph - -	A.	June 17	c. 700	64		With a church or monastery in his hand or below. In stained glass at Wiggenhall S. Mary Magdalen he is mitred, wears Mass robes, crosier turned outwards, right hand in act of benediction.
Brandan or Brendon	A.	May 16	578	2		Holding a branch and preaching.
Brice or Britius -	B. C.	Nov. 13	444	1		Carrying burning coals, which he carried unhurt to prove his innocence. With an infant in his arms or near. In a window at Wiggenhall S. Mary Magdalen he holds a staff with both hands.
Bridget or Bride of Kildare	A.	Feb. 1	523	19		Milking, or with cow by her side. Near a barn. A flame over her head. Hanging her mantle on a sunbeam. Laying her hand on the altar. Casting out a devil. With branch or with bunch of ears of corn. Restoring a man's hand cut off. On a brass at Balsham she is represented in nun's dress, with a pastoral staff in her right hand, and a book in her left.
Bridget of Sweden	Q.	Oct. 8	c. 1373	0		Nun's dress; writing; crowned; dove hovers above. See Husenbeth. On a screen at Westhall, Suffolk, she is a crowned abbess with crosier, lute, and chain.
Candida or Whyte	V. M.	Aug. 29	? 304	2		Scourged at a stake.
Cassian - -	M.	Aug. 13	359	0		A schoolmaster torn to pieces by his pupils with their iron pens.

Name		Date	Year/cent.		Page refs	Description
Cassyon or Cassian	B.	Aug. 5	4th cent.	1		
Catherine of Alexandria	V. M.	Nov. 25	290	62	22, 118, 163, 164, 165	Sumptuously dressed as princess, and crowned as martyr. Holds a sword. Tramples on Maximin. Wheel set with spikes. Palm of victory. Dove. A book in remembrance of her learning.
Catherine of Siena	V.	Apr. 30	1380	0		With heart and crown of thorns. Or with lily.
Cecilia	V. M.	Nov. 22	220	4	206	With harp, organ pipes, or violin, or lute. Wreath of red roses or white lilies. Palm of victory. Boiled in a cauldron. Deep wounds on the back of her neck.
Chad	B.	March 2	672	33		A branch of the vine. A coped bishop holding a church.
Charles	K. M.	Jan. 30	1649	5		With an arrow, or with the tower in which she was shut up by her father. Or with millstone, knife, or tongs.
Christina	V. M.	July 24	? 304	0		
Christopher	M.	July 25	250	9	59, 166, 168	A giant fording a river in which fish are seen swimming, steadying himself with a staff, and bearing the Child; on the other side a hermit, standing in front of his hermitage, holds up a lighted lantern. Or the staff may be bursting into leaf.
Clare	A.	Aug. 12	1253	2	18	In the dress of a Franciscan nun, holding in one hand an abbess' staff and closed book, and in the other a monstrance.
Clement	P. M.	Nov. 23	100	41	15, 140	With anchor. Papal tiara. Triple cross. Fountain obtained by his prayers. Lying in a marble temple in the sea.
Cleopas	…	Sept. 25	1st cent.	0		
Columba	A. C.	Nov. 21 or June 9	615	1		Taming a wild beast, or kneeling among wolves, or in a bear's den. Fountain. Sunbeams. Crucifix buds.

40

SAINTS AND THEIR EMBLEMS—*Continued*

	Title.	Day.	Date.	Ancient Dedications.	Text, Illustration.	
Constantine -	K. M.	March 11	c. 600	3		With horn, or cows, or oxen; connecting his name with "cornu." Tiara and cross.
Cornelius -	P. M.	Sept. 14	250	2	15	Attending sick man. Holding vases or phials, or pots of ointment, or surgical instruments, or medical apparatus, or the rod of Æsculapius. They were tortured and executed; and so may have arrows or sword, or be crucified. With furred robes as physicians.
Cosmas and Damian	M. M.	Sept. 27	290	3	116	Working as shoemakers. Tied to a tree and flayed for their skins to be used as leather. Thrown from a bridge with millstones tied to their necks.
Crispin and Crispinian	M. M.	Oct. 25	280	0		In a statue in Durham cathedral, and in glass at Methley, he is in episcopal costume and carries the head of S. Oswald. With otters, or swans, or loaves, or pillars of light.
Cuthbert -	B. C.	March 20	687	72	87, 89	
Cuthburga -	V. A.	Aug. 31	725	1		Burning or trampling on his books of magic; the devil flying from him; gridiron and sword; burnt in a cauldron with S. Justina.
Cyprian of Antioch	M.	Sept. 26	304	0		In episcopal robes; holds a sword and sometimes a book.
Cyprian of Carthage	Ar.	Sept. 26	258	1		Or Cyriacus or Cyr. With his mother. Riding on a boar, as he appeared to Charlemagne
Cyril -	M.	June 16	304	9		

Name		Date				Description
Cyril of Alexandria	B. C.	Jan. 28	444	0		Our Lady appears to him...
David	B. C.	March 1	c. 544	23		He stands on the hill which rose to serve as his pulpit; a dove on his shoulder.
Decuman	H. M.	Aug. 27	c. 706	1		Carrying his head, to wash it in a spring.
Denis or Dionysius	B. M.	Oct. 9	272	41	13	A headless bishop, carrying a mitred head. In glass at Methley he wears a white chasuble, and holds the nimbed head of a bishop, of which the eyes are closed in death.
Dominic	C.	Aug. 4	1221	1		Very numerous emblems, especially a lily in his hand, and a star on his head, or forehead, or breast. Or with dog and torch, the Dominicans being "Domini canes." Or with lily.
Dorothy	V. M.	Feb. 6	c. 287	0	18, 140, 180	Basket of flowers, or flowers and fruit from Paradise. Or three roses and three apples in her hand. Or bunch or wreath of flowers and palm.
Dunstan	Ar.	May 19	988	20	26, 68, 71, 157, 171	Seizing devil with pincers. With harp. With dove. Voice from crucifix. Troop of angels before him. Prostrate at the feet of Our Lord.
Eadburga of Pershore	V.	Jan. 15	960	6		May be Queen Ethelburga, wife of Ethelbert of Kent.
Eadburga of Lyminge	A.	Dec. 12	c. 647	1		Two fishes on a half hoop. Crown, crosier, and book, with a fish on either side of her.
Eanswith	V. A.	Sept. 12	c. 640	2	81	Pupil of Aidan and teacher of Cuthbert; abbot of Melrose. On Hexham screen has cope, mitre, crosier, and right hand raised in benediction.
Eata	B.	Oct. 26	685	1		
Edith of Polesworth	Q. A.	July 15	c. 964	16		In dress of abbess.

	Title.	Day.	Date.	Ancient Dedications.	Text, Illustration.	
Edith of Wilton	V.	Sept. 16	984	3		In royal robes and crosier, with Wilton church in the background.
Edmund - -	K. M.	Nov. 20	870	61	**13, 76, 127, 158**	Crowned (and so unlike Sebastian, who, moreover, is naked). May have sceptre. Pierced with arrows, or holding an arrow or arrows in his hand. Wolf guards his head.
Edmund of Pontigny	Ar.	Nov. 16	1242	1		Makes a vow before image of B.V.M. The child Christ or S. Thomas of Canterbury appears to him. Child at his feet. B.V.M. gives him a ring, or he places a ring on her finger (Husenbeth).
Edward the Confessor	K. C.	Oct. 13	1066	17	**77, 78, 117, 173**	Crowned and sceptred, and holding up a ring, or with a purse.
Edward - -	K. M.	March 18	978	5	**9, 11**	He was stabbed in the back while drinking the grace-cup on taking leave. On horseback with cup in one hand, and a dagger or short sword in the other. Or cup and serpent. Or with falcon, as he was about to hunt.
Edwin - - -	K. M.	Oct. 12	633	1		Fish with key in its mouth.
Egwin - - -	B.	Jan. 11	717	2		
Eligius - - -	...	...	...	...		See Eloy.
Elizabeth - -	...	Nov. 5	1st cent.	0		Holding the infant S. John. Dying in a desert, angels feeding her child. Saluting Our Lady.
Elizabeth of Hungary	Q.	Nov. 19	1231	0	**46**	Crowned or with double or triple crown. Giving alms or with basket of roses. Cripple clothed. In Ludlow glass with rose and sceptre

	Title.	Day.	Date.	Ancient Dedications.	Text, Illustration.	
Felicitas - - -	M.	Nov. 23	c. 160	1		Beheaded with seven sons. Emblems are sword and seven sons, or sword with seven heads on the blade.
Felix - - -	B.	March 8	646	6	104	
Firmin - - -	B.	Sept. 25	287	2		Carrying mitred head. Or sword and mitred head on the ground.
Francis of Assisi	C.	Oct. 4	1226	2	180, 182	Various; in particular a crucifix and the reception of the stigmata.
Frideswide -	V. A.	Oct. 19	735	2	18	With book and staff of abbess. Near her lies an ox, in reference to "Ox-ford."
Gabriel - -	Arch-angel	March 18	...	16	28, 29, 30	Sceptre and shield; lily in his hand and scroll AVE MARIA.
Genevieve - -	V.	Jan. 3	512	2	220	A shepherdess of Nanterre, near Paris, who was converted by S. German. Round her neck is suspended a coin stamped with a cross. She lighted her candles by her prayers, or they were lighted by an angel when they had been blown out by a devil; she is represented with a candle and a devil blowing a bellows. Or with a basket of the loaves she gave to the poor during a famine at Paris. Or as shepherdess knitting or spinning.
Gennys or Genesius	B.	June 3	662	2		A French bishop.
George - -	M.	April 23	c. 300	126	150, 151, 153	White banner and red cross. Sometimes on horseback. Generally a young knight in armour standing slaying a dragon or rescuing a maiden

318

Name		Date	Year			Description
German of Auxerre	B.	July 31	440	15		as a bishop among slain wild beasts. Or he tramples on the tyrant Maximius. Or has fetters hanging over his right arm. In stained glass at Wiggenhall S. Mary Magdalen he has a closed book and staff.
Gervase and Protasius	M. M.	June 19	1st cent.	1		Martyred by the sword, or by a scourge loaded with lead, which are their emblems.
Giles or Ægidius	A.	Sept. 1	7th cent.	162	**24, 69**	Abbot's robes and crosier. With hind and sometimes with arrow. In stained glass at Wiggenhall S. Mary Magdalen he holds a staff with plaited interlacing bands round the upper part of the shaft.
Gregory	P. D.	March 12	605	32	**102, 103**	If among the Doctors of the Church, he wears the papal tiara. A dove, i.e., the Holy Ghost, at his ear inspires him as he writes. Or holds a book or writes at a lectern. Or has tall or double-barred cross. In the Mass of S. Gregory, Christ descends from the altar with all the instruments of the Passion to convince a sceptic.
Guthlac	H.	April 1	714	9	**25**	Scourges a devil, or a dragon, or serpent.
Helena	Empress	Aug. 18	328	135	**7, 71**	With imperial crown, and holding or leaning on the True Cross; or with hammer and nail; or holding model of church of Holy Sepulchre at Jerusalem.
Henry VI.	...	...	1461	0	**195**	With white antelope.
Hilary of Poitiers	B. C.	Jan. 31	368	3		With books and treading on serpents, i.e., Arian writers; or a triangle, pen, staff, or trumpet; or child, or child in cradle.
Hilda	V. M.	Nov. 18	680	15		On the seal of Hartlepool she is represented as an abbess with crosier in her right hand; a priest is Elevating at an altar on either side; and there is a bird near the Host.
Hippolytus	B. M.	Aug. 13	255	2		He was the gaoler of S. Lawrence, whose convert he became. Has gaoler's keys, or is tied to the tails of two horses to be dragged asunder.

Title	Day	Date	Ancient Dedications.	Text, Illustration.	
Holy Innocents -	MM.	Dec. 28	...	5		Herod sitting on a throne, and soldiers slaying children.
Hubert - -	B.	Nov. 3	727	2	**15, 177, 178**	Stag with crucifix on its antlers. Stag on book. Hunting horn. May have bishop's mitre, whereas S. Cornelius has the pope's triple mitre, and S. Eustace is represented as a Roman soldier or knight.
Hugh of Lincoln -	B.	Nov. 17	1200	1		With swan. Dream of seven stars.
Hybald - -	A.	Sept. 22	685	4	**178**	
Ignatius - -	B. M.	Oct. 17	108	0		Holds a heart on which is IHS. Exposed to lions.
Isidore - -	C.	Jan. 15	5th cent.	0		In a window at Curry Rivel, Somerset, has a bowl in right hand and brushes in left. Ploughing, or obtains a fountain with his spade.
Ives - - -	V.	June 10	5th cent.	3		Fountain flows from his tomb (Cahier).
Ives or Ivo -	B.	April 25	660	...		
James the Greater	Ap.	July 25	1st cent.	414	**43, 44, 261**	Pilgrim with staff, hat, wallet, and scallop shell. Or with sword. Or charging the Moors on a white horse.
James the Less -	Ap.	May 1	1st cent.	26	**60, 261**	With a fuller's club in his hand; or with a palm, or a saw, or a toy mill.
Jerome - -	C. D.	Sept. 30	420	1	**265, 266**	In cardinal's hat and robes. Writing, with ink-horn, scroll, cross staff, and lion or skull near. Half-naked, beating his breast with a stone. Or carrying a church.

John Baptist	...	June 24 and Aug. 29	1st cent.	496	VI., 42	With lamb, or lamb on book. hair, with the camel's head sometimes hanging down. With long cross.
John Evangelist	Ap.	Dec. 27	1st cent.	181	16, 42, 44, 50, 53, 61, 135, 261	Youthful and beardless, with long flowing hair. With eagle. With poisoned chalice and serpent or dragon emerging from it. With palm.
John Evangelist, *ante portam Latinam*	...	May 6	...	0	51	Cauldron of oil.
John of Beverley	B. C.	May 7	721	7		Shrine at his side. Vested as an archbishop, with a cross-staff, in choir of York minster and on Hexham screen.
John of Bridlington	C.	...	1379	0	199	In stained glass at Morley, Derbyshire, as a canon in brown habit and a blue cloak, holding a crosier in his left hand.
Joseph of Arimathea	C.	July 27	1st cent.	1		Box of ointment. Budding staff. In Ludlow glass with thorn and vase; in Langport glass with the Holy Grail.
Jude or Thaddeus	Ap.	Oct. 28	1st cent.	0	82, 261	With a boat or a sailing ship, or loaves, or fish, or a boat hook. With a carpenter's square or a club. In glass of choir of York minster has ship and club.
Julian	B.	Jan. 27	3rd cent.	0		Fountain. Dragon. Scourges a demon on Kenn screen, Devon.
Julian Hospitaller	H.	Jan. 9	9th cent.	7		A hunted stag warned him that he would become a parricide, which came to pass. In repentance he became a ferryman, building a hospital near the ford. With a stag, or an oar, or in a ferry boat. In stained glass at Wiggenhall S. Mary Magdalen he holds a stick, perhaps a fragment of an oar.

321

SAINTS AND THEIR EMBLEMS—*Continued*

	Title.	Day.	Date.	Ancient Dedications.	Text, Illustration.	
Julitta - - -	M.	July 30	304	5		With her son, Cyril. Or with oxen. Or a fountain springs from her blood.
Justus or Just -	M.	Aug. 18	304	2		With swords. Scourged. Drowned with lead attached to his neck. Prints of his knees on a stone. Cross appears to him (Husenbeth).
Kenelm - -	K. M.	July 17	821	9	11	King holding lily. In Wells west front tramples on his stepmother, who is prostrate over an open book; it was by her orders that he was assassinated from behind while drinking a stirrup cup as he rode out with falcon on wrist.
Kentigern or Mungo	B. C.	Jan. 13	c. 600	9	105	Holding a salmon with a ring in its gills. Holding a plough drawn by two deer, or a deer and a wolf. (Husenbeth). He is represented on the seal of Glasgow.
Kyneburga -	Q. A.	March 6	c. 657	1		In dress of abbess.
Lambert - -	B. M.	Sept. 17	709	2	125	A lancet or dart. Or stabbed with javelins. Bringing hot coals in his surplice for the thurible. (See Husenbeth.)
Lawrence -	D. M.	Aug. 10	258	239	20, 112	Deacon on or holding gridiron, or dish, or bag of gold, or censer. Palm.
Leger or Leodegarius	B. M.	Oct. 2	678	5	123	Eyes plucked out and tongue cut. With borer or pickaxe, or two-pronged hook.
Leonard - -	D. C.	Nov. 6	520	177	15	Chains, or fetters, or manacles with a lock. In glass now in Durham Chapter house he holds a crosier in right hand and ...

Lô or Laud	B. C.	Sept. 21	5..	1	...	...
Louis	K. C.	Aug. 25	1270	...		Crown of thorns, nails, cross, dove, lilies, etc.
Lucian	B. M.	Jan. 8	312	1		Lying on potsherds. Consecrating. Baptizing. Carrying his head. His body brought ashore by a dolphin. Confused with S. Lucian of Antioch.
Lucy	V. M.	Dec. 13	304	2	22, 120	Eyes in a dish or on a book. Sword or palm or lamp. Sword through throat or neck. (See Husenbeth.)
Luke	E.	Oct. 18	1st cent.	28		An ox, generally winged. Or painting a picture of the Blessed Virgin. Or as a physician.
Magnus	B. M.	April 16	1104	3		
Marcellina	V.	July 17	397	1		Small cross in her hand.
Margaret of Antioch	V. M.	July 20	4th cent.	261	7, 121, 147	Piercing a dragon with a long cross. Emerging from inside a dragon. With girdle. Or pearls in her hair.
Lady Margaret of Richmond	...	June 29	1509	0		
Margaret of Scotland	Q.	Nov. 16	1093	0		Holds a black cross. Visits the sick. Prays her husband Malcolm out of purgatory (Husenbeth).
Mark	E.	April 25	1st cent.	6		Writing, with lion, winged or unwinged, near. Dragged by the neck; strangled.
Martha	V.	July 29	1st cent.	0	18, 46, 69, 93, 95, 162	With dragon or asperge. Or with ladle and keys.
Martin	B.	Nov. 11 and July 4	402	173		Dividing cloak, or as a priest or bishop, with naked beggar at his feet. Or in mail, but with mitre in his hand, and cap and cloak.

SAINTS AND THEIR EMBLEMS—Continued

	Title.	Day.	Date.	Ancient Dedications.	Text, Illustration.	
Mary Cleopas -	...	Jan. 19	1st cent.	0	52	Wife of Alphaeus. With her four children; of whom usually S. Jude has a boat; S. Simon a fish; S. James the Less a palm, club or a toy (fuller's) mill; S. Joseph Barsabas a cup or bowl, or three stones or loaves.
Mary, Blessed Virgin	...	...	1st cent.	2,305	27, 35, 39. 81, 95	Blue robe. Lily, etc. With a veil, the emblem of virginity.
Annunciation	...	March 25	...	1	28, 29, 30	
Visitation -	...	July 2	...	1		
Assumption -	...	Aug. 15	...	14	32, 281	
Nativity -	...	Sept. 8	...	12	269	
Conception -	...	Dec. 8	...	1		
Purification -	...	Feb. 2	...	1		
Mary Magdalene	...	July 22	1st cent.	187	46, 47, 48, 118	Flowing hair. Box or vase of ointment. Boat and open book.
Matthew -	Ap. E.	Sept. 21	1st cent.	33	82, 155, 261	His symbol is an angel. With table, money bag or box, inkhorn, carpenter's square, sword, halbert, or tall cross.
Matthias -	Ap.	Feb. 24	1st cent.	1	62, 63, 261	Sword or scimitar, or halbert, or lance, or axe, or stone, or carpenter's square.
Maurice -	M.	Sept. 22	280	8		Armoured knight with banner; on a Tattershall brass has a halbert.

Name		Class	Day	Year	Churches	Ref.	Emblems
							Birds flying around.
Maxentius	-	A.	June 26	515	1		
Medard	-	B.	June 8	545	1		Dove, or three white doves, or eagle above him; or he is imprinting his footsteps on a stone. In stained glass at Wiggenhall S. Mary Magdalen he holds a knife, point upwards.
Michael	-	Arch-angel.	Sept. 29	...	686	**35, 37, 39, 213**	Armoured or feathered angel; unmounted, trampling on or piercing a dragon or a devil, with spear, or cross, or sword. Weighing souls, with the Blessed Virgin Mary interceding for them.
Milburga	-	V. A.	Feb. 23	c. 700	5		Wild geese fly away by her order; or church in hand.
Mildred	-	V. A.	Feb. 20 or July 13	c. 725	3		
Modwenna or Morwenna		V. A.	July 6 or 5	c. 870	1		Teaching princess to read. Red cow by her side.
Mungo	-	B. C.	Jan. 13	601	9		See Kentigern.
Neot	-	C.	July 31	877	4		Preceptor of King Alfred.
Nicholas	-	B. C.	Dec. 6	342	437	**26, 172**	Three children in tub, or chest, or basket. Three balls, or apples, or loaves, or purses. Anchor or ship.
Nicomede	-	M.	June 1 or Sept. 15	c. 90	0		Club set with spikes.
Ninian	-	B.	Sept. 16	432	4	**96**	With crosier; heavy chain dangling from his right wrist. Staff takes root and fountain gushes from its roots.
Olave or Olaf	-	K. M.	July 29	1030	13	**13**	Crowned king seated, with cross and battle-axe, or sceptre and sword, or dagger. With a ladder which he saw in his dream. Or with a whole loaf, his Latinised name being *Holofius*, or with stones.

	Title.	Day.	Date.	Ancient Dedications.	Text, Illustration.	
Osmund - -	B.	July 16 or Dec. 4	1099	3		Book of Sarum Use, or a church in his hand.
Oswald - -	K. M.	Aug. 5	642	67	26, 88	With big cross. Or blows a horn. Or raven bears a chrismatory or a ring. In Wells west front he holds the silver dish which he gave to the beggars at Peterborough, and tramples on the heathen King Penda, by whom he was defeated and slain.
Oswin - -	K. M	Aug. 20	651	0		With spear, or spear and sceptre.
Osyth, or Sitha -	Q. M.	Oct. 7	c. 653	4		Carrying her decapitated head in glass at Long Melford.
Owen, or Ouen -	B.	Aug. 24	683	4		His coffin in a boat. Cross appearing in the air.
Pancras of Rome	M.	May 12	304	6	113	Armed youth; with book and palm; trampling on Saracen.
Pancras of Taormina	B. M.	April 3	1st cent.	10		He was stoned to death for hurling two idols into the sea.
Patrick - -	B. C.	March 17	492	8		In episcopal robes, trampling on or expelling snakes or reptiles. Near a font. Devil holding him in a fire, angel protecting him (Husenbeth).
Paul - -	Ap. M.	Jan. 25	1st cent.	43	45	Tall, dignified old man, with a bald forehead and long beard, holding a sword or sword and book. Three fountains that arose where his head bounded three times on decapitation.
With Peter -	...	June 29	...	283		

Name		Date	Year			Ref.	Description
Sebastian - -	M.	Jan. 20	288	2		**160**	Pierced with arrows, or holds an arrow or arrows or a bow. With palm.
Sexburga - -	Q. A.	July 6	699	1			She is also called Sithewella or Sithwell; and is represented decapitated with a scythe and near a well; e.g., on the piers of Sidwell's church, Exeter, and on nine Devon screens.
Sidwell, or Sativola	V. M.	Aug. 2	c. 700	2		**126**	
Silvester, or Sylvester	P. C.	Dec. 31	335	1			Tiara and double cross. Ox near. Holds chained dragon. Baptizes the Emperor Constantine.
Simon Zelotes -	Ap.	Oct. 28	1st. cent.	0		**56, 261**	With fish in his hand, or on a book. With oar. With fuller's bat or long saw.
Sitha - -	V.	April 27	1272	0		**213, 217**	Sitha or Sytha or Syth or Zita of Lucca was a maidservant and so carries pitcher or bag-purse or basket or keys. Thomas More says, "S. Sythe women get to seke their keys." And being pious, she has rosary and book. Or in her apron has loaves which turned to flowers.
Stephen - -	D. M.	Dec. 26	1st. cent.	46		**13, 53, 55**	Deacon holding stones in his hand or in a napkin or in his robe or on his shoulders or on a book. Young; tonsured, in dalmatic. With palm.
Swithun - -	B.	July 2	863	58			Emblem: a shower of rain. Represented in episcopal robes in stained glass in Winchester cathedral and Wiggenhall S. Mary Magdalen, where he has a crosier in his right hand and a closed book in
Translation -	...	July	...	...			
Paul - -	H.	...	342	0			Bearded. Bird brings loaf. Or he is dressed in leaves.
Paulinus - -	Ar.	Oct. 10	644	5			Baptizing. In glass at Methley, Yorkshire, he is vested as an archbishop and holds a staff.
Pega - -	V.	Jan. 8	c. 720	1			
Perpetua -	M.	March 7	203	1			Wild cow by her side. Ladder guarded by dragon.
Peter -	Ap. M.	June 29	1st cent.	1, 129		**33, 34, 81, 261**	With curly hair, short thick beard, and a bald spot on the top of his head. With key or keys and church or book; tiara and double-barred cross. With cock or holding a fish. In glass at Winscombe he holds staff, keys, and asperge.
Peter ad vincula	...	Aug. 1		11			
Peter Martyr -	M.	April 29	1252	0			Dominican dress; holds cross and book; dagger, or sword, or hatchet cleaving his skull.
Petronilla -	V.	May 31	1st cent.	1			With turban and key or broom and clasped book. S. Peter conversing with her.
Petrock, or Petrox	B.	June 4	564	14			
Philemon -	C.	Nov. 22	1st cent.	0			
Philip - -	Ap.	May 1	1st cent.	31		**61, 62, 63, 261**	Carries a large basket with loaves, in reference to S. John, vi. 5, 7. Or a cross, because he killed a dragon by holding up a cross. Or a pillar, because he suffered martyrdom by being suspended from a lofty column.
Polycarp -	B. M.	Jan. 26 / Feb. 23	155	0			Stabbed and burnt to death at a stake, or on a pyre, or in an oven the shape of an ox.
Pratt, or Protus	M.	Sept. 11	260	1			
Prisca - -	V. M.	Jan. 18	c. 275	0			With lion, or lions, or eagle near; holds palm or sword.

SAINTS AND THEIR EMBLEMS—*Continued*

	Title.	Day.	Date.	Ancient Dedications.	Text, Illustration.	
Radegund	Q.	Aug. 13	587	5		With royal robes, crown, and sceptre. Wolves and wild beasts that were tame with her are near. Crosier and book. Field of oats. White headdress, tunic with fleurs-de-lys, mantle with castles (Husenbeth).
Remigius, or Rémi	B.	Oct. 1	545	6		Carries the holy oils, or dove brings him chrism. Birds feed from his hand. With Clovis kneeling or in font.
Richard of Chichester	B.	April 3	1253	1		In early life he became servant to his brother, ploughing, sowing, and threshing for him. He is represented ploughing, or with chalice at his feet or before him, because he fell with the chalice in his hand, but

332

SAINTS AND THEIR EMBLEMS—*Continued*

	Title.	Day.	Date.	Ancient Dedications.	Text, Illustration.	
Theobald	H.	July 1	1150	3		Shoemaker's tools.
Thomas	Ap. M.	Dec. 21	1st cent.	46	**56, 57, 261**	With spear or lance. With carpenter's square. Handling the Saviour's wounds. Receiving girdle from Blessed Virgin Mary.
Thomas of Canterbury	Ar. M.	Dec. 29	1170	80	**130, 131, 132, 133**	Archiepiscopal cross and pallium. Crosier with battle-axe head. Sword or dagger stuck in his head. Martyred before altar. Receives red chasuble from Blessed Virgin Mary.
Translation	...	July 7	...	...		Carries in his hand the crown or corona of his skull.
Thomas of Hereford	B.	Oct. 2	1287	0		In a stained glass window at Ross, Herefordshire.
Timothy	B. M.	Jan. 24	97	0		With the club with which he was beaten to death at Ephesus for interrupting a Pagan procession.
Titus	B. M.	Jan. 4	1st cent.	0		Bright and beaming face.
Ursula	V. M.	Oct. 21	c. 450	2	**141, 142, 306**	Shot with arrows, or holds arrow or arrows. Diminutive virgins peer from mantle. With the companions of her journey. With ship.
Valentine	B. M.	Feb. 14	c. 270	0		There were two Valentines; a bishop of Terni, and a priest at Rome. The latter is represented as a priest with a sword; holding a sun; giving sight to a girl.
Vedast	B.	Feb. 6	539	2		Wolf with goose in its mouth, which S. Vedast brought to life again.

330

Name		Date	Year	No.	Page	Description
Veronica - -	V.	Jan. 13	1st cent.	...	**24**	Holds a veil or kerchief imprinted with the countenance of Our Lord.
Victor of Marseilles -	M.	July 21	303	0	**206**	With windmill or millstone; in armour.
Vigor - -	B.	Nov. 1	537	2		In bishop's vestments; with a dragon.
Vincent - -	D. M.	Jan. 22	304	6	**117**	His bowels torn with an iron hook, and his body burnt on a spiked gridiron. Millstone. Raven driving wild beasts from his body. In glass at Curry Rivel and Peylembury he holds two cruets in his right hand.
Walstan of Bawburgh	C.	May 30	1016	1		Crowned; ermine cape; sceptre and scythe. He died while he was mowing; calves below.
Wandregesilus, or Wandrille	A.	July 22	667	1		Abbot of Fontanelle or S. Wandrille, Normandy.
Wendreda of March	V.	...	? 8th cent.	1		
Werburga - -	V. A.	Feb. 3	c. 825	12		In abbess' dress and with crosier; carrying a church.
Wilfrid - -	Ar.	Oct. 12	709	48	**24, 106**	Baptizing or preaching to pagans. Breaking idols. In Mass vestments as archbishop with pallium on Hexham screen.
Wilgefortis, or Uncumber	V. M.	...	...	...	**144**	A bearded woman. Crucified with ropes.
William of Norwich	M.	...	1137	...		Child crucified; stabbed; nails, hammer and bleeding wounds.
William of York	Ar.	June 8	1154	0	**138, 139, 199**	Archbishop's vestments, mitre and cross; shield with eight lozenges. His life and miracles are depicted in the north window of the choir transept of York minster.

	Title.	Day.	Date.	Ancient Dedications.	Text, Illustration.	
Winifred -	V. M.	Nov. 3	c. 600	6	**121**	Beheaded before altar. Carrying her head. In Pierpont Morgan's catalogue, p. 94, she has a palm; is pursued by a prince on a white horse, and a stream flows out of a stone well-head. On a brass at Balsham she is in nun's dress, with a pastoral staff in her right hand and a sword in her left.
Winston, or Wyston, or Wistan	K. M.	June 1	850	3		
Withburga -	V. A.	July 8	744	1		Church in her hand. Two does.
Wulfram, or Wolfran	B.	March 20	720	2		Youthful king near him, son of Duke Rathbode, whom he is baptizing.
Wulstan, or Wolstan	B.	Jan. 19	1095	1		Fixes his crosier in S. Edward the Confessor's tomb.
Zita -	...	...	...	...		See Sitha.

INDEX OF PROPER NAMES

*N.B.—Other references will be found in the alphabetical list of saints,
pages 308 to 332*

ABBOTSBURY, 66
    Aberystwyth, 250
Abraham, 254, 275
Ælfric, 114, 128, 161, 282
Agatha, **20**, **111**, 169
Agnes, **22**, **180**, 114, 116, 169, 187
Aidan, 27, 89, 104, 124
Alban, **13**, 119, 134, 297
Aldhelm, 107
Aldington, **257**
Alford, 195
Alkelda, 79, 80, 127, 129
Alkmund, 76, 127, 215
Alleluia Victory, 68
All Hallows, 60
All Saints, 60, 191, 204, 208
All Souls, 60
Alphege, 127, 129, 194, 209
Alphington, 197
Ambrose, **24**, **85**, **265**, **267**, 84, 134,
    238, 264
Amphibalus, 190
Anderson, Sir Charles, 177
Andrew, **40**, **261**, 148, 154, 186, 206
Andrewes, 241
Angelo, S., 38
Angers, 66
Anglo-Saxon Church, 80, 222
Anne, *frontispiece*, **58**, **59**, 58, 170, 219
Antholin, 70
Anthony, **13**, **85**, **141**, **153**, 141, 157,
    195, 277
Apollonia, **123**, 123, 159
Apostles, **261**, 262
Apulia, 38
Arilda, 80
Armel, **93**, 146
Arnold, 186
Ashby de la Launde, 208
Ashby S. Leger, 124

Ashton, **140**, **141**, **213**, **267**, 40, 66,
    75, 84, 123, 143, 153, 154, 159, 212
Assumption, **32**, **281**, 31, 191
Athanasius, 138, 238
Attercliffe, 6
Augustine of Canterbury, 6, 27, 41,
    101, 114, 192, 193, 209
Augustine of Hippo, **15**, **265**, **267**, 1,
    10, 153, 256, 264
Autun, 122
Auxerre, 94
Ave Maria, 219
Avranches, 39

BALTHAZAR, 267
    Bamburgh, 104
Barbara, **7**, **22**, **47**, **144**, **149**, 122, 148
Barlow, 241
Barming, **273**
Barningham, 291
Barrow, 97
Bartholomew, **63**, **134**, **135**, **261**, 135,
    136, 206
Barton, 252
Barton Turf, 195
Basilissa, **189**
Basingstoke, 8
Bean, 176
Beaulieu, **189**
Beauvale, 111
Beckford, 66
Becon, 240
Bede, 10, 138, 185, 223, 224, 240
Bees, **189**
Bega, **189**
Bell, 296
Benedict of Cassino, **68**, 174
Benedict Biscop, 47
Benedictines, 67, 107

333

GENERAL INDEX

A LB, 293
   Almond, mystic, 256
Almuce, 297
Alphabets, mystic, 241
Alternative dedications, 14, 193
Amice, 293
Anchorites, 86
Angels, 40
Anglo-Saxon Church, 222
Anglo-Saxon consecration of churches, 240
Anglo-Saxon missioners, 105-107
Anglo-Saxon royalties, 76-78
Anglo-Saxon saints, 137
Animals, stories about, 176-182
Annunciation, 31
Apostles, emblems of, 262
Apparel, 293
Apparitions of S. Michael, 38
Archangels, 36
Ark as emblem of Church, 269
Ascetic life, 86
Asperge, 297
Assumption, 31
Aureole, 282
Austerities, 86
Axis, deviation of, 247

B ARE feet, 256
   Bearded lady, 143
Bells, dedications of, 167-169, 217-219
Bible, little known, 86
Biblical saints, 28-64, 191
Birthday saints, 70
Building methods in Middle Ages, 249

C ALENDARS, 220-225
   Calendar of Church of Ireland, 223
Calendar of Church of Scotland, 223
Calendar of Eastern Church, 224
Canonisation, popular, 198
Canonisation, procedure of, 194
Canons of credibility, 183

Captives, 173
Cassock, 297
Celtic consecration of churches, 239
Celtic dedications, 10, 25, 33, 39, 80, 81, 83, 97-99, 192, 193, 204, 205, 212, 216, 221, 222, 225; and see *Bibliography*
Celtic mission, 104
Chancels, deviation of axis, 247
Change of dedications, 190, 191
Charity, praise of, 174
Chasuble, 294
Child saints, 170
Christ in glory, 254
Cluster dedications, 70
Colours, symbolism of, 288
Compound dedications, 12, 189
Consecration of churches, procedure of, 238-242
Consolidation of dedications, 190
Contemplative religion, 86
Continental missioners, 100
Continental saints, 65
Conversion of England, 79, 101
Cope, 297
Coronation of Virgin, 261
Credibility of legends, 183
Crosier, 277, 297
Cross, discovery of true, 6, 75
Cross, forms of, 277
Cross of bishop, abbot, archbishop, and pope, 276, 277, 296
Cross-staff, 297
Crown of thorns, 277
Crucifix, 277
Cruciform churches, symbolism of, 246
Crusades, 151

D ALMATIC, 295
   Day, dedication, 192
Dedication, meaning of, 1
Dedications—
   Alternative, 193
   Change of, 191
   Compound, 189

341

Printed at THE DARIEN PRESS, *Edinburgh*.

Church Art in England

A Series of Books edited by

FRANCIS BOND, M.A., F.G.S., Hon. A.R.I.B.A.

HUMPHREY MILFORD, OXFORD UNIVERSITY PRESS
LONDON, NEW YORK, TORONTO, MELBOURNE, & BOMBAY

BY FRANCIS BOND

SCREENS AND GALLERIES IN ENGLISH CHURCHES

Demy 8vo, containing 204 pages, with 152 Illustrations reproduced
from Photographs and Drawings. Strongly bound in cloth. Price
6s. net ($2.40).

Screen in Scarning Church

SOME PRESS NOTICES

New York Nation.—"It is not easy to praise too highly the simple and effective presentation of the subject and the interest of the book to all persons who care for ecclesiology or for decorative art."

Daily Graphic.—"Mr Bond has produced a work on our ecclesiastical screens and galleries which, like his larger work on the 'Gothic Architecture of England,' is

Screen in Holbeton Church

in the first degree masterly. His knowledge of his subject, exact and comprehensive, is compressed into a minimum amount of space, and illustrated by a series of photographs and measured drawings which render the work of permanent value."

Bulletin Monumental.—"Après avoir analysé, aussi exactement que possible, l'intéressant étude de M. Bond, nous devons le féliciter de nous avoir donné ce complément si utile à son grand ouvrage."

3

FONTS & FONT COVERS

Demy 8vo, containing 364 pages, with 426 Illustrations reproduced from Photographs and Measured Drawings. Strongly bound in cloth. Price 12s. net ($4.80).

Font at Stanton Fitzwarren

Font at Belton

PRESS NOTICE

Font at Bodmin

BY FRANCIS BOND

Wood Carvings in English Churches
I. Misericords

Demy 8vo, containing 257 pages, with 241 Illustrations reproduced from Photographs and Measured Drawings. Strongly bound in cloth. Price 7s. 6d. net ($3.00).

Misericords at Stratford-on-Avon

SOME PRESS NOTICES

New York Herald.—" One of the quaintest, most fascinating, and at the same time most learned volumes that a reader would happen upon in a lifetime."

Antiquary.—" An authoritative, and at the same time delightful and instructive volume."

Church Times.—" An indispensable guide to the subject. The illustrations are worthy of all praise."

Yorkshire Post.—" Another of the valuable series of monographs on Church Art in England, and the most entertaining of all."

Misericord at Worcester

Misericord at Beverley Minster

Liverpool Courier.—" Another of the admirably written and illustrated art handbooks for which the author is famous."

Birmingham Post.—" This well illustrated volume is not only a valuable technical monograph, but also an important contribution to the history of social life and thought in the Middle Ages. Mr Bond's treatment of the subject is exceptionally charming and successful."

Outlook.—" Many there must be to whom Mr Bond's new book will be welcome. Into all the details of this varied and most puzzling subject he goes with thoroughness and a pleasant humour. The bibliography and indices, as in all the volumes in this series, are admirable."

autre par noms des lieux, viennent faciliter les recherches et permettre au lecteur de tirer bénéfice des vastes resources d'une érudition informée et sure."

Stalls at Manchester

The Cabinet Maker.—"Every lover of woodwork should possess this series, which contains beautiful illustrations and most interesting descriptions of the noble heritage of magnificent work handed down to us by the mediæval Church."

BY FRANCIS BOND

WESTMINSTER ABBEY

Demy 8vo, containing 348 pages, with 270 Illustrations reproduced
from Photographs and Measured Drawings. Strongly bound in
cloth. Price 10s. net ($4.00).

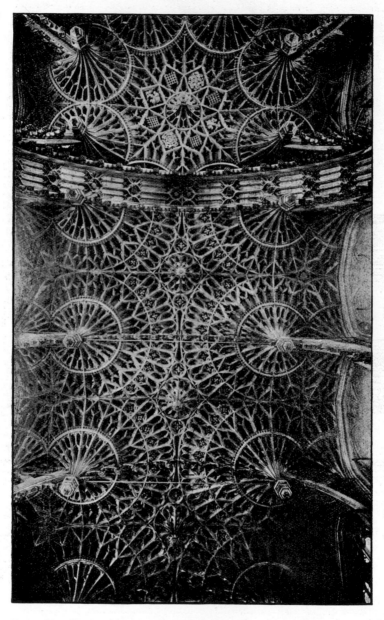

Fan Vault of Henry VII.'s Chapel in Westminster Abbey

VISITORS' GUIDE TO WESTMINSTER ABBEY

93 pages of text, abridged from the larger work on "Westminster Abbey."
Fcap 8vo, with 15 Plans and Drawings and 32 Photographic Illustrations.
Price 1s. net (40 c.).

Chapter House at Westminster

BY H. B. WALTERS

Church Bells of England

Demy 8vo, containing 420 pages, with 170 Illustrations
reproduced from Photographs and Drawings. Strongly
bound in cloth. Price 7s. 6d. net ($3.00).

Times.—"It is by far the most complete work of its kind in existence and the
most accurate . . . a treatise as readable as it is erudite."

Cross and Letters on Lincolnshire Bells (1423-1431)

Military Architecture in England During the Middle Ages

By A. Hamilton Thomson, M.A., F.S.A.

Demy 8vo, containing 406 pages, with 200 Illustrations reproduced from Photographs, Drawings, and Plans. Strongly bound in cloth. Price 7s. 6d. net ($3.00).

Bodiam : North Front and Gatehouse

SOME PRESS NOTICES

Church Times.—" Not only those who are specially interested in military architecture, but also everyone who desires, on visiting an ancient castle, to view it with intelligent appreciation, must needs add this work to his library."

Guardian.—" This volume at once steps into the position of a classic ; it will be long before it is superseded."

English Historical Review.—" This monograph is compressed into about four hundred pages, and copiously illustrated, yet it contains a wealth of detail that could easily have been expanded into a much longer work. . . . Its author is not writing a guide to castles, but a history of military architecture ; yet the work might usefully be taken as a guide to many of the castles described in it."

Country Life.—" The book could scarcely be bettered as a concise survey of a difficult and complex subject."

Journal des Savants. — " Le livre de M. Thompson sera . . . le bienvenu. Il le sera d'autant plus qu'il donne un aperçu très complet des transformations de l'architecture militaire outre-Manche depuis les temps les plus anciens. . . . Ce n'est pas seulement au point de vue anglais, c'est également a notre point de vue français que ce livre offre un réel intérêt."

Two Volumes, Demy Quarto; 1000 Pages; 1400 Illustrations
Price Two Guineas net ($16.75).

An Introduction to English Church Architecture

From the Eleventh to the Sixteenth Century

By FRANCIS BOND

SOME PRESS NOTICES

Athenæum.—"These volumes form a worthy sequel to the important work on 'Gothic Architecture in England,' by the same author, published in 1905. They represent a vast amount of orderly labour, and show an astonishingly wide grasp of a great subject. It is a big undertaking; 1000 quarto pages, with 1400 illustrations. One of the pleasant features of the work is the sparing use of exceptional or technical terms, the exact meaning of which is grasped as a rule only by a professed architect. For the use of the unlearned, the first volume opens with a tersely-written glossary of terms, and this is followed by a most useful explanatory list of French words and phrases of an architectural character. But for the most part there is a breezy freshness about Mr Bond's phrases which at once rivets the attention."

Westminster Gazette.—"We know Mr Bond as a careful student, of sound scholarship, but if we had no other evidence, this 'Introduction' of his would mark him also as a writer of imagination who has not allowed the infinite detail of his subject to obscure his sight of the building. 'It is good for those who are to be introduced to mediæval church architecture,' he writes in his preface 'to know not only how a church was built, but why it was built, who built it, who served in it, who worshipped in it, and what manner of worship was theirs—Ancient or Modern.' Already we are beginning to regard such an attitude as perfectly natural, forgetting that the text-books of the last century took no more account of the human impulse than a treatise on trigonometry takes of the private life of Euclid. . . . The book is magnificently illustrated."

Yorkshire Observer.—"Mr Bond shows, step by step, how the church varied from age to age, structure following need, so that an ancient parish church as we see it now is not a mere bit of ingenious or clumsy designing, plain or beautiful by caprice, but a living organism reflecting the lives, the faith, and indeed the material fortunes of the people who built and used it. It is in the realisation of this soul of a building more than in anything else that the difference lies between the old guide-book antiquarianism and the new archæology which Mr Bond represents. . . . If it were not so easy and lucid to read, one might compare it with Darwin's 'Origin of Species.'"

Connoisseur.—"An unrivalled record of English ecclesiastical architecture. It is difficult to speak in too high praise of the work. Mr Bond has explored his subject from end to end."

14

Western Mail.—"Splendidly bound and well printed, with a glossary of terms which will prove most useful to the lay reader, it is a work of the greatest value to all who are in any way interested in the construction, details, and uses of our ancient and beautiful churches."

Antiquary.—"The student or the general reader who wishes to have an intelligent grasp of principles and of their illustration and exemplification in the

Vault of Choir of Gloucester Cathedral

details of construction has here provided for him an ideal book. Mr Bond's pages are likely, however, to fascinate the expert as well as the beginner. . . . For this valuable book the author will receive the grateful thanks of students, not only those of the present time but those of many a day to come. . . . Every chapter and every section is lavishly illustrated, not at random, but by a carefully chosen set of examples closely related to the text; the wealth of illustration is so great that a full half of the thousand pages of the two volumes is occupied by pictures."

IN PREPARATION

Uniform with the above Volumes of the English Church Art Series

PULPITS AND LECTERNS IN ENGLISH CHURCHES

By Rev. J. CHARLES COX, D.D.

Author of "Churches of Derbyshire," "How to Write the History of a Parish,"
"English Church Furniture," "Churchwardens' Accounts," "Parish Registers,"
"Royal Forests of England," "Sanctuaries," etc.

ENGLISH CHURCH PLATE

By Rev. J. T. EVANS, M.A.

Editor of "Church Bells of Gloucestershire, Cardiganshire, Pembroke," etc.

CHURCH CHESTS, DOORS, COLLECTING AND POOR BOXES, PRESSES, ETC.

By PHILIP MAINWARING JOHNSTON
F.S.A., F.R.I.B.A.

Author of numerous Papers in the "Surrey and Sussex Archæological Collections,"
and in the "Archæological Journal."

THE ENGLISH CHANCEL

The Altar, Reredos, Communion Table, Altar Rails, Piscina, Sedilia, Easter Sepulchre, etc.

By FRANCIS BOND

Author of "English Church Architecture," etc.

TOMBS AND MONUMENTS IN ENGLISH CHURCHES

By F. E. HOWARD

Author of papers on "Fan Vaulting," "English Chantry Chapels,"
"Devon Churches," etc.

OXFORD UNIVERSITY PRESS

16